Bloom's Modern Critical Views

Bloom's Modern Critical Views

ERNEST HEMINGWAY
New Edition

Edited and with an introduction by
Harold Bloom
Sterling Professor of the Humanities
Yale University

BLOOM'S
LITERARY CRITICISM
An imprint of Infobase Publishing

Bloom's Modern Critical Views: Ernest Hemingway—New Edition

Copyright © 2011 by Infobase Publishing
Introduction © 2011 by Harold Bloom

Bloom's Literary Criticism
An imprint of Infobase Publishing
132 West 31st Street
New York NY 10001

Library of Congress Cataloging-in-Publication Data
Ernest Hemingway / edited and with an introduction by Harold Bloom. — New ed.
    p. cm. — (Bloom's modern critical views)
    Includes bibliographical references and index.
    ISBN 978-1-60413-364-6 (hardcover)
    1. Hemingway, Ernest, 1899–1961—Criticism and interpretation. I. Bloom, Harold.
    PS3515.E37Z586553 2011
    813'.52—dc22

                          2010036211

Contributing editor: Pamela Loos
Cover designed by Takeshi Takahashi
Composition by IBT Global, Troy NY
Cover printed by IBT Global, Troy NY
Book printed and bound by IBT Global, Troy NY
Date printed: January 2011
Printed in the United States of America

10 9 8 7 6 5 4 3 2 1

Contents

Editor's Note

My introduction acknowledges Hemingway's genius at composing the short story, while questioning his achievement as a novelist.

George Monteiro offers an extended treatment of Hemingway's relationship to the Bible and biblical utterance, after which Donald E. Hardy examines the function of presupposition in the dialogue in three of the short stories.

Margot Norris explores veracity and the ethical awareness Hemingway brought to the writing of *A Farewell to Arms*. Robert Paul Lamb then credits Hemingway with a radical transformation of the role and art of dialogue.

Norman Friedman argues that the protagonist of "The Snows of Kilimanjaro" is a projection of the author, a figure who absorbs and corrects Hemingway's ambiguous relationship to his vocation. Susan F. Beegel then studies aspects of gendering in *The Old Man and the Sea*, which I myself read as involuntary self-parody.

David Savola posits *The Sun Also Rises* as a critique of the pastoral mode, after which Philip Melling appraises the cultural concerns orbiting *The Old Man and the Sea*. The volume concludes with an analysis by Donald A. Daiker of the representational distortions of Lady Brett Ashley.

HAROLD BLOOM

Introduction

Hemingway freely proclaimed his relationship to *Huckleberry Finn*, and there is some basis for the assertion, except that there is little in common between the rhetorical stances of Twain and Hemingway. Kipling's *Kim*, in style and mode, is far closer to *Huckleberry Finn* than anything Hemingway wrote. The true accent of Hemingway's admirable style is to be found in an even greater and more surprising precursor:

> This grass is very dark to be from the white heads of old mothers,
> Darker than the colorless beards of old men,
> Dark to come from under the faint red roofs of mouths.

Or again:

> I clutch the rails of the fence, my gore drips, thinn'd with the ooze
> of my skin,
> I fall on the weeds and stones,
> The riders spur their unwilling horses, haul close,
> Taunt my dizzy ears and beat me violently over the head with
> whip-stocks.
> Agonies are one of my changes of garments,
> I do not ask the wounded person how he feels, I myself become
> the wounded person,
> My hurts turn livid upon me as I lean on a cane and observe.

1

Hemingway is scarcely unique in not acknowledging the paternity of Walt Whitman; T.S. Eliot and Wallace Stevens are far closer to Whitman than William Carlos Williams and Hart Crane were, but literary influence is a paradoxical and antithetical process, about which we continue to know all too little. The profound affinities between Hemingway, Eliot, and Stevens are not accidental but are family resemblances due to the repressed but crucial relation each had to Whitman's work. Hemingway characteristically boasted (in a letter to Sara Murphy, February 27, 1936) that he had knocked Stevens down quite handily: " . . . for statistics sake Mr. Stevens is 6 feet 2 weighs 225 lbs. and . . . when he hits the ground it is highly spectaculous." Since this match between the two writers took place in Key West on February 19, 1936, I am moved, as a loyal Stevensian, for statistics' sake to point out that the victorious Hemingway was born in 1899 and the defeated Stevens in 1879, so that the novelist was then going on 37 and the poet verging on 57. The two men doubtless despised each other, but in the letter celebrating his victory Hemingway calls Stevens "a damned fine poet," and Stevens always affirmed that Hemingway was essentially a poet, a judgment concurred in by Robert Penn Warren when he wrote that Hemingway "is essentially a lyric rather than a dramatic writer." Warren compared Hemingway to Wordsworth, which is feasible, but the resemblance to Whitman is far closer. Wordsworth would not have written, "I am the man, I suffer'd, I was there," but Heming-way almost persuades us he would have achieved that line had not Whitman set it down first.

It is now a half century since Hemingway's suicide, and some aspects of his permanent canonical status seem beyond doubt. Only a few modern American novels seem certain to endure: *The Sun Also Rises*, *The Great Gatsby*, *Miss Lonelyhearts*, *The Crying of Lot 49*, and at least several by Faulkner, including *As I Lay Dying*, *Sanctuary*, *Light in August*, *The Sound and the Fury*, and *Absalom, Absalom!* Two dozen stories by Hemingway could be added to the group, indeed perhaps all of *The First Forty-Nine Stories*. Faulkner is an eminence apart, but critics agree that Hemingway and Fitzgerald are his nearest rivals, largely on the strength of their shorter fiction. What seems unique is that Hemingway is the only American writer of prose fiction in this century who, as a stylist, rivals the principal poets: Stevens, Eliot, Frost, Hart Crane, aspects of Pound, W.C. Williams, Robert Penn Warren, and Elizabeth Bishop. This is hardly to say that Hemingway, at his best, fails at narrative or the representation of character. Rather, his peculiar excellence is closer to Whitman than to Twain, closer to Stevens than to Faulkner, and even closer to Eliot than to Fitzgerald, who was his friend and rival. He is an elegiac poet who mourns the self, who celebrates the self (rather less effectively) and who suffers divisions in the self. In the broadest tradition of

American literature, he stems ultimately from the Emersonian reliance on the god within, which is the line of Whitman, Thoreau, and Dickinson. He arrives late and dark in this tradition and is one of its negative theologians, as it were, but as in Stevens the negations, the cancellings, are never final. Even the most ferocious of his stories, say "God Rest You Merry, Gentlemen" or "A Natural History of the Dead," can be said to celebrate what we might call the real absence. Doc Fischer, in "God Rest You Merry, Gentlemen," is a precursor of Nathanael West's Shrike in *Miss Lonelyhearts,* and his savage, implicit religiosity prophesies not only Shrike's satanic stance but the entire demonic world of Pynchon's explicitly paranoid or Luddite visions. Perhaps there was a nostalgia for a Catholic order always abiding in Hemingway's consciousness, but the cosmos of his fiction, early and late, is American Gnostic, as it was in Melville, who first developed so strongly the negative side of the Emersonian religion of self-reliance.

Hemingway notoriously and splendidly was given to overtly agonistic images whenever he described his relationship to canonical writers, including Melville, a habit of description in which he has been followed by his true ephebe, Norman Mailer. In a grand letter (September 6–7, 1949) to his publisher, Charles Scribner, he charmingly confessed, "As a man without any ambition, except to be champion of the world, I wouldn't fight Dr. Tolstoi in a 20 round bout because I know he would knock my ears off." This modesty passed quickly, to be followed by, "If I can live to 60 I can beat him. (MAYBE)." Since the rest of the letter counts Turgenev, de Maupassant, Henry James, even Cervantes, as well as Melville and Dostoyevski, among the defeated, we can join Hemingway himself in admiring his extraordinary self-confidence. How justified was it, in terms of his ambitions?

It could be argued persuasively that Hemingway is the best short-story writer in the English language from Joyce's *Dubliners* until the present. The aesthetic dignity of the short story need not be questioned, and yet we seem to ask more of a canonical writer. Hemingway wrote *The Sun Also Rises* and not *Ulysses,* which is only to say that his true genius was for very short stories and hardly at all for extended narrative. Had he been primarily a poet, his lyrical gifts would have sufficed: We do not hold it against Yeats that his poems, not his plays, are his principal glory. Alas, neither Turgenev nor Henry James, neither Melville nor Mark Twain provide true agonists for Hemingway. Instead, de Maupassant is the apter rival. Of Hemingway's intensity of style in the briefer compass, there is no question, but even *The Sun Also Rises* reads now as a series of epiphanies, of brilliant and memorable vignettes.

Much that has been harshly criticized in Hemingway, particularly in *For Whom the Bell Tolls,* results from his difficulty in adjusting his gifts to the demands of the novel. Robert Penn Warren suggests that Hemingway is successful when his "system of ironies and understatements is coherent." When incoherent, then, Hemingway's rhetoric fails as persuasion, which is to say, we read *To Have and Have Not* or *For Whom the Bell Tolls* and we are all too aware that the system of tropes is primarily what we are offered. Warren believes this not to be true of *A Farewell to Arms*, yet even the celebrated close of the novel seems now a worn understatement:

> But after I had got them out and shut the door and turned off the light it wasn't any good. It was like saying good-by to a statue. After a while I went out and left the hospital and walked back to the hotel in the rain.

Contrast this to the close of "Old Man at the Bridge," a story only two and a half pages long:

> There was nothing to do about him. It was Easter Sunday and the Fascists were advancing toward the Ebro. It was a gray overcast day with a low ceiling so their planes were not up. That and the fact that cats know how to look after themselves was all the good luck that old man would ever have.

The understatement continues to persuade here because the stoicism remains coherent and is admirably fitted by the rhetoric. A very short story concludes itself by permanently troping the mood of a particular moment in history. Vignette is Hemingway's natural mode, or call it hard-edged vignette: a literary sketch that somehow seems to be the beginning or end of something longer, yet truly is complete in itself. Hemingway's style encloses what ought to be unenclosed, so that the genre remains subtle yet trades its charm for punch. But a novel of 340 pages (*A Farewell to Arms*), which I have just finished reading again (after 20 years away from it), cannot sustain itself on the rhetoric of vignette. After many understatements, too many, the reader begins to believe that he is reading a Hemingway imitator, like the accomplished John O'Hara, rather than the master himself. Hemingway's notorious fault is the monotony of repetition, which becomes a dulling litany in a somewhat less accomplished imitator like Nelson Algren and sometimes seems self-parody when we must confront it in Hemingway.

Nothing is got for nothing, and a great style generates defenses in us, particularly when it sets the style of an age, as the Byronic Hemingway did. As with Byron, the color and variety of the artist's life become something of a veil between the work and our aesthetic apprehension of it. Hemingway's career included four marriages (and three divorces); service as an ambulance driver for the Italians in World War I (with an honorable wound); activity as a war correspondent in the Greek-Turkish War (1922), the Spanish civil war (1937–39), the Chinese-Japanese War (1941), and the war against Hitler in Europe (1944–45). Add big-game hunting and fishing, safaris, expatriation in France and Cuba, bullfighting, the Nobel Prize, and ultimate suicide in Idaho, and you have an absurdly implausible life, apparently lived in imitation of Hemingway's own fiction. The final effect of the work and the life together is not less than mythological, as it was with Byron and with Whitman and with Oscar Wilde. Hemingway now is myth and so is permanent as an image of American heroism, or perhaps more ruefully the American illusion of heroism. The best of Hemingway's work, the stories and *The Sun Also Rises*, are also a permanent part of the American mythology. Faulkner, Stevens, Frost, perhaps Eliot, and Hart Crane were stronger writers than Hemingway, but he alone in his American century achieved the enduring status of myth.

The Sun Also Rises

Rereading *The Sun Also Rises* provides a few annoyances, particularly if one is a Jewish literary critic and somewhat skeptical of Hemingway's vision of the matador as messiah. Romero seems to me about as convincing a representation as Robert Cohn; they are archetypes for Hemingway in 1926 but hardly for us 60 years after. Brett and Mike are period pieces also; Scott Fitzgerald did them better. But these are annoyances only; the novel is as fresh now as when I first read it in 1946, when I was 16. Like *The Great Gatsby*, *The Sun Also Rises* ages beautifully. Why? What are the qualities that save this novel from its own mystique, its self-intoxication with its own rhetorical stance? What does it share with Hemingway's best stories, like those in the fine collection *Winner Take Nothing*?

A great style is itself necessarily a trope, a metaphor for a particular attitude toward reality. Hemingway's is an art of evocation, hardly a singular or original mode, except that Hemingway evokes by parataxis, in the manner of Whitman or of much in the English Bible. This is parataxis with a difference, a way of utterance that plays at a withdrawal from all affect, while actually investing affect in the constancy of the withdrawal, a willing choice of the void as object, rather than be void of object, in Nietzschean terms. Not that Hemingway is spurred by Nietzsche, since Conrad is clearly the largest precursor of the author of *The Sun Also Rises*. The stance of Marlow in *Lord Jim* and *Heart of Darkness* is the closest analogue to Hemingway's own rhetorical stance in *The Sun Also Rises* and *A Farewell to Arms*.

Erich Auerbach and Angus Fletcher are among the notable modern critics who have illuminated the literary uses of parataxis. Fletcher lucidly summarizes parataxis as a syntactic parallel to the symbolic action of literature:

This term implies a structuring of sentences such that they do not convey any distinctions of higher or lower order. "Order" here means intensity of interest, since what is more important usually gets the greater share of attention.

Fletcher, without implying childlike or primitive behavior, indicates the psychological meaning of parataxis as being related to "the piecemeal behavior of young children or primitive peoples." As Fletcher notes, this need not involve the defense Freud named as regression, because a paratactic syntax "displays ambiguity, suggesting that there is a rhythmic order even deeper in its organizing force than the syntactic order." Hemingway's parataxis is worthy of the full-length studies it has not yet received. Clearly it is akin to certain moments in Huck Finn's narration, Walt Whitman's reveries, and even Wallace Stevens's most sustained late meditations, such as *The Auroras of Autumn*. John Hollander usefully compares it also to "an Antonioni shooting script in the relation of dialogue and shots of landscape cut away to as a move in the dialogue itself, rather than as mere punctuation, and ultimately in the way in which dialogue and uninterpreted glimpse of scene interpret each other." I take it that the refusal of emphasis, the maintaining of an even tonality of apparent understatement, is the crucial manifestation of parataxis in Hemingway's prose style. Consider the celebrated conclusion of *The Sun Also Rises*:

> Down-stairs we came out through the first-floor dining-room to the street. A waiter went for a taxi. It was hot and bright. Up the street was a little square with trees and grass where there were taxis parked. A taxi came up the street, the waiter hanging out at the side. I tipped him and told the driver where to drive, and got in beside Brett. The driver started up the street. I settled back. Brett moved close to me. We sat close against each other. I put my arm around her and she rested against me comfortably. It was very hot and bright, and the houses looked sharply white. We turned out onto the Gran Via.
>
> "Oh, Jake," Brett said, "we could have had such a damned good time together."
>
> Ahead was a mounted policeman in khaki directing traffic. He raised his baton. The car slowed suddenly pressing Brett against me.
>
> "Yes," I said. "Isn't it pretty to think so?"

The question of Jake's impotence is more than relevant here. It is well to remember Hemingway's description of authorial intention, given in the interview with George Plimpton:

Actually he had been wounded in quite a different way and his testicles were intact and not damaged. Thus he was capable of all normal feelings as a man but incapable of consummating them. The important distinction is that his wound was physical and not psychological and that he was not emasculated.

The even, understated tone at the end of *The Sun Also Rises* depends on a syntax that carries parataxis to what might have been parodistic excess, if Hemingway's art were less deliberate. Sentences such as "It was hot and bright" and the sly "He raised his baton" are psychic images of lost consummation, but they testify also to Jake's estrangement from the earlier intensities of his love for Brett. Reduced by his betrayal of the matador-messiah to Brett's rapacity, Jake is last heard in transition toward a less childlike, less primitive mode of reality testing: "'Yes.' I said. 'Isn't it pretty to think so?'" One remembers Nietzsche's reflection that what we find words for is something we already despise in our hearts, so that there is always a sort of contempt in the act of speaking. Kenneth Burke, in *Counter-Statement*, rejoined that the contempt might be in the act, but not contempt for speaking. Jake, as the novel ends, is in transition toward Burke's position.

Hemingway possessed both a great style and an important sensibility. He was not an original moralist, a major speculative intellect, a master of narrative, or superbly gifted in the representation of persons. That is to say, he was not Tolstoy, whom he hoped to defeat he said, if only he could live long enough. But style and sensibility can be more than enough, as *The Sun Also Rises* demonstrates. Style alone will not do it; consider Updike or Cheever. We go back to *The Sun Also Rises* to learn a sensibility and to modify our own in the process of learning.

A Farewell to Arms

If *A Farewell to Arms* fails to sustain itself as a unified novel, it does remain Hemingway's strongest work after the frequent best of the short stories and *The Sun Also Rises*. It also participates in the aura of Hemingway's mode of myth, embodying as it does not only Hemingway's own romance with Europe but the permanent vestiges of our national romance with the Old World. The death of Catherine represents not the end of that affair but its perpetual recurrence. I assign classic status in the interpretation of that death to Leslie Fiedler, with his precise knowledge of the limits of literary myth: "Only the dead woman becomes neither a bore nor a mother; and before Catherine can quite become either she must die, killed not by Hemingway, of course, but by childbirth!" Fiedler finds a touch of Poe in this, but Hemingway seems to me far healthier. Death, to Poe, is after all less a metaphor for sexual fulfillment than it is an improvement over mere coition, since Poe longs for a union in essence and not just in act.

Any feminist critic who resents that too-lovely Hemingwayesque ending, in which Frederic Henry gets to walk away in the rain while poor Catherine takes the death for both of them, has my sympathy, if only because this sentimentality that mars the aesthetic effect is certainly the mask for a male resentment and fear of women. Hemingway's symbolic rain is read by Louis L. Martz as the inevitable trope for pity and by Malcolm Cowley as a conscious symbol for disaster. A darker interpretation might associate it with Whitman's very American confounding of night, death, the mother, and the sea, a fourfold mingling that Whitman bequeathed to Wallace Stevens, T.S. Eliot, and Hart Crane, among many others. The death of the beloved woman in Hemingway is part of that tropological cosmos, in which the moist element dominates because death the mother is the true image of desire. For Hemingway, the rain replaces the sea and is as much the image of longing as the sea is in Whitman or Hart Crane. Robert Penn Warren, defending a higher estimate of *A Farewell to Arms* than I can achieve, interprets the death of Catherine as the discovery that "the attempt to find a substitute for universal meaning in the limited meaning of the personal relationship is doomed to failure." Such a reading, though distinguished, seems to me to belong more to the literary cosmos of T.S. Eliot than to that of Hemingway. Whatever nostalgia for transcendental verities Hemingway may have possessed, his best fiction invests its energies in the representation of personal relationships and hardly with the tendentious design of exposing their inevitable inadequacies. If your personal religion quests for the matador as messiah, then you are likely to seek in personal relationships something of the same values enshrined in the ritual of bull and bullfighter: courage, dignity, the aesthetic exaltation of the moment, and an all but suicidal intensity of being—the sense of life gathered to a crowded perception and graciously open to the suddenness of extinction. That is a vivid but an unlikely scenario for an erotic association, at least for any that might endure beyond a few weeks.

Wyndham Lewis categorized Hemingway by citing Walter Pater on Prosper Merimée: "There is the formula . . . the enthusiastic amateur of rude, crude, naked force in men and women. . . . Painfully distinct in outline, inevitable to sight, unrelieved, there they stand." Around them, Pater added, what Merimée gave you was "neither more nor less than empty space." I believe that Pater would have found more than that in Hemingway's formula, more in the men and women, and something other than empty space in their ambiance. Perhaps by way of Joseph Conrad's influence on him, Hemingway had absorbed part at least of what is most meaningful in Pater's aesthetic impressionism. Hemingway's women and men know, with Pater, that we have an interval, and then our place knows us no more. Our one chance is to pack that interval with the multiplied fruit of consciousness, with the solipsistic truths of perception and sensation. What survives time's ravages in *A Farewell to Arms* is precisely Hemingway's textually embodied knowledge that art alone apprehends the moments of perception and sensation and so bestows on them their privileged status. Consider the opening paragraph of chapter 16:

> That night a bat flew into the room through the open door that led onto the balcony and through which we watched the night over the roofs of the town. It was dark in our room except for the small light of the night over the town and the bat was not frightened but hunted in the room as though he had been outside. We lay and watched him and I do not think he saw us because we lay so still. After he went out we saw a searchlight come on and watched the beam move across the sky and then go off and it was dark again. A breeze came in the night and we heard the men of the anti-aircraft gun on the next roof talking. It was cool and they were putting on their capes. I worried in the night about some one coming up but Catherine said they were all asleep. Once in the night we went to sleep and when I woke she was not there but I heard her coming along the hall and the door opened and she came back to the bed and said it was all right she had been downstairs and they were all asleep. She had been outside Miss Van Campen's door and heard her breathing in her sleep. She brought crackers and we ate them and drank some vermouth. We were very hungry but she said that would all have to be gotten out of me in the morning. I went to sleep again in the morning when it was light and when I was awake I found she was gone again. She came in looking fresh and lovely and sat on the bed and the sun rose while I had the thermometer in my mouth and we smelled the dew on the roofs and then the coffee of the men at the gun on the next roof.

The flight of the bat, the movement of the searchlight's beam and of the breeze, the overtones of the antiaircraft gunners blend into the light of the morning to form a composite epiphany of what it is that Frederic Henry has lost when he finally walks back to the hotel in the rain. Can we define that loss? As befits the aesthetic impressionism of Pater, Conrad, Stephen Crane, and Hemingway, it is in the first place a loss of vividness and intensity in the world as experienced by the senses. In the aura of his love for Catherine, Frederic Henry knows the fullness of "It was dark" and "It was cool," and the smell of the dew on the roofs, and the aroma of the coffee being enjoyed by

the antiaircraft gunners. We are reminded that Pater's crucial literary ancestors were the unacknowledged Ruskin and the hedonistic visionary Keats, the
Keats of the "Ode on Melancholy." Hemingway, too, particularly in *A Farewell to Arms*, is an heir of Keats, with the poet's passion for sensuous imme-
diacy, in all of its ultimate implications. Is not Catherine Barkley a belated
and beautiful version of the goddess Melancholy, incarnating Keats's "Beauty
that must die"? Hemingway, too, exalts that quester after the melancholy,

> whose strenuous tongue
> Can burst Joy's grape against his palate fine;
> His soul shall taste the sadness of her might,
> And be among her cloudy trophies hung.

The Old Man and the Sea

Hemingway's greatness is in his short stories, which rival any other master
of the form, be it Joyce or Chekhov or Isaak Babel. Of his novels, one is
constrained to suggest reservations, even of the very best: *The Sun Also
Rises*. *The Old Man and the Sea* is the most popular of Hemingway's later
works, but this short novel alas is an indeliberate self-parody, though less
distressingly so than *Across the River and Into the Trees*, composed just before
it. There is a gentleness, a nuanced tenderness, that saves *The Old Man and
the Sea* from the self-indulgences of *Across the River and into the Trees*. In an
interview with George Plimpton, Hemingway stated his pride in what he
considered to be the aesthetic economy of *The Old Man and the Sea*:

> *The Old Man and the Sea* could have been over a thousand pages
> long and had every character in the village in it and all the
> processes of the way they made their living, were born, educated,
> bore children, etc. That is done excellently and well by other writers.
> In writing you are limited by what has already been done satisfacto-
> rily. So I have tried to learn to do something else. First I have tried
> to eliminate everything unnecessary to conveying experience to the
> reader so that after he or she has read something it will become
> part of his or her experience and seem actually to have happened.
> This is very hard to do and I've worked at it very hard.
>
> Anyway, to skip how it is done, I had unbelievable luck this
> time and could convey the experience completely and have it be
> one that no one had ever conveyed. The luck was that I had a
> good man and a good boy and lately writers have forgotten there
> still are such things. Then the ocean is worth writing about just
> as a man is. So I was lucky there. I've seen the marlin mate and

known about that. So I leave that out. I've seen a school (or pod) of more than fifty sperm whales in that same stretch of water and once harpooned one nearly sixty feet in length and lost him. So I left that out. But the knowledge is what makes the underwater part of the iceberg.

The Old Man and the Sea unfortunately is too long, rather than exquisitely curtailed, as Hemingway believed. The art of ellipsis, or leaving things out, indeed is the great virtue of Hemingway's best short stories. But *The Old Man and the Sea* is tiresomely repetitive, and Santiago the old fisherman is too clearly an idealization of Hemingway himself, who thinks in the style of the novelist attempting to land a great work:

> Only I have no luck anymore. But who knows? Maybe today. Every day is a new day. It is better to be lucky. But I would rather be exact. Then when luck comes you are ready.

Contemplating the big fish, Santiago is even closer to Hemingway the literary artist, alone with his writerly quest:

> His choice had been to stay in the deep dark water far out beyond all snares and traps and treacheries. My choice was to go there to find him beyond all people. Beyond all people in the world. Now we are joined together and have been since noon. And no one to help either one of us.

Santiago's ordeal, first in his struggle with the big fish, and then in fighting against the sharks, is associated by Hemingway with Christ's agony and triumph. Since it is so difficult to disentangle Santiago and Hemingway, this additional identification is rather unfortunate in its aesthetic consequences, because it can render a reader rather uncomfortable. There is a longing or nostalgia for faith in Hemingway, at least from *The Sun Also Rises* until the end of his career. But if *The Old Man and the Sea* is a Christian allegory, then the book carries more intended significance than it can bear. The big fish is no Moby Dick or Jobean adversary; Santiago loves the fish and sees it as his double. What can we do with Santiago-as-Christ when we attempt to interpret the huge marlin?

William Faulkner praised *The Old Man and the Sea* as being Hemingway's best work, but then Faulkner also considered Thomas Wolfe to be the greatest American novelist of the century. The story, far from Hemingway's best, cannot be both a parable of Christian redemption and of a novelist's triumph, not so much because these are incompatible, but because so repetitive and self-indulgent a narrative cannot bear that double burden. Sentimentality, or emotion in excess of the object, floods *The Old Man and the Sea*. Hemingway himself is so moved by Hemingway that his famous, laconic style yields to uncharacteristic overwriting. We are not shown "grace under pressure" but something closer to Narcissus observing himself in the mirror of the sea.

GEORGE MONTEIRO

Ernest Hemingway, Psalmist

The subject of Ernest Hemingway and the Bible has been touched on here and there in Hemingway scholarship and occasionally acknowledged by the critics, yet the matter continues to call for extended treatment. It is clearly the subject for a book. Here, however, it may be worthwhile to sketch out one small segment of such a study: Hemingway's reading of one well-known piece of Scripture and its effect on his writings in the late twenties and early thirties. The Biblical text is King David's "Twenty-Third Psalm," and the Hemingway texts are "Neothomist Poem," published by Ezra Pound in *The Exile* in 1927, *A Farewell to Arms* (1929), and "A Clean, Well-Lighted Place" (1933). By examining, in some detail, Hemingway materials—in manuscript and typescript—at the John F. Kennedy Library, we can trace the genesis of an idea and relate it to Hemingway's vision.

I

Among the Hemingway papers at the Kennedy there are five texts included in four numbered documents that are relevant: documents 597a, 597b, 597c, and 658a. Two of these are typescripts (597a and 658a), the other two (597b and 597c) are penciled manuscripts in Hemingway's hand. Of the typescripts, 658a presents Hemingway's "Neothomist Poem" as we know it from publication in *The Exile*. The only one of these five texts that carries the poem's title,

From *Journal of Modern Literature* 14, no. 1 (Summer 1987): 83–95. Copyright © 1987 by Indiana University Press.

it now rests as part of a sheaf of Hemingway's poems, eighteen in all, including the seventeen poems that appear in the several unauthorized editions in which Hemingway's poetry has circulated for decades. The eighteenth poem entitled "They All Made Peace—What Is Peace?" does not appear in those pirated chapbooks. The second typescript (597a), untitled, is a single sheet of ten lines. A clean copy of the longer version of Hemingway's poem, this text is reproduced in facsimile on page 82 of Nicholas Gerogiannis' edition of *Ernest Hemingway: 88 Poems*.[1] The manuscripts survive in two notebooks. Item 597b, the flyleaf of which contains the signature and address "Ernest Hemingway/Note Book/113 Rue Notre Dame des Champs/Paris VI,"[2] offers two tries—the earliest of those at Kennedy—at the longer version of the poem. The second half of the first of these two (on the second manuscript page) is reproduced in facsimile in *88 Poems* (also page 82), along with the complete second attempt at the longer version on the third page. These versions are untitled. Item 597c is also an untitled manuscript in pencil in Hemingway's hand. It appears in a lined notebook with writing on the first five leaves. The front flyleaf is signed "Ernest Hemingway/69 Rue Froidevaux/155, Boul^d Saint-Germain/Paris G." At the Kennedy this item is described, in part,

> 597c Manuscript. Untitled pencil manuscript beginning "The Lord is My Shepherd I shall not want . . ." 1 p. Also one page of sentences on the dust and dew in the dark in Italy.

This manuscript offers, in some ways, the most intriguing of the five versions available at Kennedy. The description of it, as I shall argue later on, is misleading—as is, I think, the numbering. For reasons that I hope to establish, I now list the five texts contained in these manuscripts and typescripts in their order of composition and/or recording:

> Version 1, 597b (first and second pages);
> Version 2, 597b (third page);
> Version 3, 597a (typescript of ten lines);
> Version 4, 597c; and
> Version 5, 658a ("Neothomist Poem").

To begin at the beginning as we can best know it from the extant materials, here is Version 1, before Hemingway's cancellations:

> The wind blows in the fall
> and it is all over
> The wind blows the leaves

from the trees
and it is all over
They do not come back
And if they do
  are
We're gone.
You can start it any time
But you in————
It will flush its self.
When it goes it takes
everything with it
The Lord is my shepherd
I shall not want him long.
He maketh me to lie down in
green pastures
And lo there are no green pastures
He leadeth me beside still waters
And still waters run deep.
Surely goodness and mercy shall
follow me all the days of
my life   And I shall
never escape them
Though I walk through the
vale
shadow of the shadow
of death I shall return
to do evil.
For thou art with me
In the morning and the evening
Especially in the evening
The wind blows in the fall
And it is all over
When I walk through the valley
of the shadow of death
I shall (feel) fear all evil
For thou art with me.

In revising this version, Hemingway crossed out the first thirteen lines, as
well as lines 21–29. He also rearranged lines 30–33 so that they would come
at the end of the poem.

The temporarily final poem that emerges from these revisions reads:

The Lord is my shepherd
I shall not want him long.
He maketh me to lie down in
green pastures
And lo there are no green pastures
He leadeth me beside still waters
And still waters run deep.
When I walk through the valley
of the shadow of death
I shall fear all evil
For thou art with me.
In the morning and the evening
Especially in the evening
The wind blows in the fall
And it is all over.

My first observation is that the poem appears not to have been conceived, if the opening thirteen lines constitute its true beginning, as a parody of the "Twenty-Third Psalm." Yet when, with line fourteen, the poet moves in that direction, he remains on target for the remainder of the poem with the single exception of lines 29–33, which return the poem to its opening motif—the blowing wind. These four lines would remain in the poem, in some form or other, through the ten-line typed version (597a). Purged of its first thirteen lines, the poem reads as a rather straightforward if a trifle lachrymose rewriting of David's "Twenty-Third Psalm":

The Lord is my shepherd; I shall not
    want.
He maketh me to lie down in green pastures: he leadeth me
    beside the still waters.
He restoreth my soul: he leadeth me in the paths of
    righteousness for his name's sake.
Yea, though I walk through the valley of the shadow of death,
    I will fear no evil: for thou art with me; thy rod and
    thy staff they comfort me.
Thou preparest a table before me in the presence of mine
    enemies: thou anointest my head with oil; my cup
    runneth over.
Surely goodness and mercy shall follow me all the days of my
    life: and I will dwell in the house of the Lord for ever.

This version of Hemingway's poem parodies the "Psalm" only at certain points, namely verses one and two, and only the first three quarters of verse four. It does not touch verses three, five, and six. In the next version of the poem Hemingway makes several changes in wording and phrasing, adds lines (later canceled), and inserts a treatment of verse six of the "Psalm" (also largely canceled). Some of the changes and additions are significant:

1. In the line "And still waters run deep" he crosses out "run deep," replacing it with "reflect thy face."
2. As an alternative to the line "For thou art with me" he writes, "you are not with me," only to cross it out.
3. He writes and then crosses out "In the morning and in the evening." He then adds the line, "In the morning nor in the evening," which he changes, by adding "Neither" and crossing out "nor," to "Neither In the morning and in the evening"; and then he crosses out "Neither." (There may be a step here that I have left out.)
4. He writes and then crosses out the line, "Nor in the valley of the shadow of death." (It will not reappear in later versions.)
5. He writes "And," crosses it out, and then begins again, "In the night the wind blows and you are not with me," only to change, first, "you" to "thou" and "are" to "art," then interpolating the clause, "I did not hear it for" so that the line reads: "In the night the wind blows and I did not hear it for thou art not with me," and finally, puzzlingly, he crosses out "thou" and "not."
6. He writes, "You have gone and it is all gone with you," only to cross it out.
7. He writes, "Surely goodness and mercy shall follow me all the days of my life and I shall never escape them. For thou art with me"—all of which he cancels.

Here is what is left, the second extant version of the poem:

The Lord is my shepherd
I shall not want him long
He maketh me to lie down in
green pastures
And there are no green pastures.
He leadeth me beside still
waters

And still waters reflect thy face.
For thou art with me
In the morning and in the evening
In the night the wind
blows and I did not hear it for [thou] art
[not] with me.
The wind blows in the fall
and it is all over

The next version of the poem is the ten-line version in typed clean copy. My hunch is that the poem went through additional intermediate stages, but at this late date we can only speculate idly as to the nature and the number of steps by which Hemingway arrived at the shape of the last four lines.

The Lord is my shepherd
I shall not want him for long
He maketh me to lie down in green pastures
  and there are no green pastures
He leadeth me beside still waters
  and still waters run deep
the wind blows and the bark of the trees is wet from the rain
the leaves fall and the trees are bare in the wind
Leaves float on the still waters
There are wet dead leaves in the basin of the fountain

(In the eighth line, incidentally, Hemingway had first written "bare in the rain," crossed out "rain" and written in "fall," and then crossed out "fall" in favor of "wind."[3])

Between the final revisions of the second manuscript version and the typing of this version Hemingway reinstated some of the first version's cancellations. Hence the second version's "And still waters reflect thy face" becomes here (once again) "and still waters run deep," while the second-version lines "In the night the wind blows" and "The wind blows in the fall" are replaced (with a specific echo of the first version's reference to "leaves") by "the wind blows and the bark of the trees is wet from the rain / the leaves fall and the trees are bare in the wind / Leaves float on the still waters / There are wet dead leaves in the basin of the fountain."

The poem, too, is wet and dead. Fortunately, Hemingway did not publish it in this form, although it is possible that it was this version that was first offered to Pound for *The Exile*. If so, it might well have been Pound, famous for his editorial blue pencil, who cut the poem down to its published form and who made the crucial decision on how to arrange the words of the poem on the page:

> The Lord is my shepherd, I shall not
> want him for long.[4]

It is of course in this "truncated" form that the poem appears in typescript (658a) in the sheaf of eighteen poems that constitutes, chronologically, the final text of this poem at Kennedy, a text the preparation of which, I suspect, came after the publication of the poem in *The Exile* and was undertaken for the possible purpose of an authorized collection of Hemingway's verse that never materialized.

II

In this chronological consideration of the extant texts of "Neothomist Poem," I have so far skipped document 597c, even though I would place its date of composition somewhere between that of the ten-line typescript (597a) and that of the published version in *The Exile* in 1927. I consider it now, seemingly out of order, mainly because in manuscript 597c this "text" is squeezed in at the top of the first page of Hemingway's notebook in this form: "The Lord Is My Shepherd I Shall Not Want / him / for / long," with the last three words written down the right margin horizontally, one word to the line. Crammed in as it is, with each word in the top full line showing an initial capital, it is obvious to me that this is not the text of a poem but the title for the piece of fragmentary writing that follows it. And what is that piece of fragmentary writing? Whatever it is, it is not a parody of the "Twenty-Third Psalm," one might be surprised to learn, but an entirely different text unmistakably in prose:

> Now that I know that I
> am going to die none of it
> seems to make much difference
> there are a few things that
> I would like to think about.
> When you have them you can
> not keep them y but maybe
> after you have gone away they
> are still there. You can not
> keep them but if you try but
> later, when they have gone, they
> return

come
come again and sometimes
they will stay.
You can not keep them but
after you are gone they are
still there. In the fall the leaves
fell from the trees, and we walked
    It was very dusty
    Toward evening it was not
so hot but it was still
dusty and the dust
rose from the road

    When it was dark the
dew came and settled the
dust on the road that
we marched on.
    In Italy when it was
dark the dew came settled the
dust on the road and
the men that the troops
marched on in the dark
and beside the road there
were poplar trees in the
dark
    In Oak Park Illinois

Hemingway would cross out all but two of the first thirteen lines, expunge the whole of lines eighteen, thirty, thirty-one, and thirty-five, and cancel individual words and phrases in lines seventeen, twenty-eight, and twenty-nine, thereby leaving this residual text:

The Lord Is My Shepherd I Shall Not Want
    him for long.
When you have them you can
not keep them y
You can not keep them but
after you are gone they are
still there. In the fall the leaves
fell from the trees
    Toward evening it was not

so hot but it was still
dusty and the dust
rose from the road
      When it was dark the
dew came and settled the
dust on the road that
we marched on.

In Italy when it was
dark the dew settled the
dust on the road
and beside the road there
were poplar trees in the
dark

To Hemingway's attentive readers there will be something undoubtedly familiar about this unpublished text, crude as it is, with multiple starts. Dating from 1926, it is the forerunner (quite possibly the very first version), I would propose, of that famous text with its memorable opening lines:

> In the late summer of that year we lived in a house in a village that looked across the river and the plain to the mountains. In the bed of the river there were pebbles and boulders, dry and white in the sun, and the water was clear and swiftly moving and blue in the channels. Troops went by the house and down the road and the dust they raised powdered the leaves of the trees. The trunks of the trees too were dusty and the leaves fell early that year and we saw the troops marching along the road and the dust rising and leaves, stirred by the breeze, falling and the soldiers marching and afterward the road bare and white except for the leaves.[5]

Here, with its evocative references to falling leaves and dust rising from the road (there are three attempts at getting the imagery right in the manuscript numbered 597c), we have the ur-text for the opening of *A Farewell to Arms* (as well as the opening of Chapter 25, with its echoing imagery of "bare trees" and "wet dead leaves"), one that can be dated considerably earlier than any so far suggested.[6] In any case, if I am right in seeing this as the ur-text for the novel, we would do well to mull over the fact that Hemingway had originally begun his book with the clear indication that the narrator (and hero) is convinced that his death (suicide, perhaps) is imminent. Taken in combination with the sardonic title (crammed in at the top after, as I have already suggested, the author had sat down the prose text), this rejected text suggests even more strongly that the context in which ex-Lieutenant Frederic Henry sets down his own retrospective narrative of his losses in war and love is one of personal despair and acedia.[7] As such, then, the line, "The Lord Is My Shepherd I Shall Not Want Him For Long" should not merely be acknowledged as another of the titles, considered and rejected, for the novel that would eventually be called *A Farewell to Arms* but recognized as the very first of that string of titles (at least the earliest one so far uncovered) to be set down.[8] In this case, I suspect that the author would have rejected the title soon after crossing out the opening six lines about the narrator's impending death as sounding too orthodox a religious note. But having considered the opening lines of his poem parodying the "Twenty-Third Psalm" as a title for a work of fiction he proposed to write and isolating them for that purpose, he may well have discovered, I would venture, the poem he (or Pound) would later entitle "Neothomist Poem."[9]

III

Echoes of the "Twenty-Third Psalm" and Hemingway's parodies of that Old Testament poem would resurface still again. And they would reappear creatively in combination with the dual themes of death and suicide in what would turn out to be one of Hemingway's finest stories: "A Clean, Well-Lighted Place."

Consider that in this dark parable there are not only nihilistic parodies of "The Lord's Prayer," and the Catholic prayer to the Virgin recited by the so-called older waiter, but also a context for those culminating prayers, the conversation between the two waiters about an old man (a "client") and his unsuccessful attempt at suicide: his failure to commit, in short, the unpardonable sin against the Holy Ghost, an act undertaken in the first place because, as the older waiter explains, the old man was in the state of despair. "He was in despair," the waiter says wryly (in what is, after all, a privately grim joke), about "Nothing."[10] Three times on the opening pages of this story we are told that the old man, in a deliberate echoing of the shadow image of the "Twenty-Third Psalm" ("though I walk through the valley of the shadow of death"), is sitting there in the "shadow" made by the leaves of the tree (17–18). (But note as well the even closer echo of Luke 1:79 on the purpose of John the Baptist: "To give light to them that sit in darkness and in the shadow of death.") The old man, deaf and alone, orders another drink of brandy. The younger waiter pours him one, filling up his glass. But then, in a remarkable literalization into action of one of the most familiar metaphors employed in the "Twenty-Third Psalm"—"my cup runneth over"—Hemingway writes, "The old man motioned with his finger. 'A little more,' he said. The waiter poured on into the glass so that the brandy slopped over and ran down the stem into the top saucer of the pile" (19).

If the talk of suicide and the imagery of shadows caused by the leaves of trees recall the discarded opening for *A Farewell to Arms* the second sentence of the story echoes closely the opening of the novel as published. Here is *A Farewell to Arms*: "the dust they (the troops) raised powdered the leaves of the trees. The trunks of the trees too were dusty and the leaves fell early that year and we saw the troops marching along the road and the dust rising ..." (17).

At one point in "A Clean, Well-Lighted Place," the older waiter tries to spell out just how his situation differs from that of his fellow-waiter. When the latter asserts, "'I have confidence. I am all confidence,'" he replies, "'you have youth, confidence, and a job'" (22). As for himself, he is no longer young, he acknowledges, and he has never had "confidence." Even as it was for Herman Melville, "confidence" is a key term here. If it can mean something like self-assurance (as it does, undoubtedly, for the younger waiter), it also means "faith"—the Spanish term *confidencia*. Indeed, if the older waiter has never had such *confidencia*, such "faith," then I am even more certain that his expressions of nihilism are a form of displaying his acedia. The consolations to the believers—to men of faith—that are the "Lord's Prayer" and the prayer to the Virgin Mary are not available to those who lack "confidence," even as the "Twenty-Third Psalm"—sometimes described as "David's confidence in the grace of God"—serves only as a repository of sentiments and images that can only be taken ironically by the author who not only constructed parodies of the "Twenty-Third Psalm," but also wrote *A Farewell to Arms* and "A Clean, Well-Lighted Place." To the expansive pastoral consolations of the "Twenty-Third Psalm"—its "still waters," "paths of righteousness," the "table" prepared "in the presence of mine enemies," and the promise of anointment—man can only counter with the narrow virtues of a localized cleanliness and man-made light. For the "house of the Lord" in which the psalmist, confident in the grace of God, shall "dwell ... for ever," Hemingway's older waiter offers only the café, "clean, well-lighted," which, though he would "stay late," will perforce close each night while the night is still dark and will remain so long, ostensibly, after the first glimmer of "daylight." "It is probably only insomnia," the waiter says to himself; "Many must have it" (24). And indeed they must in Hemingway's peopled world, from the rattled Nick Adams of "Now I Lay Me" (with its ironic titular reference to still another prayer) to the author who himself compulsively parodied the "Twenty-Third Psalm" in the late 1920s, both in his poem and in his fragmentary first try at writing his novel about the loss of confidence in war, love, and self.

Yet the story is not a simpler re-treatment of the implosive matter of the novel. Although the themes of faith and *confidencia* appear and reappear thematically in the novel, the emphasis there is more secular than in the story. In fact, the novel and story differ in this matter nowhere more distinctly than in the way each of the texts handles the shared matter of empty high-mindedness, bankrupt idealism, and the words and beliefs attending both. Although it is not common to relate the two passages, I shall juxtapose here two of the best known excerpts in all of Hemingway. I have in mind the passage from *A Farewell to Arms* in which Lt. Henry identifies the words that embarrass him, along with those that do not, and the sentences from "A Clean, Well-Lighted Place," in which the older waiter utters his prayer to "*nada*." The first quotation comes from the novel:

> I was always embarrassed by the words sacred, glorious, and sacrifice and the expression in vain. We had heard them, some-times standing in the rain almost out of earshot, so that only the shouted words came through, and had read them, on proclama-tions that were slapped up by billposters over other proclama-tions, now for a long time, and I had seen nothing sacred, and the things that were glorious had no glory and the sacrifices were like the stockyards at Chicago if nothing was done with the meat except to bury it. There were many words that you could not stand to hear and finally only the names of places had dignity. Certain numbers were the same way and certain dates and these with the names of the places were all you could say and have them mean anything. Abstract words such as glory, honor, courage, or hallow were obscene beside the concrete names of villages, the numbers of roads, the names of rivers, the numbers of regiments and the dates. (184–85)

In "A Clean, Well-Lighted Place," it should be noted, there are no words that seem to convey "dignity." Indeed, the first time the word "dignity" appears in the story, it is used to describe the old man, who, as the waiter watched him, "walk[ed] unsteadily" down the street "but with dignity," while later the word is used to indicate not its existence but its absence: "Nor can you stand before a bar with dignity." As for the reality behind "words," here is the older waiter's utterance of the "Lord's Prayer":

> Our *nada* who art in *nada*, *nada* be thy name thy kingdom *nada* thy will be *nada* in *nada* as it is in *nada*. Give us this *nada* our daily *nada* and *nada* us our *nada* as we *nada* our *nada*s and *nada* us not into *nada* but deliver us from *nada*; *pues nada*. (23–24)

To make clear just what is at stake in this prayerful blasphemy of a prayer, we need only recall the Catholic prayer itself. I have underlined the words the older waiter has replaced by his *nadas* to bring to the fore just what he is denying:

Our <u>Father</u> who art in <u>heaven</u>, <u>hallowed</u> be Thy name; Thy Kingdom <u>come</u>; Thy will be <u>done</u> on <u>earth</u> as it is in <u>heaven</u>. Give us this <u>day</u> our daily <u>bread</u>: and forgive us our <u>trespasses</u> as we <u>forgive those who trespass</u> against us; and <u>lead</u> us not into <u>temptation</u>, but deliver us from <u>evil</u>. <u>Amen</u>.[11]

Denied here—not just their value but their very existence—are not the abstract words of *A Farewell to Arms*—such as sacred, glorious, and sacrifice, along with the virtues encoded in the expression in vain—but words such as *Father, heaven, hallowed* ("hallow" does appear in Lt. Henry's litany), *earth, day, bread, trespasses, forgive[ness], temptation,* and *evil.* Father, heaven and hell, in this context, might well be considered conceptualized abstractions, but surely earth, day, and bread would be considered by most to be at least as real as those proper names and nominative numbers that still carry meaning for Frederic Henry. If it can be said that the strongest subtext of *A Farewell to Arms* is religious, it is equally clear that in "A Clean, Well-Lighted Place" Hemingway makes that theme fully explicit. In the story he again succeeded in drawing on the same emotional pressure and spiritual capital that had energized his novel about a young soldier's acetic experience of war and love.

NOTES

1. *Ernest Hemingway: 88 Poems*, ed. Nicholas Gerogiannis (Harcourt Brace Jovanovich/Bruccoli-Clark, 1979).

2. This and all quotations from Hemingway's manuscripts and typescripts at the John F. Kennedy Library, Boston, Massachusetts, have been permitted by Mary Hemingway with the consent of the Library.

3. The aesthetic/biographical function of the echoes here of two other texts—although of sufficient significance to call for close investigation—cannot be taken up at this time. I refer to (1) the anonymous sixteenth-century poem beginning: "O Western wind, when wilt thou blow / That the small rain down can rain?" (for an analysis of the way allusions to this text—already present in this discarded opening—work at certain points in *A Farewell to Arms*, see Charles R. Anderson's "Hemingway's Other Style," *Modern Language Notes*, LXXVI [May 1961], 434–42); and (2) Ezra Pound's "In a Station of the Metro"—"The apparition of these faces in the crowd; / Petals on a wet, black bough"—a poem which, suffice it to say here, also resulted (as in Hemingway's case) from its author's success, to quote Hugh Kenner, "after several decreasingly wordy attempts, over a period of months . . . in boiling

away the contingent distractions of the original experience" (*The Poetry of Ezra Pound* [New Directions, n.d.], p. 73).

4. *The Exile*, I (Spring 1927), 21. If the layout of the poem cannot be definitively attributed to either the author or his editor, we can nevertheless find the precedent for so breaking the opening line of the "Twenty-Third Psalm." The line is so broken, of course, in the King James Version of the Old Testament: "The Lord is my shepherd; I shall not / want." This traditional line-break is maintained even in the New International Version of the Holy Bible: "The Lord is my shepherd, I shall lack / nothing."

5. Ernest Hemingway, *A Farewell to Arms* (Scribner's, 1929), p. 3. All further references to the novel will be to this edition and will be indicated in the text by page number.

6. See Michael S. Reynolds, *Hemingway's First War: The Making of "A Farewell to Arms"* (Princeton University Press, 1976), p. 285, who suggests that Hemingway began the novel in early March 1928.

7. Reynolds devotes an appendix to rejected titles (*Hemingway's First War*, pp. 295–97). To this list, Bernard Oldsey adds three other titles in his *Hemingway's Hidden Craft: The Writing of "A Farewell to Arms"* (Pennsylvania State University Press, 1979), pp. 21–22. Paul Smith presents a still longer list, one numbering forty-three titles in "Almost All Is Vanity: A Note on Nine Rejected Titles for *A Farewell to Arms*," *The Hemingway Review*, II (Fall 1982), 74–76. I wish to take this opportunity to thank Paul Smith for his advice regarding the manuscripts at the Kennedy Library.

8. My reading of this discarded opening is not at all at odds, in my opinion, with Millicent Bell's telling interpretation of *A Farewell to Arms*. "The novel is about neither love nor war; it is about a state of mind, and that state of mind is the author's," asserts Bell. "Already on the opening page, in 1915, the voice that speaks to us exhibits that attitude psychoanalysts call 'blunting of affect,' the dryness of soul which underlies its exquisite attentiveness" ("*A Farewell to Arms*: Pseudobiography and Personal Metaphor," in James Nagel, ed., *Ernest Hemingway: The Writer in Context* [University of Wisconsin Press, 1984], pp. 111 and 112).

9. No one seems to have paid sufficient attention to the fact that it was Ezra Pound who explained in *The Exile* that "Mr. Hemingway's POEM refers to events in what remains of the French world of letters" (91–92). It's possible that Pound actually got this notion from Hemingway himself, but the early manuscripts/typescripts of the longer version of the poem indicate nothing of the sort. That these drafts are untitled as well suggests that it was not until 1927 that either Hemingway or Pound thought up the title. When the poem appeared, its title was garbled: "Nothoemist Poem." Pound penciled in a correction in every copy of *The Exile*, an act that perhaps indicated that he was the true author of the poem's title. (See Philip Young, *Ernest Hemingway* [Rinehart, 1952], p. 236.) Later Hemingway would seemingly echo Pound's explanation in *The Exile* by insisting: (1) that this title referred to the "temporary embracing of church by literary gents" (Louis Henry Cohn, *A Bibliography of the Works of Ernest Hemingway* [Random House, 1931], p. 89); and (2) that (in a letter to Philip Young, June 23, 1952) "his poem was meant to 'kid' Jean Cocteau, who had then just switched from opium to Neo-Thomism. He added that the poem did not express his own personal beliefs." (Carlos Baker, *Ernest Hemingway: A Life Story* [Scribner's, 1969], p. 596.)

Even before Hemingway sent in his poem, however, Pound had assured him that in his projected magazine "there shall be absolootly no neo-Thomism (will thot content you?)." In this letter dated 3 November 1926 (and only recently published: Jacqueline Tavernier-Courbin, "Ernest Hemingway and Ezra Pound," *Ernest Hemingway: The Writer in Context*, p. 194), Pound goes on to describe the sort of contribution he would like from Hemingway: "Re yr own stuff as I sez, there is no use me paying a printer for to set up stuff you can sell to Scribner. What one wants fer this kind of show, is short stuff, so short that space rates cant make it worth while carrying to market; and odd sizes, and unvendable matter."

10. *Winner Take Nothing* (Scribner's, 1933), p. 17. All further references to the story will be to this edition and will be indicated in the text by page number.

11. *New Baltimore Catechism No. 1*, Official Revised Edition (Benziger Brothers, n.d.), p. 3.

DONALD E. HARDY

Presupposition and the Coconspirator

Although presupposition has a long history of extensive study in philosophy and linguistics, it has been almost entirely ignored in literary studies except in a few scattered essays and book chapters.[1] This neglect is not for lack of analytically crucial examples occurring in literature. Consider the following:

(1a) I'll forget what you did for me though.

(1b) I won't forget what you did for me though.

(2a) Well, Doc, that's a nice lot of timber you've stolen.

(2b) Well, Doc, that's not a nice lot of timber you've stolen.

(3a) I just meant the coloring of their skin through the trees.

(3b) I didn't just mean the coloring of their skin through the trees.

Examples (1b), (2a), and (3a), which will serve as the basis for much of our discussion later, are from dialogue in three different short stories by

From *Style* 26, no. 1 (Spring 1992): 1–11. Copyright © 1992 Northern Illinois University Department of English and College of Liberal Arts & Sciences.

Hemingway: "The Short Happy Life of Francis Macomber," "The Doctor and the Doctor's Wife," and "Hills Like White Elephants," respectively. These sentences and their respective affirmative or negative forms contain examples of presupposition, all italicized, because the pairs of sentences share semantic content that is not affected by the negation of the affirmative, the standard test for presupposition.

Presupposition is encoded in examples (1–3) by a wh-complement clause, relative clause, and definite reference, respectively. There are many other possible syntactic and lexical encodings for presupposition, but our concern here is primarily the semiotic function of presupposition in literary dialogue. In (1a) and (1b), it is presupposed that the addressee has done something for the speaker. What is at issue in the assertions of both sentences is simply whether or not the speaker will forget it. In (2a) and (2b), it is presupposed that the doctor has stolen something. In (2a), the assertion is that the stolen something is a "nice lot of timber." In (2b), the assertion is that the stolen something is a not-so-nice lot of timber or a nice lot of something that is not timber, depending on the scope of the negative. And in (3a) and (3b), it is presupposed that there are trees and that their specific identity is known to the hearer. The assertions concern whether or not the speaker intended to refer in an earlier utterance to the "coloring of their skin." There are many other presuppositions in each of these sentences. For example, in (3a) and (3b), the skin of something is presupposed to exist, making possible a crucial metaphor in "Hills Like White Elephants," the story from which (3a) is excerpted. In this essay, I shall examine presupposition in the dialogue of the three Hemingway short stories quoted in (1–3) in order to demonstrate that dialogic presupposition can signal what Roland Barthes calls the hermeneutic code, one of the five codes Barthes identifies in *S/Z* as semiotic strategies for reading texts (18–21).[2]

The work that has been done on presupposition in literature concerns narrative, not dialogic, presupposition. Gerald Prince, in a call for detailed study of presupposition in narrative, identifies presupposition as a device by which the narrator's relationship with the narratee can be manipulated. Presupposition is recognized by Seymour Chatman as a device available to covert narrators that allows them to assume what they cannot assert without giving themselves up as overt (209–11). Roger Fowler identifies presupposed generic sentences as a device for signaling Barthes's referential/cultural code. And Jonathan Culler argues that logical presupposition—the type illustrated in examples (1–3) above—is a crucial way that poets can assume rather than assert poetic worlds but that it is perhaps not as important as what he calls pragmatic presupposition, which, as he describes it, is closer to what linguists and language philosophers refer to as felicity conditions for speech acts (100–18).

Although logical presupposition may be used to signal Barthes's referential/cultural code, as Fowler demonstrates at length in his analysis of generic sentences in *Sarrasine*, it may also be used to signal the hermeneutic code, whereby the enigmas of a narrative are established and pursued either by the narrator or by the characters themselves. These enigmas are questions that characters consciously or unconsciously strive to answer during the course of the story. For example, is Francis Macomber a coward, is Doctor Adams dishonest, and what does the woman want from the man in "Hills Like White Elephants"? We will not be concerned here with the establishing of the enigmas, but rather with the pursuit of the answers to them, which of course is not a straight line to truth. Presuppositions in literary dialogue frequently contain the promise of answer, the snares that mislead, the equivocations, the jamming due to an admission of defeat, the answers suspended or deferred, and the partial answers that Barthes outlines as steps on the crooked path to truth, or elements of the "hermeneutic sentence" (209–10).

I intend to show here that logical presupposition is frequently used in literary dialogue to signal an attempt on the part of the speaker to establish a conspiratorial relation between speaker and addressee in an effort to solve an enigma. Presupposition is used in these cases because the speaker attempts to implicate the addressee in judgments or solutions to enigmas which the addressee would likely reject if they were asserted rather than presupposed. This attempt to create a conspiracy can have at least three results. The first is that the conspiracy can be accepted by the addressee; second, it can be disputed; and third, it can be ignored. Only the first result creates an actual conspiracy in the sense that the speaker and addressee share presuppositions that other characters, the narrator, and reader typically would not accept. The presuppositions shared between speaker and addressee, then, unite them in answering (or attempting to answer) the enigmas, or hermeneutic questions, that the narrative raises. The presuppositions are denied and ignored in the second and third possibilities, but these cases are just as interesting as the first since in the second case the character typically rejects an answer to an enigma because he or she presupposes a different answer and in the third the character ignores a solution because he or she is too stupid, morally nearsighted, or preoccupied to accept the answer.

In our first story to be examined, a conspiracy is created, though it is not a very long-lasting conspiracy. One of the important questions of "The Short Happy Life of Francis Macomber" is whether Francis Macomber is a coward. Macomber did bolt from the lion, but as in so many Hemingway short stories, the major test of courage is how one reacts to a challenge; perhaps in "The Short Happy Life," Macomber's real challenge is to face his already demonstrated cowardice and overcome it. The story begins, "It was now lunch time and they were all sitting under the double green fly of the dining tent pretending that nothing had happened" (Hemingway 3). This, then, is one of Macomber's choices: that is, to ignore the fact that he "had just shown himself, very publicly, to be a coward" (4). The conflict between this solution and the solution that Macomber's wife, Margot, favors makes the first impossible to follow for long. Margot believes Francis is a coward and always will be, partly because it makes him less likely to leave her for a younger woman. If Macomber cannot simply ignore his cowardly act and if he does not want to accept Margot's answer to the question of whether he is indeed a coward, he must find another answer.

Lacking the strength to answer the question by himself, he turns to the red-faced Robert Wilson, his hunting guide on the safari, in conspiracy. The following conversation occurs after Margot goes to her tent in tears when she becomes too upset over her husband's cowardice to stay in his and Wilson's company:

> (4) "Women upset," said Wilson to the tall man. (5) "Amounts to nothing. (6) Strain on the nerves and one thing'n another."

> (7) "No," said Macomber. (8) "I suppose that I rate that for the rest of my life now."

> (9) "Nonsense. (10) Let's have a spot of the giant killer," said Wilson. (11) "Forget the whole thing. (12) Nothing to it anyway."

> (13) "We might try," said Macomber. (14) "I won't forget what you did for me though."

> (15) "Nothing," said Wilson. (16) "All nonsense." (Hemingway 5–6)

In this conversation, Wilson, who is not under the power of Margot, sticks to the first solution in (4–6) and (9–12) in asserting that Margot's behavior and even "the whole thing" of the hunting incident that morning is best forgotten. In (13), Macomber indicates that they could try to forget the whole thing, but he knows as well as Wilson that it cannot be forgotten. Later, the narrator lets us know Wilson's real thoughts about the possibility of forgetting the morning:

> "But, of course, you couldn't. The morning had been about as bad as they come" (8).

If the incident cannot be forgotten, it must be remembered. But there are at least two parts of the incident that can be remembered or forgotten independently of each other. First, Francis Macomber bolted from his wounded and charging lion. Second, Robert Wilson shot the lion. As the affirmative and negative in (1a) and (1b) show, the wh-complement clause in Macomber's (14) presupposes that Wilson did something for Francis. Macomber does not want to remember his cowardice, so he says in (14) that he will never forget the favor that Wilson did for him. He does not name this favor specifically, but the most likely possibility is saving his life in shooting his lion, although it is questionable that with Wilson and the two gun bearers between the lion and the fleeing Macomber the lion would have gone after Macomber. Hemingway's narrator tells us that the lion was waiting in the grass so that the men would "bring the crashing thing close enough so he could make a rush and get the man that held it" (Hemingway 15). Wilson was the only one with a crashing gun when the lion came out of the grass. Macomber's solution to the enigma of his cowardice, then, is not to forget that anything happened, but to reconstruct the incident so that what is remembered is Wilson's saving Macomber's life, which was not in danger once he bolted from the lion. Wilson accepts Macomber's presupposed revisionist history of (14) since he has an interest in the safari continuing with no more major upsets. There is no doubt that Wilson shot the lion, but there is room to argue about whether Wilson did this for rather than to Francis: that is, whether Francis is purely a benefactee or at least partially a malefactee of Wilson's action.

To realize the magnitude of the conspiracy that Wilson and Macomber create here, remember that Wilson not only shot Macomber's lion but accepted a kiss from Margot after he did so. In (15) and (16), Wilson appears to shrug off the thanks that Macomber offers in (14), but obviously, these sentences can be read as ambiguous comments to the effect that Macomber's assumption that his life was in danger is nonsense. That Macomber's presupposed clause is not a permanent answer is indicated by the narrator's comment in the very next paragraph that Macomber and Wilson "avoided one another's eyes while the boys set the table for lunch." Macomber's presupposed solution to the question of his cowardice lasts only moments. It falls apart completely when he asks Wilson whether anyone has to hear about the incident. Then Margot comes back from her tent and in telling them that she has "dropped the whole thing" (Hemingway 6) reminds them in a hundred ways that Macomber acted as a coward that morning.

In "The Short Happy Life," Wilson accepts the conspiracy of Macomber's presupposed clause since he has an interest in maintaining the peace. Presupposition is not always so peacefully accepted however. Consider the following conversation between Dick Boulton and Doctor Adams in "The Doctor and the Doctor's Wife":

(17) "Well, Doc," he said, "that's a nice lot of timber you've stolen."

(18) "Don't talk that way, Dick," the doctor said. (19) "It's driftwood."

(20) Eddy and Billy Tabeshaw had rocked the log out of the wet sand and rolled it toward the water.

(21) "Put it right in," Dick Boulton shouted.

(22) "What are you doing that for?" asked the doctor.

(23) "Wash it off. (24) Clean off the sand on account of the saw.

(25) I want to see who it belongs to," Dick said. . . .

(26) "It belongs to White and McNally," he said, standing up and brushing off his trousers knees.

(27) The doctor was very uncomfortable.

(28) "You'd better not saw it up then, Dick," he said, shortly.

(29) "Don't get huffy, Doc," said Dick. (30) "Don't get huffy.

(31) I don't care who you steal from. (32) It's none of my business."

(33) "If you think the logs are stolen, leave them alone and take your tools back to the camp," the doctor said. (34) His face was red.

(35) "Don't go off at half cock, Doc," Dick said.

(36) He spat tobacco juice on the log.

(37) It slid off, thinning in the water.

(38) "You know they're stolen as well as I do. (39) It don't make any difference to me."

(40) "All right. (41) If you think the logs are stolen, take your stuff and get out."

(42) "Now, Doc—"

(43) "Take your stuff and get out."

(44) "Listen, Doc."

(45) "If you call me Doc once again, I'll knock your eye teeth down your throat."

(46) "Oh, no, you won't, Doc." (Hemingway 100–01)

Perhaps the most important question of "The Doctor and the Doctor's Wife" is whether Doctor Adams is honest. The narrator tells us that Adams always "assumed" that the logging company would not come for the logs that they regularly lost in transporting them down the river. Thus, just as the question of Macomber's bravery centers on how he will face his act of cowardice in running from the charging lion, the question of Adams's honesty revolves around how he will face his theft of the logs. As the affirmative and negative in sentences (2a) and (2b) show, the relative clause in Boulton's (17) presupposes that Adams stole the timber that he hired Boulton to cut up for firewood. Thus, Boulton's solution to the hermeneutic enigma of Adams's dishonesty is that Adams must admit his dishonesty to be honest. If Adams participated in the conspiracy of honesty-in-dishonesty here that Boulton makes possible through presupposition, the question of Adams's honesty would be answered. (But, then, there would be no story.) Adams's (18) and (19) show that he rejects Boulton's conspiracy and prefers to defend his absolute honesty.

Now that we have two answers to the enigma of Adams's honesty, we read to find out whose view wins. In (25), Boulton presupposes that the logs belong to someone. The threat that this presupposition poses to Adams is best understood as a Gricean conversational implicature generated through the violation of the maxim of relevance. If the logs are driftwood, as Adams asserts in (19), then it is irrelevant to presuppose that they belong to someone. The implicature is, of course, that Adams is not only a thief but now a liar as well.[3] And in (26) Boulton asserts that the timber belongs to White and McNally. Adams again rejects Boulton's attempts at conspiracy in (28), this time by pretending that he has just been informed by Boulton that it belongs to someone and implying that he does not want timber that belongs to someone else. The doctor is still adhering to his solution to the honesty enigma.

He maintains his absolute honesty. In (31) Boulton again presupposes in the wh-complement clause that Adams steals and asserts that he does not care whom he steals from. Boulton mercilessly pursues his solution to the honesty enigma here in deliberately assuming that Adams implicitly admits to being a thief and is only concerned about whom he steals from. Adams distances himself in (33) from Boulton's conspiracy by implying through the use of "you" that it is only Boulton who thinks that the logs are stolen. And in (38) Boulton flatly asserts what he has been presupposing all along, that Adams knows that the logs are stolen. If Adams is to maintain his facade of absolute honesty, he has no choice but to attempt to throw Boulton off his land once Boulton has made the conspiracy impossible by actually asserting what he has been presupposing all along. Even though Boulton's presuppositions in (17), (25), and (31) are threatening to Adams, they are not as threatening as the assertion in (38) that Adams knows that the presuppositions are accurate whether or not he will admit it. The answer to the question of Adams's honesty is evident in his reactions to Boulton's presuppositions. The presuppositions contain the hint that he is dishonest. Paradoxically, it is his refusal of the conspiracy of petty theft that demonstrates a much more fundamental dishonesty, both with Boulton and with himself.

An outright denial of presupposition, as in "The Doctor and the Doctor's Wife," is not the only way a conspiracy based on presupposition can fail. The presuppositions can be ignored as happens in "Hills Like White Elephants." Here, I want to examine in some depth just two presuppositions in one of the woman's sentences and the man's reactions to those presuppositions. Consider the woman's sentence in (3a) above: "I just meant the coloring of their skin through the trees." The existential presuppositions, signaled by definite reference, are italicized. The context for the story is that the man and woman, lovers who have been traveling together throughout Europe, are sitting in a bar in a train station in Spain's Ebro valley waiting for a train that will take them to Madrid so that the woman can have an abortion. The alternatives of an abortion versus having the child, as well as their relationship, are the subjects of their argument. The woman apparently wishes to have the child; the man wants the woman to have an abortion. The woman apparently loves the man and wants some sort of commitment of love from him. One of the major enigmas of the story is what it is exactly that she wants from the man. The woman's love for the man is complex, minimally compounded with concerns for fertility and nature. Thus, the presuppositions that encode her questioning of the man relate to these concerns. To understand how crucial to their relationship the woman's statement about "the coloring of their skin through the trees" really is, we have to examine closely the setting for the story, as Hemingway's narrator has described it.

The hills of the valley of the Ebro occur not only in the title of the story but also in the first sentence of the story: "The hills across the valley of the Ebro were long and white. On this side there was no shade and no trees and the station was between two lines of rails in the sun." The proximate deictic marker "this" signals that the man and the woman are on the side of the station on which there are no trees. The man and woman sit at "a table in the shade." And the shade is described as being "[c]lose against the side of the building." After the man and woman order beers, she looks out to the line of hills. The narrator reports, "They were white in the sun and the country was brown and dry" (Hemingway 273). There is, then, a very good chance that the man and the woman cannot see the other side of the valley, on which there are trees. Later in the story when the woman gets up, walks to the end of the station, and looks over to the other side of the valley, the narrator reports, "Across, on the other side, were fields of grain and trees along the banks of the Ebro. Far away, beyond the river, were mountains. The shadow of a cloud moved across the field of grain and she saw the river through the trees" (276). If there are no trees through which to see the white hills on the side of the valley visible to the man and woman from where they sit, then the woman's statement containing the presuppositions that we have pointed out is problematic: "'They're lovely hills,' she said. 'They don't really look like white elephants. I just meant the coloring of their skin through the trees'" (274). We will discuss later the white elephant metaphor and the presupposition of "their skin." The more immediate question is the location of the trees of which she is presupposing the existence here. Even if the man and woman can see the other side of the valley on which there are trees, the narrator does not say that there are hills there that can be seen through the trees. The narrator mentions only mountains. And even these are not seen through trees. Only the river is seen through the trees.

One can come to one or more of at least three conclusions about the woman's presupposition. First, one might conclude that the trees are actually there and that the man and woman can see them. Second, one might decide that Hemingway made a mistake, that the narration makes it clear that the man and woman cannot see the trees and that the imagery of "their skin through the trees" is striking but inconsistent within the story. Third, one might come to the conclusion that the trees are not there on the side of the valley on which the man and woman sit, that they cannot see the other side of the valley, and that the woman deliberately presupposes in her sentence the existence of trees where she knows they do not exist. If we come to the third conclusion, there are at least two other questions. Why does the woman do this, and why does the man not ask the woman something like "What trees, dear?" when she presupposes trees where they do not exist. Instead, he replies, "'Should we have another drink?'" The woman's presupposition of the trees and her presupposition signaled by "their skin" are partial answers to the question of what she wants from the man. And the man's response to the woman's presuppositions is, in turn, an answer to her question of whether the man can give her what she wants.

Before we identify the woman's needs buried in the presuppositions and how the man's response in effect tells her that he will not meet her needs, we must make one detour to the beginning of the story. Just after the man and the woman order two beers, we are told:

> The girl was looking off at the line of hills. They were white in the sun and the country was brown and dry.
> "They look like white elephants," she said.
> "I've never seen one," the man drank his beer. (Hemingway 273)

The man's response to the woman's figurative language is revealing of his character since it is abruptly literal and since Hemingway uses the phrase "the man drank his beer" instead of the usual quote formula "the man said." The implication is that the man makes his remark into his beer and does not look up and outwards to identify the referent for "they."

Throughout the story the woman repeatedly attempts to get the man to see the emotional costs of the abortion and the man's alienation from her. In part she does this by introducing and reintroducing the image of the hills like white elephants, which at once evokes through the "white elephant" metaphor the child that the man does not want and the world of nature from which they are both alienated by traveling around on a train looking at things and trying new drinks. The woman makes two calculated attempts to get the man to look up and out to this revealing image. Her first introduction of the major image of the story does not accomplish this, even though she uses the referent "they," which the man would not be able to identify without looking out to the hills. In her second attempt she tries something more daring by referring to trees that do not exist and making the simile a tighter and stronger metaphor by presupposing the existence of "their skin." The man's failure to look up for the referent of "trees" is consistent with his alienation from the woman and from nature itself. The two presuppositions that we have discussed in the woman's "the coloring of their skin through the trees" provide partial answers to the question of what the woman wants from the man: an acceptance of her pregnancy and a closer communion with nature. The man's refusal to accept her presuppositions is an indication that he will not or cannot give the woman what she wants.

It is a commonplace to argue that Hemingway effaces himself in his narrative, although critics are still involved in the project of discovering just how it is that Hemingway does this. Fowler notes an absence of generic sentences or any other formal markers of authorial judgment in Hemingway's fiction (149–51). Hemingway achieves this effacement not only by the absence of generic sentences but by a relative lack of the use of any type of presupposition to manipulate the reader's sympathy. This is not to say that presupposition is not important in Hemingway's fiction. Although Hemingway's narrators might in many (but not all) cases be uninvolved spectators, many of Hemingway's characters are highly involved with one another and show their involvement through the use of presupposition, which at least implies shared knowledge and belief. Thus, much of the dramatic interest in the short stories that we have examined in this essay lies in seeing how presupposition helps settle the basic enigmas of the stories. Hemingway's narrator may not tell us that Francis Macomber does not have the strength to face his cowardice and overcome it, but Francis himself does when he imposes on Robert Wilson with his presupposition that Wilson did him a favor in shooting his lion. The narrator does not tell us that Doctor Adams is a thief. Merely given the narrator's comments, it is difficult to categorize Adams as a thief simply because he takes advantage of a lumber company's loss. Given the same circumstances, the narrator and readers might themselves decide to assume that the logging company would never come for the drift logs. It is Adams's reactions to Dick Boulton's unrelenting presuppositions that convince the reader of Adams's fundamental dishonesty. And the man's insensitivity to the significance of the woman's metaphorical and referential presuppositions in "Hills Like White Elephants" tells us more surely than any narrator could that the man really does not love the woman, at least not in any way that would satisfy her emotional or spiritual needs. All of the presuppositions that we have examined in these stories, whether accepted, rejected, or ignored, provide the basis for a conspiracy to answer an enigma of the hermeneutic code.

Barthes argues in *S/Z* that all five of his codes are "already-written" in the sense that they are background knowledge that we draw on in reading texts (20–21). Since I have been arguing that presupposition is used in Hemingway's dialogue as part of the hermeneutic code, it seems important to distinguish the sort of already-written intertextuality of the codes from another sense of being already written, the already-written of presuppositions. Barthes's five codes are intertextual, the result of a particular cultural literacy, so that one knows when one reads literature to look for the proairetic code (the plot), the semic code (characterization and setting), the symbolic code (the theme), the cultural code (the background cultural knowledge), and, of course, the hermeneutic code. Presupposition is not intertextual, but interpersonal, whether between narrator and reader or character and character. That Fowler has discovered that presupposition may be used to signal the cultural code indicates that presupposition may be an important formal device for encoding all of Barthes's codes. As Barthes outlines it, the cultural code signals that background cultural knowledge, which can be "physical, physiological, medical, psychological, literary, historical, etc." (20). One of the remarkable characteristics of the narrator of *Sarrasine* is that he indulges himself frequently in generic pronouncements of the following type: "J'étais plongé dans une de ces rêveries profondés ... qui saisissent tout le monde, même un homme frivole, au sein des fêtes les plus tumultueuses" ["I was deep in one of those profound reveries ... that may grip anyone, even a frivolous man, in the midst of a most entertaining party"] (Barthes 25; qtd. in Fowler 133). As Barthes comments, the narrator's references to tumultuous parties and deep daydreams are part of the cultural code (17–18). Fowler comes to the conclusion that in this and other presupposed generic sentences like it, the narrator of *Sarrasine* "invites our complicity by assuming that we share the values he announces.... The values of the in-group are worldliness, mature sexuality, hedonism, *savoir-faire*, scepticism, selfish irony" (135). And given that the reader of *Sarrasine* hears the story of Sarrasine's amorous pursuit of Zambinella as it was told, also with the use of presupposed generic sentences, to a young woman that the narrator intended to seduce, we might find in a much more detailed and extensive inspection of presupposition in both narrative and dialogue that an attempted conspiracy of some sort underlies all literary uses of presupposition, regardless of which code the presupposition might signal.

Notes

1. For an introduction to presupposition and the history of its study in philosophy and linguistics, see Levinson.

2. In the time since this paper was accepted for publication, I have had published or accepted for publication essays on metaphor in "Hills Like White Elephants" (Hardy and Hardy) and the linguistic pragmatics of politeness strategies in "The Short Happy Life of Francis Macomber" (Hardy) and "The Doctor and the Doctor's Wife" (Hardy). Presupposition is touched on in each of these essays but not from a semiotic perspective.

3. See Grice for his discussion of conversational maxims and implicatures.

Works Cited

Barthes, Roland. *S/Z*. Paris: Seuil, 1970.

———. *S/Z*. Trans. Richard Miller. New York: Hill, 1974.

Chatman, Seymour. *Story and Discourse: Narrative Structure in Fiction and Film*. Ithaca: Cornell UP, 1978.

Culler, Jonathan. *The Pursuit of Signs: Semiotics, Literature, Deconstruction.* Ithaca: Cornell UP, 1981.

Fowler, Roger. "The Referential Code and Narrative Authority." *Language and Style* 10 (1977): 129–61.

Grice, H. Paul. "Logic and Conversation." *Speech Acts.* Ed. Peter Cole and Jerry Morgan. Syntax and Semantics 3. New York: Academic, 1975. 41–58.

Hardy, Donald E. "Politeness Strategies and the Face of Honesty in Hemingway's 'The Doctor and the Doctor's Wife.'" *Language and Style* (forthcoming).

———. "Strategic Politeness in Hemingway's 'The Short Happy Life of Francis Macomber.'" *Poetics* 20 (1991): 343–62.

Hardy, Donald E., and Heather K. Hardy. "Love, Death and War: Metaphorical Interaction in Hemingway's 'Hills Like White Elephants.'" *Language and Literature* 15 (1990): 1–56.

Hemingway, Ernest. *The Short Stories of Ernest Hemingway.* New York: Scribner's, 1966.

Levinson, Stephen C. *Pragmatics.* Cambridge: Cambridge UP, 1983.

Prince, Gerald. "On Presupposition and Narrative Strategy." *Centrum* 1 (1973): 23–31.

MARGOT NORRIS

The Novel as War: Lies and Truth in Hemingway's A Farewell to Arms

The project of reevaluating Modernism in terms of the political interests that informed its formalistic claims has particularly questioned the
aesthetics of the American moderns—Pound, Eliot, Stein, Fitzgerald, and
Hemingway. Hemingway's style has suffered an especially damaging trans-
lation into its ideological determinants—for example, Walter Benn Michaels
reading the signature of simplicity ("nice" "good" "true") in Hemingway's
miraculously clean prose as the transformation of racism ("breeding") into
aesthetics (196). While revisionary skepticism has, of course, regularly
followed praise of Hemingway throughout his publication history, contemporary ideological criticism—in which New Historicism has taken the
lead—proposes a much broader challenge of the formalist New Critical can-
onization ("It is the discipline of the code that makes man human, a sense
of style or good form" [Warren 80])[1] of Modernism. At this stage a project
both impelled by this revisionary impulse, yet poised to challenge its cruder
political indictments of Hemingway, might productively launch a sharply
focused interrogation of the rhetorical and narrative maneuvers that constitute his troubled and troublesome ethic. By using textualist strategies that
revisit the tensions between narrative unreliabilities (that have traditionally
been recognized) and their function to alert the reader to their own power
of rhetorical manipulation, one can demonstrate in Hemingway's novelistic

From *Modern Fiction Studies* 40, no. 4 (1994): 689–710. Copyright © 1994 by the Purdue
Research Foundation.

treatment of World War I a series of thoughtful and shrewd maneuvers to challenge the desires and resistances that readers bring to war novels. By treating plotting and style, narrative and dialogue, as self-conscious exercises by which Hemingway recognizes (and *shows* that he recognizes) that even novelistic writing is inevitably enmeshed in an ethical function (veracity, lying, self-deception, misdirection, etc.), Hemingway's textual practices lose some of their transparency and take on the self-reflexive sophistication more usually imputed to his modernist contemporaries. While this does not solve the problem of judging the residues of either authenticity or bad faith that survive in writing when the courage to tell the truth is transformed into the courage to betray that one is lying, the Hemingway who writes *A Farewell to Arms* brings to his text an ethical sophistication that contrasts sharply with that of his character and narrator, Frederic Henry.

In *A Farewell to Arms* the stakes of "writing truly" take on special seriousness as a fictive witness to the unknowabilities of war. The novel therefore provides an excellent opportunity for testing for patterns of self-reflection that reveal an authorial willingness to problematize the ethical status of modernistic poetics. What can be demonstrated, I believe, is that Hemingway inscribes attention to ethical discourse into speech acts within and outside the narrative—an inscription that relates discrepancies between *speaking truly* and *writing truly* to problems of reception that plague ideologically invested fiction—particularly novels of love and war. We can begin by noting in *A Farewell to Arms* a moment in which Hemingway appears to stage the obverse of Walter Benn Michaels' formulation, when he shows figures transforming aestheticism into racism. When Catherine Barkley produces the lovely Shakespearean locution, "Othello with his occupation gone" (257), Frederic Henry transforms her poetry according to the modernistic poetic into the form of the short declarative sentence, whose valued simplicity is here a stark brutality: "Othello was a nigger" (257). But without attempting to separate Frederic's ugly sentiment from Hemingway's own demonstrable racism, this dialogue with its poetic juxtapositions can be read as a complex set of speech acts intended to foreground, rather than ignore or excuse, a hatefulness of character in the protagonist.[2] Catherine's Shakespearean lines, intended as a tactful reference to the lassitude brought on by Frederic's desertion, inadvertently places him in painfully embarrassing moral contrast to the courageous, victorious Moor. The vicious epithet with which he responds is meant to assault and negate the ground of contrast, but serves instead to foreground Frederic's cowardice, desertion, racism, and bad faith. But the dialogue supplements this tacit moral with a generic gloss. Catherine's poetry textualizes Frederic and interpolates him into a Shakespearean play in which—as in *A Farewell to Arms* itself—the war story and the love story are peculiarly implicated in each other. The allusion complicates the generic question which has plagued the novel since its publication[3] by raising the possibility that Hemingway here, as elsewhere, makes a self-reflexive gesture to foreground the mutually seductive relationship of war and love stories that ultimately corrupts and perjures both. *Othello* and *A Farewell to Arms* are, of course, opposites: in the former a war story is used for seduction in love; in the latter a love story seduces readers into misreading a war story.

As I will argue in a moment, Hemingway produces, and uses, critical resistance to facing and censuring Frederic Henry's hatefulnesses, in order to demonstrate reception's power to warp and suborn texts—especially fictions of love and war. He thereby has *A Farewell to Arms* perform, or stage, the lying about war induced by reception, by the desire of listeners or readers to evade its truths, that in earlier war texts he merely thematized. "Krebs found that to be listened to at all he had to lie" (243), Hemingway wrote of the returning veteran in his sketch "Soldier's Home." In telling and writing his own war story, he feels he faces a similar problem—namely that in order to be listened to, in order to give the novel a popular reception in the United States, he has to mask his war story as a love story. He thereby subordinates his preferred style, the philosophical naturalism he tests in his sketch "A Natural History of the Dead," to the signature simplicity that seems to disavow rhetorical intentions, by appearing to absorb rhetoric so completely into representation that what remains is a residue of guileless and "true" discourse. In "A Natural History of the Dead," published three years after the novel as a satirical disquisition in chapter 12 of *Death in the Afternoon*, Hemingway effectively demonstrates why he wrote *A Farewell to Arms* as he did. One is tempted to construe the essay's displacement, its being somewhat "out of place" in its textual homes (it was later included as a short story in *Winner Take Nothing*)[4], as symptomatic of its moral exile as an unwanted and transgressive text that should have found its proper place and function in Hemingway's World War I novel.

In its version in *Death in the Afternoon*, which includes the comments of the *Old lady*, "A Natural History of the Dead" may be read as an allegory of modern reading, supplementing the satirical treatment of the ideologies of eighteenth and nineteenth century naturalists and twentieth century New Humanists, for which the essay is usually read (Beegel). In the mock dialogue with the *Old lady*, the mock *Author* sets out to shock her with increasingly horrific descriptions of the physiology of dead male and female bodies, of battlefield trauma, euthanasia, and sadistic doctors, under the guise of empirical objectivity and detachment ("war has been omitted as a field for the observations of the naturalist" [133]). This mock Socratic dialogue is figured as a combat of reciprocal violence between an author prepared to assault the

reader's sensibility with brutal truths and little tact, and a passively aggressive bourgeois reader whose complacency insulates her from being disturbed
by his story's provocations. In this exteriorized truth-telling of the hidden
coercions and aggressions that govern the compact of narrative reception,
the author presents a version of the true story of war as he would actually
like to tell it, and dramatizes the responses that make it clear why he cannot:
readers are less interested in the violence and cruelty that is the truth of war
than in their own comfort and pleasure as readers. Thus the *Old lady* does not
much like the title of "A Natural History of the Dead"—"You may very well
not like any of it," (133) he tells her—nor his justification for the graphic
descriptions of body fragments he picked from the barbed wire around the
exploded Milan munitions factory. To her "This is not amusing" (137), the
Author snaps, "Stop reading it then. Nobody makes you read it" (137). But
in practice, *A Farewell to Arms* gives the *Old lady* exactly the war novel she
desires: "I like it whenever you write about love" (138).

However urgent Hemingway's sense of war as requiring a special testi-
monial veracity—"It was one of the major subjects and certainly one of the
hardest to write truly of" (*Green Hills of Africa* [70])—he perhaps promises
less to write of war truly than to write truly about what makes it "one of the
hardest to write truly of." The answer lies deeply embedded in the phenom-
enology of war itself, and in the essential disjunction between its discourses
and its activity, its ideologies and its materiality, its justifications and its facts.
"The essential structure of war, its juxtaposition of the extreme facts of body
and voice, resides in the *relation* between its own largest parts, the relation
between the collective casualties that occur *within* war, and the verbal issues
(freedom, national sovereignty, the right to a disputed ground, the extra-
territorial authority of a particular ideology) that stand *outside* war," Elaine
Scarry writes (63). Hemingway, of course, seems to thematize just this point,
when he has his narrator, Frederic Henry, declare "I was always embarrassed
by the words sacred, glorious, and sacrifice . . . I had seen nothing sacred, and
the things that were glorious had no glory and the sacrifices were like the
stockyards at Chicago if nothing was done with the meat except to bury it"
(184). But we should be wary of trusting Frederic's demystification of patri-
otic cant, however seductive its allegiance to the hard, concrete words of the
modernistic poetic ("Abstract words such as glory, honor, courage, or hallow
were obscene beside the concrete names of villages, the numbers of roads,
the names of rivers, the numbers of regiments and the dates" [185]). It fails
as a warrant of the kind of truth-telling we feel promised by the fiction of
rhetorical self-identity associated with Hemingway's style ("the facts shall be
so rightly ordered that they will speak for themselves" [Beach 82]). For all the
verbal purity it thematizes, *A Farewell to Arms* is riven with inconsistencies

and ruptures that call attention to themselves—between words and actions, words and words (particularly those of Frederic Henry the character and Frederic Henry the narrator), genres and genres. These inconsistencies are designed, I believe, to test the reader's resistance to other hypocrisies, cant, and bad faith. This ethical focus on war as a rhetorical problem—as a site of contradictions and disjunctions between its language and its unadorned material "reality" as violence—will shape the specialized, and perhaps inevitably reductive, sense of the term "war" as it is used in this essay. Insofar as it belongs to the rhetorical structure of war to mask and disavow its violence and cruelties with sentiment and idealism, the layering of the love story and the war story in *A Farewell to Arms* can be treated as an analogue to the duplicitous discourses often produced by war. Looked at in this way, *A Farewell to Arms* becomes less a novel *about* war than a novel *as* war, a text whose own relationship between what is said (or not said) and what is shown (or not shown) is constructed on the model of war's own possibilities of bad faith.

In writing *A Farewell to Arms*, Hemingway achieved a double maneuver whose outcome is a deliberate, if deliberately ineffectual, textual self-betrayal. He will have it both ways, writing the war novel readers want (a love story that transforms war casualties into the more sentimental forms of maternal and infant mortality) while thematizing and dramatizing his "lying" in a way that both discloses and conceals the narrative perjury delivered in its testimony about World War I. "How many had I killed?" Frederic Henry is asked about the Austrians. "I had not killed any but I was anxious to please—and I said I had killed plenty" (94). In fact, he kills (with help) only one man—the Italian sergeant who refuses to help him move his truck. But the narration of that act makes it very clear that this particular war casualty is produced by an act of cold-blooded murder. Readerly resistance to accepting this point (and its larger ramification, that the violence of war permits and produces much such murder) was clearly understood not only by Hemingway, but by Fitzgerald as well. Fitzgerald patently had no compunction about pointing the narration of war in the direction of readerly reception and readerly desire:

> I had a long letter sent over by F. Scott Fitzgerald in which among other things he said I must *not* under any circumstance let Lt. Henry shoot the sergeant and suggesting that after Catherine dies Frederick [sic] Henry should go to the cafe and pick up a paper and read that the Marines were holding in Chateau Thierry. This, Scott said, would make the American public understand the book better. He also did not like the scene in the old Hotel Cavour in Milano and wanted changes to be made in other places 'to make it more acceptable'. (Letter to Charles Poole, 23 January 1953 in Baker, 800)

Fitzgerald was right: the shooting of the sergeant would require much tortured critical apology to keep Frederic a hero, and critics of the 1980's were no more comfortable with the passage than Fitzgerald—"How we meet our fate is everything in Papa's world, and it is unlikely that he would have made his protagonist in this, one of his best novels, anything but honorable. Frederic Henry shoots the sergeant because, by the cold logic of war, that is what is required of him" (Nolan 274).

Hemingway seems to have set up a double system of testimony in which his style determines its ethical value in a perverse test against readerly desire. Truth is less a fidelity to experience than an act of narrative aggression: a willingness to frustrate and disappoint readers by telling them not what they want to hear, but what they don't want to hear. A story that would make Frederic Henry dishonorable is intolerable to a reader and critic like Charles Nolan. But Papa's concern with how we meet our fate extends to readers as well as soldiers. In his writing, therefore, the warrant of truth is not a historical referent, a fact, but the courage to inflict a cruelty (in the form of a cruel truth) that rhetorically replicates the aggression of combat. Insofar as it embeds this cruel truth in an ideology that American soldiers must, at all costs, be portrayed as honorable, the novel also replicates the "cold" logic (that can mask murder as duty and honor) of war. That is why I say *A Farewell to Arms* is less a novel about war than (figuratively) a novel as war.

Because "writing truly" seemed to imply claims to historical accuracy, Hemingway's World War I experience has been consistently tested for its ethical reliability as a script to the novel—in spite of Hemingway's own disclaimers ("Remember Charlie in the first war all I did mostly was hear guys talk; especially in hospital and convalescing. Their experiences get to be more vivid than your own. You invent from your own and from all of theirs" [Letter to Charles Poole, Baker, 800]). Hemingway's stylistic ethic was thought to have placed a great burden on the discursive proportion and economy with which war experience is narrated (Beach, 82), because it has displaced the heroic from soldierly action onto writerly action, and situated heroism in the act of truth-telling and veracious witness. James Nagel's 1989 "Hemingway and the Italian Legacy" (Villard and Nagel) is perhaps the most rigorous and convincing examination of this period of Hemingway's life, and his meticulous sifting of fact and fiction produces much precise information and correction of the biography, and biographical idolatry (compare *Ernest Hemingway, Man of Courage*). Nagel confirms that Hemingway was not a lieutenant in the Italian army ("Hemingway was in the Red Cross at all times, never in any army or combative position" 252) and "Contrary to many people's impressions, Hemingway did not receive his injuries while serving as an ambulance driver" (22). He was, in fact, a dispenser of refreshments, hit after only six days of canteen service while handing out chocolate to soldiers. Nagel treats as unverifiable Hemingway's account in his 18 August 1918 letter to his parents, that he carried a wounded Italian on his back while his legs were full of shrapnel ("The 227 wounds I got from the trench mortar didn't hurt a bit at the time. . . . They couldn't figure out how I had walked 150 yards with a load with both knees shot through and my right shoe punctured two big places [sic]. Also over 200 flesh wounds" [*Selected Letters* 14]). According to Nagel, "Ernest's suggestion that even after he was hit by machine-gun bullets he still assisted a wounded soldier, walking 150 yards, cannot be confirmed with certainty" (221).

Whether or not the wounded Hemingway carried the wounded soldier on his back, he clearly understood—in translating the story to fiction—the ambiguous ethical economy of the equivocal story. Heroism is not served by a perjured testimony that fails to compel belief, and Hemingway decides to have Frederic Henry earn his moral credit by truth-telling rather than by self-sacrifice—"'They say if you can prove you did any heroic act you can get the silver. . . . Did you do any heroic act?' 'No,' I said. 'I was blown up while we were eating cheese'" (63). Frederic's candor earns his narrative a credulity that would serve the reader better by strain—particularly because his motives are themselves undecidable. For example, Frederic may have resisted fabricating false heroic tales because he feared skepticism of their implausibilities—"Gordini says you carried several people on your back but the medical major at the first post declares it is impossible" (63). In the end, in spite of his disclaimers ("I didn't carry anybody. I couldn't move" [63]), Frederic receives the undeserved decorations ("'Did you get the boxes with the medals?' . . . 'The boxes will come later'" [164]) and like Hemingway (who received his medal in the mail rather than from the hand of the Italian King or from General Diaz, as his brother Leicester claimed [Nagel, 253–254]) he wears them ("I opened my cape so he could see the two ribbons" [164]). Is wearing an unearned decoration a *lie*? If so, does the falsity of Frederic the character impugn the honesty of Frederic the narrator, to whose credibility we are subject as readers? The question is important because the text continually invites us to match Frederic's words, both as character and as narrator, with his experiences and his deeds, and the two are not always in accord.[5]

The critical tradition has long invested ethical value in Hemingway's stylistic strategy of verbal economy, whose quantitative calculus is one of reduction and subtraction, and whose qualitative form is one of containment and the prevention of excess or spillage.[6] Less is more, in the stylistic morality of the Hemingway discourse, and truth is invested in silence rather than speech. Unlike the voluble Italians in *A Farewell to Arms* who always say too much, and whose excess produces the inflation and the lie that damage credibility, the laconic Frederic practices a stoicism in which the suppression of truth and its investment in conspicuous silence are simultaneously equated with a manly virtue. "We have heroes too," Catherine Barkley sniffs at the boasting Ettore Moretti, "But usually, darling, they're much quieter" (124). The problem this specific ethical coding of language creates in the text is that it privileges gaps and omissions as signs of candor and courage by denying their opposite functions as lies or deceptions. The modernistic poetic of simplicity depends on formal principles of selection that are not purely aesthetic and ethically neutral. They depend, indeed, on the rigorous rhetorical control of a variety of unaesthetic contents (pain, excessive feeling, erratic behaviors, filth and poverty, masses and crowds, etc.).[7] The equation of verbal form with moral control creates an ethical economy in which truth in the modernistic poetic is itself reckoned as a disfiguring addition—an excess, excrescence, and waste—that must be expelled from discourse and occluded. Hemingway chooses to have the text of *A Farewell to Arms* perform or act out the thematized relationship between containment and truth.

In the novel, the narrative describing Catherine's preparation of Frederic for surgery rigorously suppresses the procedure named in Hemingway's early sketch for the novel called "A Very Short Story" ("When they operated on him she prepared him for the operating table; and they had a joke about friend or enema" [239]). In describing this operation, the discourse of Frederic the narrator obeys Catherine's injunction that Frederic the character censor his thoughts and words, while Catherine's actions perversely reverse her words: while violating the containment of Frederic's bowels, she enjoins him not to violate his verbal containment—"And, darling, when you're going under the ether just think about something else—not us. Because people get very blabby under an anaesthetic" (103). Instead of describing the action, the enema he receives at Catherine's hands, Frederic doubles or repeats her interdiction: his censorship thus fronts itself with her censorship to shield the reader from an unaesthetic and unerotic image. This novelistic moment might be seen as paradigmatic of the novel as a whole, as the tightly controlled and contained love story—that articulates its own control and containment—is offered to shield the reader from unappealing and appalling images of war. The narration, like the text, enacts a euphemism—("Now you're all clean inside and out" [104]; "I was clean inside and outside and waiting for the doctor" [105])—to avoid naming the figurative excrements—the moral squalor and cruelties—we would rather deny as a feature of war.

By juxtaposing dirty and clean with truth and lying, the text puts in place a tropology of discourse that constitutes the "clean" prose of Modernism by expelling the dirty and embarrassing truths of love and war, and by expelling the realism of its more vulgar and obscene discourses ("they had a joke about friend or enema"). At the same time, the text does not lie as much as it performs or stages the logic and practice of lying. Thus the narration performs the lovers' discourse at the same time that it thematizes it as a compact of lying. When Catherine asks Frederic how many women he has had, he says "None":

> "You're lying to me."
> "Yes."
> "It's all right. Keep right on lying to me. That's what I want you to do. . . ." (104)

Catherine, of course, wants a lie spoken that she herself does not believe, and she asks Frederic to extend his lying to other discourses of love— between men and their prostitutes, for example—"Does she say she loves him? Tell me that. . . ." "Yes. If he wants her to." The complicity of lying is extended to the point where it turns back on itself and can no longer speak a truth. When Catherine asks Frederic if he ever told other women that he loved them, he, of course, lies about having lied to them:

> "But you never did? Really?"
> "No."
> "Not really. Tell me the truth."
> "No," I lied. (105)

The result of the compact of lying between Catherine and Frederic is that he tells her lies that she knows, and desires, as lies.

The echoic structure of the novel's dialogues (like the mirrored structure of some of its incidents, as I will discuss later) makes discourse reciprocal on many textual levels: between the lovers, between the love story and the war story, between the text and its readers as the text tells readers what they want to hear and readers interpret the text as the narration prompts them to interpret it. The structure borrows, as Hemingway is no doubt perfectly aware, from the narcissism of Romanticism—both in its Shelleyan versions of having lovers constructed as siblings, twins, or symmetrical types, and its Victorian revisitations most prominent in the passions of *Wuthering Heights* ("I am Heathcliff")—the novel that Catherine and Frederic, in naming their unborn offspring "young Catherine," appear tacitly to claim as their eponym. By thematizing the lovers' narcissism as constructed on the principle of the mirror and the echo—Catherine's "I do anything you want" [106] and its dialogical version of "I say anything you want" in the novel—Hemingway maps the politics of the male author onto the representations within the text.

Female representation (and self-representation) is thematically staged as a product of male desire constructed as a double mirror (men creating women as conforming themselves to male fantasies of women). If Catherine, the character, is a male construction, a male lie about what women say to men, she at least announces that she is a construction of male desire, a product of doing, saying, and being whatever Frederic wants, or whatever she imagines Frederic wants—"I'll be a fine new and different girl for you" (304). The precious quality of some of Catherine and Frederic's "love talk" results from the mirror-like quality of the reciprocity produced by the mandate to say what the other wants to hear. During their tryst in the Milan hotel room before Frederic is shipped back to the front, they engage in a dialogue in which his part consists largely of a catalogue of terms of endearment prompted by Catherine's need to avert the argument ("Oh, hell, I thought, do we have to argue now?" [152]) threatened by her feeling of degradation ("I never felt like a whore before" [152]). Her corrective—"Come over, please. I'm a good girl again" (152)—is repeated by Frederic ("You're my good girl" [153]) and elaborated throughout their talk with a set of aesthetic adjectival variations ("You're a lovely girl" ..."You're a grand girl" ..."You're a fine simple girl" [153]) that Catherine herself affirms at the end of the set, "I am a simple girl" (153). The product of this reductive and repetitive amorous taxonomy is to make Catherine an empty girl, a cipher (Millicent Bell calls her an "inflated rubber woman available at will to the onanistic dreamer" [114]). The text refuses to divulge or even imagine a "true" content for Catherine or to break the discursive containment that makes her a mere vessel for an imagined male desire. Her fate is virtually allegorical: to deliver only a dead male, a male form rather than the reincarnated version of her female self ("young Catherine") that she desired. Catherine dies as though her only rhetorical content or self had been spilled by her delivery, in a gesture cruelly figurative of her poetic status as male echo in this text.

But my purpose in exploring the mirrored and echo-like structures of the love story and its discourses is less to judge its politics than to make visible the role discursive symmetries and reciprocities play in reception. The lovers are *shown* creating a set of scripts that textualize their situation, that turn their communications into a poetic dialogue geared to appease each other's sense of aesthetic pleasure, and each other's expectations of how lovers speak in love stories. The ethical issues of the novel's sexual politics are thereby located more interestingly in its manipulation of the reader and the novel's reception than in its role as either representation or behavioral model for the sexes. Furthermore, by focusing the crux of the love story on its effects *as a story*, I plan to argue that in thematizing itself as an instrument for producing and controlling readerly desire, it makes visible the far more obscure and disturbing politics of the war story's narrative effects. In this way, the love story and the war story can be read against each other, as forming an interpretive system that opens alternatives and challenges to more traditional thematic and philosophical readings. For example, in addition to interpreting love as the "separate peace" that permits escape and redemption in a world of war, or love as entrapment and subjection to the malevolent fate that governs war, love may also be seen as an experience that parallels war in its obligation to conform to the idealistic and aesthetic expectations of those to whom it is *told*. By treating love and war as narrations by the same voice, the same figure and subjectivity, the reader can test the ideology and philosophy of one against the other, and thereby identify astounding contradictions, disjunctions, and hypocrisies that confound both sentimental and nihilistic readings of the novel's ending.

Specifically, Frederic's narration offers us two intimate testimonies to the fact of death—the Italian sergeant's and Catherine's—that test both his logic and his ethics, his sense of conceptual order and his sense of responsibility and justice. Frederic's failure to acknowledge that both deaths (not only the one he suffers, but also the one he inflicts) must be weighed as evidence in his philosophical meditations on fate and cosmic justice, produces a corresponding refusal and resistance in the reader to deprivilege and demythify certain habits of reading and interpretation. The result is that the novel is read much as war itself is frequently read or understood: with philosophical and ideological rationalizations denying and occluding both violence and responsibility. But before comparing Frederic's comportment toward death in his double role—how he acts, and what he says, in relation to the deaths that surround him—it is necessary to examine three episodes of the Caporetto retreat as tests of self-presentation and narrative consistency: the soldiers and the virgins, Frederic's killing of the sergeant, and his desertion in the face of execution.

By having the love story frame the Caporetto retreat, Hemingway surrounds the war story with the love story in a way that causes the conventions of one to contaminate and distort the conventions of the other. Readers interpret the war incidents through the filter of the love story, and submit both narratives to a moral ideology that conflates *eros* and *agape* to equate the lover, the man with the ability to love, with the goodness of the good man. But in *A Farewell to Arms*, this conventional pressure will warp the moral equation in such peculiar and sinister ways that one overlooks the lover's equivocal relation to wartime rape, and *un*equivocal relation to wartime murder. Frederic's treatment of vulnerable women at the front participates in a brutal and ugly ritual of war: threatening very young girls with rape. Frederic's narrative account of this incident gives the reader ample information to assess the extent to which the provincial pubescent sisters are being terrorized: "Every time he said the word the girl stiffened a little. Then sitting stiffly and looking at him she began to cry. I saw her lips working and then tears came down her plump cheeks. . . . The older one, who had been so fierce, began to sob" (196). Yet the text implicitly allows Frederic's tenderness to Catherine to carry over as a dubious warrant for their safety, as though he would let nothing happen to the girls. As a result we are barely prompted to remark Frederic's own threatening gestures toward the girls—"'All right,' I said and patted her knee. I felt her stiffen away when I touched her. . . . Aymo put his hand on the elder girl's thigh and she pushed it away. He laughed at her" (196). Nor does the text encourage us to notice Frederic's refusal to intervene, as commanding officer, in the menacing conduct of his men, or to grasp the import of his sleepy thoughts: "Those were a couple of fine girls with Barto. A retreat was no place for two virgins. Real virgins. Probably very religious. If there were no war we would probably all be in bed. In bed I lay me down my head. Bed and board. Stiff as a board in bed. Catherine was in bed now" (197). "Stiff" had been used repeatedly by the narration to describe the girls' fear and resistance to the men's vulgar verbal and manual aggressions. "Stiff as a board in bed" therefore alludes to Frederic's discomfort and fatigue without ceasing to serve as a code for a sexual erection, and the virgins' terrified resistance to what he knows they perceived as a threat of rape ("I felt her stiffen away when I touched her" [196]). The girls are saved neither by Frederic's chivalry nor his authority as commanding officer, but by their own mistrustful and fearful instincts—"'Come on,' Aymo said to the girls. . . . The older sister shook her head. They were not going into any deserted house. . . . 'They are difficult,' Aymo said" (200). Frederic, the character, never interferes with the designed rape, just as Frederic the narrator never disapproves. The love story has blotted out or erased the earlier Frederic who patently favored Catherine as a free whore ("This was better than going every evening to the house for officers where the girls climbed all over you" [30]), but brings him back, fleetingly, in his unguarded descent into sleep during the retreat. The narrative both disavows and affirms the legitimacy of Catherine's feelings about her ambiguous sexual status ("I never felt like a whore before" [152]) by leaving the unregenerate Frederic in place as a textual memory.

Hemingway further uses the moral credit as a loving and decent man that Frederic's love for Catherine earns him, to work a complex double ethical maneuver in writing the episode of Frederic's killing of the Italian sergeant. Hemingway conjoins two narrative strategies—a detailed and virtually unambiguous description of the action with an utterly impersonal, objective narrative that betrays no emotion. This action without affect places the reader in a position of judgment without a clear moral compass, and with the necessity of judging both an action and an act of narration. Since this episode confronts readers with behavior that violates norms of decency and honor in their protagonist, they are placed under immense hermeneutical pressure to rationalize and justify that behavior if the story is to sustain itself as Fitzgerald's kind of war story: one in which our boys are heroic and gallant, and all the atrocities and cruelties are committed by the other side. Charles Nolan exemplifies this pressure, as he continually begs the question by taking as his premise ("As a decent man and a man of honor" [272]; "As a man of honor, Frederic will keep his commitments and do his duty" [273]; "To make Frederic less than heroic is to undercut his character and diminish Hemingway's meaning" [273]) the very point in dispute in reading the episode. The critical situation is thus one of double jeopardy: while the episode places readers under obligation to conduct a hermeneutical court martial of Frederic's acts, readers are themselves placed on trial in a test of their ethics of reading. Hemingway's text functions to act on the reader, prodding readers into committing a series of interpretive outrages that simultaneously allow them to transform *A Farewell to Arms* into an ideologically acceptable war story, but only at the price of colluding with the specific deeds and their tacit disavowals in the narrative.

By designing the shooting of the sergeant to serve as the mirror image of Frederic's desertion, Hemingway places the reader in the excruciating hermeneutical position of recognizing, yet desperately wanting to resist, the troubling, silent countertext to the war story and the love story that we have come to expect and want. With the killing of the sergeant, the novel splits into the two novels adumbrated by the epigraph from Marlowe's *The Jew of Malta*— "Thou hast committed—/ Fornication—but that was in another country; and besides, the wench is dead." Hemingway, who titled the short stories prefatory to the novel "In Another Country," and "In Another Country—Two" (a late title for "Now I Lay Me"), can be seen as having inscribed two versions of the same novel within *A Farewell to Arms*. The love story invites us to assimilate Frederic's killing to itself, as an alternate example of the soldier's honor—perhaps the unspecified thing that Krebs in "Soldier's Home" calls "the only thing for a man to do, easily and naturally" (244)—some sort of traditional test of his intestinal fortitude to be able to kill in war when he must. But Frederic's shooting of the sergeant can (and I would argue, ultimately must) also be read and named as the transgression—Murder—committed in another moral country than that of the ideologically ingratiating version of the novel that has, chiefly, been canonized. If one has no brief for exonerating Frederic, every element of the incident can be discerned as carefully chosen to make Frederic's shooting of the sergeant indefensible. The victim is an Italian, an ally, not an enemy soldier. He is an engineer rather than a warrior. He has no military connection to Frederic's small troop, to which he is attached accidentally, temporarily, involuntarily, to hitch a ride during the retreat. He in no way threatens Frederic or any of the soldiers or civilians in his charge, and there is no indication in the narrative that the sergeant is even armed. He is shot in the back while walking, then running, away. The killing is not done in panic, or without premeditation: when the sergeant is not dead, Frederic gives Bonello his gun to finish him off, and when it fails to fire, tells him how to cock it to make it shoot. Although the retreat certainly makes it perilous and stressful, the situation is neither combat, nor self-defense, nor a life and death crisis: Hemingway contrives it to resemble as much as possible a civilian traffic jam ("Still, traffic could tie up in cities when every one was awake" [197]) in which the sergeant is an ungrateful hitchhiker who refuses, in a stressful road emergency, to help the people who gave him a ride. Frederic quite simply shoots in the back a soldier who wants to leave an *ad hoc* situation that has come to seem very dangerous to him.

There is no ambiguity in the text about the existential "facts" of the killing of the sergeant. What makes the shooting troubling for the reader is the incident's relation to the speech act in which it is embedded. Since neither the Frederic of the action, nor the Frederic of the narration, attempt to interpret the killing or draw it into a symbolic or moral order, the text fails to identify its significance. The "facts" are "cold"—embedded in the silence of an emotional and cognitive vacuum that makes it impossible to apply even Hemingway's hedonistic morality, "what is moral is what you feel good after and what is immoral is what you feel bad after" (*Death in the Afternoon* 4). There is no indication of remorse, regret, pleasure, satisfaction, or even memory past the point of narration in the narrative discourse, and Nolan infers that "To his credit, his action makes him feel bad" (274) purely from Frederic's indecipherable refusal to laugh with Bonello about the killing. The narrative account of the killing stops at an empirical level, giving evidence but no witness, no testimony of the self's vision or feeling that could endow the incident with significance or meaning in the story. Meaning emerges elsewhere—in the text's dialogical manipulation of the plot that obliges readers to adjudicate similarities and differences between two incidents with a sharply reciprocal structure: Frederic's shooting of the Italian, and the Italians' threat to shoot him. The second incident provides us with feelings and principles of action and judgment that can be applied retrospectively to the first. The exercise becomes a court martial of Frederic's good faith as excuse is matched against excuse, outrage against outrage, transgression against transgression.

Hemingway addresses the most compelling justification for the killing of the sergeant, that Frederic lawfully executed a deserter under military law or code, through its narrative reflection in the act of the carabinieri "executing officers of the rank of major and above who were separated from their troops"

(224). Frederic's jurisdiction over the two Italian sergeants is no clearer than the battle police's right to discipline him. The sergeant's desertion is as questionable as Frederic's; he too may have been merely attempting to rejoin his unit as surely as Frederic was attempting to rejoin his at Pordenone. Nor does Frederic's action receive ready extratextual support. Although military law in most Western nations provides for summary as well as for judicial punishment of soldiers,[8] such discipline is left to the commanding officers of military units ("In the majority of countries, summary penalties can be inflicted only by officers not lower than the rank of captain" [*The New Encyclopaedia Britannica* 12:195]). Even in case of the most serious breaches of discipline on the battlefield, "mortal punishment" has historically required some sort of tribunal, like the "drumhead court" invoked by analogy in Melville's *Billy Budd*. Indeed, Hemingway insures that if Frederic mistakenly thought he had an obligation to shoot a deserter under some mysterious military code,[9] his action becomes arbitrary and inconsistent when—even before his mistreatment by the carabinieri, he decides not to report the desertion of Bonello. The judicial and transgressive situation of Bonello is much clearer than that of the sergeant: Bonello is formally under Frederic's command, and Bonello explicitly deserts in order to give himself up to the enemy. Piani further makes it clear that in pleading for Bonello, he recognizes that he is asking Frederic to abrogate a military responsibility: "'Can't you just put him down as taken prisoner?' 'I don't know.' 'You see if the war went on they would make bad trouble for his family.'... 'I won't make a report that will make trouble for his family,' I went on with our conversation" [219]. This conversation raises the possibility of a troublesome gap in the narrative logic: namely, that Frederic agrees to hush up the desertion of Bonello because he is afraid that Piani (and Bonello) could in turn report him for shooting the sergeant.

The reader is blinded to the ethical perversities of Frederic's acts by the ethical warrant seemingly bestowed on the narration by his silence. Frederic's silence appears to guarantee both courage (lack of justification, defense, apology, or contrition) and truth (lack of self-serving feeling or explanation), while averting other possibilities, such as blind fear and panic. When Frederic is captured by the carabinieri, he loses his cool both as a character ("'Why isn't there somebody here to stop them?' I said. 'Why haven't they blown the bridge up? Why aren't there machine guns along this embankment?'" [211]), and as narrator ("I was very angry" [211]). Frederic is also very frightened: beneath the mock-officiousness of his protest he can't control his voice ("'What's the meaning of this?' I tried to shout but my voice was not very loud" [222]). His appeal to military protocol ("Don't you know you can't touch an officer?" [222]) precisely mirrors the sergeant's earlier appeal to him ("You can't order us. You're not our officer" [204]), just as the carabinieri's rationale for killing

("*A basso gli ufficiali*'! Down with the officers!" [219]) precisely mirrors Bonello's rationale for killing the sergeant ("all my life I've wanted to kill a sergeant"
[207]). In his bitter judgment of the carabinieri, Frederic the narrator delivers—without irony or recognition—a perfect if inadvertent self-indictment
of his own comportment in shooting the sergeant, "The questioners had all
the efficiency, coldness and command of themselves of Italians who are firing
and are not being fired on" (223).

Frederic's narration does not explicitly lie, but its factualism riddles
it with holes and blindnesses. For example, his mourning of the desertion
of Bonello is marked by a significant oversight that he catches neither at
the time of his rumination, nor during its reportage: "It seemed so silly for
Bonello to have decided to be taken prisoner. There was no danger. We had
walked through two armies without incident. If Aymo had not been killed
there would never have seemed to be any danger. No one had bothered us
when we were in plain sight along the railway. The killing came suddenly and
unreasonably" (218). There was no danger? For the Italian sergeant he and
Bonello killed there was surely quite mortal danger, and to the sergeant the
killing must have come as suddenly and unreasonably as the killing of Aymo.
Frederic's erasure of this shooting in his thinking about the war and about
death persists throughout his subsequent narration. In tracking how Frederic processes his experiences philosophically, this erasure or amnesia about
the shooting becomes visible as a problem of reading, as Frederic's refusal
to assimilate this incident to the remaining text of his war experience. His
"separate peace" depends on a reading protocol of his experience that permits
him an unruffled self-righteousness. In constructing the critical register of his
narrative, Frederic banishes his shooting of the sergeant from the categories
of senseless deaths (Catherine's, Aymo's) that become the philosophical "evidence" for his famous stoical fatalism.

The peculiar and suspect philosophical outcome of this selectively muti-
lated reading process is the nihilism that assigns war and death to a motive-
less cosmic malignancy: "Now Catherine would die. That was what you did.
You died. You did not know what it was about. You never had time to learn.
They threw you in and told you the rules and the first time they caught you
off base they killed you. Or they killed you gratuitously like Aymo" (327). The
syntactic peculiarities of Frederic's language—the shift from passive to active
constructive ("You died . . . they killed you") with its unreferenced pronomial
agent—are marked, by the preceding novelistic events, with the silent echo
of the grammar of the now perjured truth of agency ("You died" [*you were
killed*]; "they killed you" [*I killed him*]; "they killed you gratuitously like Aymo"
[*I killed the sergeant gratuitously*]). Frederic's thoughts are textually haunted by
the ghost of the counternarrative from another ethical country whose story

tells him (and us) that he committed murder, and the man is dead. At the end of the novel, the reader becomes witness to the witness, and catches the witness in a perversion of logic that amounts to a lie about the truth of war. Frederic knows, as the reader knows from Frederic's own account, that the killing of war is not done by an agent-less, will-less, corporate machine—a deific, irresponsible, unresponsive "they" stripped of purpose, necessity, reason, or heart. The killing of war was done, at least in this instance, without purpose, necessity, reason, or heart by the American soldier, Frederic Henry.

The philosophical climax of the novel, Frederic Henry's theological parable about the ants on the burning log, invokes a patently false analogy that uses two modes of dying to illustrate two modes of inadvertency in the killing of people in wartime. The fire represents combat death, with soldiers like ants incapable of directing their movements towards a place of safety where there is no danger. The water Frederic tossed on the log (not to save the ants, but to rinse his whiskey cup) deftly figures his aquatic desertions, alone and with Catherine, his attempts to escape the fires of war by water only to have Catherine 'steamed' to death, as it were—the fire of war coloring, or heating, her own fate to die in the rain ("I'm afraid of the rain because sometimes I see me dead in it" [126]). Frederic's parable is designed to neutralize agency by absorbing the deaths war produces, or encompasses, into inevitability, inadvertency, and indifference. The novel's philosophical conclusion summarizes the novel's final generic self-contradiction. *A Farewell to Arms* ends as a love story masking and protecting a war story from the truth of its own violence, and its own lies. If from classical times, literature reflects how war lies about itself—as Wilfred Owen claimed ("The old Lie")—then Hemingway's own separate peace with his resistant readership is to give us a novel that textually performs just this function of war.

Notes

1. Robert Penn Warren's 1951 essay on Hemingway exemplifies the New Critical need to privilege form and style into an ethic ("It is more important because, ultimately, it is a moral achievement" 80). Style supplemented the dreaded *nada* engulfing the modern world ("This is Hemingway's world, too, the world with nothing at center" 82).

2. Mine is a more extreme and polemical statement of the disjunction between narrator and text that James Phelan calls *distance*—"the relation between Hemingway as author and Frederic as narrator; it is a function of the extent to which Hemingway endorses Frederic's understanding of and judgments about the events he reports" (Donaldson 53–54).

3. See the early reviews of the novel published in *Stephens* 69–104, which are, in general, marked by the tension of attempting to evaluate the crossing of the war story and the love story, and the strange disjunctions of tone, sentiment,

and philosophy this fusion or superimposition produces. My own response to this generic dilemma is to twist Robert Penn Warren's description of *A Farewell to Arms* as "the great romantic alibi for a generation" (76) by arguing that this operation of the romantic alibi, of translating one kind of story into another so that cruelties or moral bankruptcies can be disguised by romance and love, is immanent in the text and produced by its narrative and stylistic performance.

4. Susan Beegel's extensive and useful treatment of the piece explores its critical neglect as a generic problem: "Yunck in particular dislikes this combination of genres, and objects to Hemingway's using a short story as 'a vehicle for miscellaneous criticism'" (32).

5. My argument adds textual incrimination to such excellent readings of the problem of narrative unreliability as James Phelan's, and Gerry Brenner's ("it is because he is preoccupied with his feelings and experience, rather than with our understanding, that Frederic is an inconsiderate, and ultimately an untrustworthy, narrator" (35). My aim is to demonstrate that the text is contaminated by, and replicates, Frederic's narrative pliability as a character—his tendency to tell people what they want to hear—because the narrative issues of love and war exert tremendous ideological pressures both within and outside the text.

6. See, for example, Smith, Beegel, and Brenner.

7. Maud Ellmann's brilliant analysis of "The Waste Land" elaborates the implication of the war dead in the obsessional formal strategies ("The text's integrity dissolves under the invasion of its own disjecta" [98]) through which modernism sought to grapple with the abjection of filth, bodily effluvia, and verbal trash.

8. "In Great Britain, the United States, and other common-law countries, there is usually a right of appeal against summary punishment awarded through the military chain of command and extending to the highest authority. In other countries, the appeal will lie to [sic] a tribunal" (*The New Encyclopaedia Britannica* 195).

9. If casual execution, like the sergeant's, is unimaginable for a debatable desertion, still less can it be justified for looting. Hemingway, anticipating that the sergeant's looting would elicit a highly charged response ("Looting, Frederic knows, is a despicable act of greed" [Nolan 271]), carefully writes in Bonello's counter-looting to test the ethics of adjudicating this issue. When Charles Nolan writes "As a decent man and a man of honor, Frederic recognizes the inappropriateness of the sergeant's stealing and reprimands the engineer for it" (272), he fails to note that as a decent man and a man of honor, Frederic does not reprimand Bonello for looting the dead man's pockets. "Bonello, sitting behind the wheel, was looking through the pockets of the sergeant's coat. 'Better throw the coat away,' I said" (206). Frederic does not tell him to restore its contents first.

WORKS CITED

Baker, Carlos, ed. *Ernest Hemingway: Selected Letters 1917–1961.* New York: Charles Scribner's Sons, 1981.

Beach, Joseph Warren. "Style in *For Whom the Bell Tolls.*" *Ernest Hemingway: Critiques of Four Major Novels.* Ed. Carlos Baker. New York: Charles Scribner's Sons, 1962.

Beegel, Susan F. *Hemingway's Craft of Omission: Four Manuscript Examples.* Ann Arbor: UMI Research P, 1988.

Bell, Millicent. "*A Farewell to Arms*: Pseudoautobiography and Personal Metaphor." *Ernest Hemingway: The Writer in Context.* Ed. James Nagel. Madison: The U of Wisconsin P, 1984. 107–128.

Brenner, Gerry. *Concealments in Hemingway's Works.* Columbus: Ohio State UP, 1983.

Ellmann, Maud. *The Poetics of Impersonality: T. S. Eliot and Ezra Pound.* Cambridge: Harvard UP, 1987.

Hemingway, Ernest. *Death in the Afternoon.* New York: Charles Scribner's Sons, 1960.

———. *A Farewell to Arms.* New York: Charles Scribner's Sons, 1957.

———. *Green Hills of Africa.* New York: Charles Scribner's Sons, 1963.

———. *The Short Stories of Ernest Hemingway.* New York: The Modern Library, 1938.

Michaels, Walter Benn. "The Souls of White Folk." *Literature and the Body.* Ed. Elaine Scarry. Baltimore: Johns Hopkins UP, 1988. 185–209

"Military Law." *The New Encyclopaedia Britannica.* 15th Edition. Vol. 12. Chicago: U of Chicago P, 1984. 194–197.

Nolan, Charles J., Jr. "Shooting the Sergeant—Frederic Henry's Puzzling Action." *College Literature.* Fall 11:3 (1984): 269–275.

Phelan, James. "Distance, Voice, and Temporal Perspective in Frederic Henry's Narration: Successes, Problems, and Paradox." *New Essays on 'A Farewell to Arms'.* Ed. Scott Donaldson. New York: Cambridge UP, 1990. 53–73.

Scarry, Elaine. *The Body in Pain.* New York: Oxford UP, 1985.

Singer, Kurt, and Jane Sherrod. *Ernest Hemingway, Man of Courage: A Biographical Sketch of a Nobel Prize Winner in Literature.* Minneapolis: T. S. Denison & Company, Inc., 1963.

Smith, Julian. "Hemingway and the Thing Left Out." *Ernest Hemingway: Five Decades of Criticism.* Ed. Linda Welshimer Wagner. Michigan State UP, 1974. 188–200.

Stephens, Robert O., ed. *Ernest Hemingway: The Critical Reception.* Burt Franklin & Co., Inc., 1977.

Villard, Henry Serrano, and James Nagel, eds. *Hemingway in Love and War: The Lost Diary of Agnes von Kurowsky, Her Letters, and Correspondence of Ernest Hemingway.* Boston: Northeastern UP, 1989.

Warren, Robert Penn. "Ernest Hemingway." *Five Decades of Criticism.* Ed. Linda Welshimer Wagner. Michigan State UP, 1974. 75–102.

ROBERT PAUL LAMB

Hemingway and the Creation of Twentieth-Century Dialogue

[Hemingway's] is an obscuring and at the same time a revealing way to write dialogue, and only great skill can manage it—and make us aware at the same time that communication of a limited kind is now going on as best it can.

Eudora Welty (90)

As a writer I was astonished by Hemingway's skill. . . . I have never understood, to this day, how Hemingway achieved his powerful dialogue. . . . [W]hat Hemingway offered . . . was not dialogue overheard, but a concentrate of it, often made up of superficially insignificant elements—mere fragments of everyday phrases, which always managed to convey what was most important.

Ilya Ehrenburg (20)

[T]here is not a living writer in England who has been unaffected by the laconic speed of his dialogue, the subtle revelation of character that lies behind a spoken phrase.

Alan Pryce-Jones (21)

From *Twentieth Century Literature* 42, no. 4 (Winter 1996): 453–80. Copyright © 1996 by *Twentieth Century Literature*. Revised for *Art Matters: Hemingway, Craft, and the Creation of the Modern Short Story*, pp. 169–203. Copyright © 2010 Louisiana State University Press.

Hemingway's most original and influential contribution to the art of fiction was his creation of an entirely new role for dialogue. Between the completion of his sixth story, "Indian Camp," in February 1924 (the first new story written for *In Our Time*) and his thirtieth story, "Hills Like White Elephants," in May 1927 (the last story written for *Men Without Women*), he so thoroughly revolutionized dialogue that, had he done nothing else, this accomplishment alone would have secured his reputation in literary history. But although critics have frequently commented on his distinctive dialogue, the exact nature of his achievement remains rudimentarily explored.[1] I can posit only two reasons why. First, since the academy is dismissive of scholarship on articulated technique in fiction studies—if not in poetry, music, or art criticism—an examination of the craft of dialogue is, unfortunately, of far greater interest to writers, the direct beneficiaries of Hemingway's achievement, than to critics. Second, as renowned novelist Anthony Powell observes, "Hemingway systematized a treatment of dialogue in a manner now scarcely possible to appreciate, so much has the Hemingway usage taken the place of what went before" (110).

How, then, did Hemingway forever change an entire element of fiction? Before the mid-nineteenth-century advent of realism, dialogue served a limited set of functions. For instance, in romances and sentimental fiction, it was confined to melodramatic speeches, the communication of information, commonplace exchanges, and displays of the author's erudition and verbal wit. It was rarely used for characterization, especially since, as Mark Twain's "Fenimore Cooper's Literary Offences" makes devastatingly clear, characters either tended to talk alike, or else speak in a way, often ad nauseam, that was meant to be illustrative (180–81, 189–90). Frequently, there was little difference between their speech and that of the author or narrator, and even the speeches of the same character would vary widely throughout a text. Worse, with a few notable exceptions such as Jane Austen in her novels of manners or Nathaniel Hawthorne in his romances, dialogue lacked subtlety: characters said what they consciously thought, meaning lay on the surface, and their words were remarkably free from the sorts of inner conflicts and psychological complexities inherent in the speech of real people.

With the emergence of realism and its focus on character, the art of dialogue advanced. As characters became consistent, so too did their speech; different characters spoke differently, and many of the intricacies of real-life speech emerged in fiction. Additionally, due to a new interest in regional differences in America stimulated by the Civil War and a thriving postwar market for national magazines, the accurate depiction of dialect became a convention, not only in the works of such masters as Twain, William Dean

Howells, Harriet Beecher Stowe (in her later works), Sarah Orne Jewett, Mary Wilkins Freeman, Charles W. Chesnutt, Stephen Crane, and Kate Chopin, but across the literary landscape (see Jones). As dialogue moved from the overwrought speeches of Poe's characters, the high rhetoric of Melville's Shakespearean sailors, the commonplaces of the domestic novel, and the schizophrenic verbosity of Cooper's Natty Bumppo to the shrewdly calculating speeches of Twain's Jim, Huck, Hank Morgan, and Roxy, the idiosyncratically specific and characterizing speeches of Howells' Lapham family, and the brilliantly modulated registers in the verbal battlefields of James's and Wharton's novels of manners, dialogue benefited from Howells's realist mandates of fidelity to experience and probability of motive. In short, one of the consequences of the movement toward verisimilitude was that fictional characters began to sound as though they were actual human beings.

But even as the quality of dialogue improved immeasurably, its role in fiction changed very little. For James, whose theory of dialogue was exemplary in the late nineteenth century, dialogue was purely complementary; its proper and only function was to be "directly illustrative of something given us by another method" of presentation ("London" 1404). The idea that dialogue could crystallize situation or advance plot was, to James, ludicrous. Complaining that the "fashion of our day" is "an inordinate abuse of the colloquial resource" (too much quoted speech), he believed that "there is a *law*" governing the use of fictional dialogue, and that while "admirable for illustration, functional for illustration, dialogue has its function perverted, and therewith its life destroyed, when forced . . . into the constructive office" ("Balzac" 137). Any attempt to have dialogue play more than this limited illustrative role he termed "singularly suicidal" ("London" 1404). The notion of "really constructive dialogue, dialogue organic and dramatic, speaking for itself, representing and embodying substance and form" was an "abhorrent thing," appropriate to the theater, which "lives by a law so different," but never to fiction (*Awkward Age* 1127; "Balzac" 137). Moreover, James, for whom mimesis and a direct impression of life were the paramount goals of fiction, did not believe that direct speech was even capable of being mimetically reproduced, and so he called for writers to recognize "the impossibility of making people both talk 'all the time' and talk with the needful differences." To get characters to do that, he frankly admitted, "is simply too hard. There is always at the best the author's voice to be kept out. It can be kept out for occasions, it can not be kept out always. The solution therefore is to leave it its function, for it has the supreme one" ("London" 1404).

In truth, James wrote dialogue superbly and used it liberally. But he could not countenance allowing it out of its box. Take, for instance, this brief passage from *The Portrait of a Lady* (1881), in which young Ned Rosier comes to Gilbert Osmond's house in pursuit of Pansy, Osmond's daughter, unaware, as is the reader at this point, that Osmond already knows the purpose of the visit:

> "I saw a jolly good piece of Capo di Monte to-day."
>
> Osmond answered nothing at first; but presently, while he warmed his boot-sole, "I don't care a fig for Capo di Monte!" he returned.
>
> "I hope you are not losing your interest?"
>
> "In old pots and plates? Yes, I am losing my interest."
>
> Rosier for a moment forgot the delicacy of his position. "You are not thinking of parting with a—a piece or two?"
>
> "No, I am not thinking of parting with anything at all, Mr. Rosier," said Osmond, with his eyes still on the eyes of his visitor.
>
> "Ah, you want to keep, but not to add," Rosier remarked, brightly.
>
> "Exactly. I have nothing that I wish to match."
>
> Poor Rosier was aware that he had blushed, and he was distressed at his want of assurance. "Ah, well, I have!" was all that he could murmur; and he knew that his murmur was partly lost as he turned away. (Ch. 37, 569–70)

Here we see many of the distinguishing features of James's dialogue. Rosier and Osmond speak in character and, as do all James characters, they speak with skill. Rosier, torn between his predisposition to diffidence and his desire for Pansy, attempts to soften up his auditor by addressing a subject of which Osmond is fond but is caught short by his host's unforeseen rudeness. Perhaps consciously, perhaps not, he tips his hand by continuing to talk ostensibly about china when the real subject of the conversation is Pansy, and he is more seriously rebuffed when Osmond substitutes "anything" for "a piece or two." With his blushing indicating a dawning awareness, Rosier attempts a witty rejoinder, verbally pursuing his goal from a slightly different angle. But Osmond's use of the verb *match* in his final rebuff (to Rosier's cleverly implied notion of "adding" a son-in-law) makes it unambiguously clear to Rosier that both know what the conversation is really about and that Osmond has strong feelings on the subject. The suitor turns away, feebly protesting, with diffidence momentarily overcoming desire.

For an author who abhorred "the colloquial resource," James included a great deal of dialogue in *The Portrait of a Lady*. Nevertheless, none of it conflicts with James's theory. This brief, dramatic confrontation is embedded in paragraphs in which James's narrator probes the consciousnesses of the characters, and, for all its artful execution, the dialogue merely illustrates what is given us by that other, main method of presentation. In the paragraph preceding this passage, James prepares us for Rosier's performance by stating that Rosier "was not quickly resentful, and where politeness was concerned he had an inveterate wish to be in the right" (569). Even in the passage itself, James tells us that Rosier "forgot the delicacy of his position" rather than allowing the dialogue to make that clear on its own, and Rosier's final remark only illustrates the distress that James's narrator describes instead of allowing Rosier's words to indicate that discomfiture on their own.

Ezra Pound first directed Hemingway to the works of James, and Hemingway's first wife, Hadley, was a James enthusiast. Although Hemingway alternately ridiculed and praised James and was loath to acknowledge any influence (his usual response to any writer who had truly mattered to his development), and although the impact of James on his work would not reach full fruition until the late 1940s and 1950s when Hemingway was trying to write Jamesian novels, nevertheless early in his career his predecessor's texts had shown him, as Michael Reynolds has insightfully noted, that the significance of "dialogue appears frequently in the white space between the lines" and that "it is what the characters do not say that is highlighted by their conversation" (30). In this manner, James's dialogue served as a powerful model for Hemingway in its indirection, ambiguity, and portrayal of communication as veiled, partial, and difficult. As Sheldon Norman Grebstein observes, both authors "employed a technique of brief exchanges which tended to refer obliquely to the subject under discussion rather than to name it outright" (96). Carlos Baker terms this technique "the hovering subject":

> Another remarkable similarity in the conduct of dialogue by James and Hemingway is what may be called the hovering subject. James often establishes the subject of a conversation by hint and allusion rather than overt statement. At other times he introduces the subject briefly (often it is a single word at the end of a sentence), and then conducts the dialogue by reference to it, while it hovers, helicopter-like, over the surface of the conversation. In either instance the neuter pronoun *it*, or its unuttered equivalent, is the index to what is being talked about. *It* is the apex of a pyramid whose base is the dialogue, and the real subject is the star at which the apex points. (185, n. 32)

In addition, both authors share a technique that Grebstein calls "incremental repetition" or a "type of stichomythia": "In this rhetorical scheme each speaker will pick up a word or phrase from the other's speech and utilize it as the basis for his own remarks, but adding, subtracting, or changing, so that the dialogue continuously rehearses itself yet evolves as it proceeds" (96). Note for example, in the James passage, the repetitions of "Capo di Monte," "losing ... interest," "not thinking of parting," and "I have," and also such substitutions as: "I don't care a fig" for "I saw a jolly good piece"; "old pots and plates" for "Capo di Monte"; "anything" for "a piece or two"; "nothing that I wish to match" for "want to keep, but not to add"; and "I have [something that I wish to match]" for "I have nothing that I wish to match."

It sometimes seems as though the main difference in their dialogue—aside from James's pervasive use of access to his characters' consciousnesses—consists of Hemingway's complete abandonment of James's stage directions. Hemingway's favorite identification tag is the simple "he said" or "she said," and even these he often eliminates. But in James, as Baker observes, "the phrases range from 'I gaily confessed' through 'she rather inscrutably added' and on to 'I attempted the grimace of suggesting.' Like his use of italicized words [in dialogue], these phrases are meant to mark the tone and emphasis, the special ring, of a particular speech. James is in effect gesturing silently from the prompt-box." Baker concludes by demonstrating how, if we remove the prompts from a James passage, "the dialogue proceeds in a manner scarcely distinguishable from Hemingway's" (183). Here, though, I must demur, for however much Hemingway learned about dialogue from James, his decision to let it play the constructive role that James considered inappropriate—to remove the author's voice and allow dialogue to speak solely for itself—was revolutionary.

James's theories of fiction—despite his movement toward increased dramatization, foreshortening, and the effacement of the narrator—derived from his work in the nineteenth-century novel of manners. The sine qua non of that genre was the dense depiction of social texture and the representation of temporality. James asserted that the novelist's most difficult, and therefore most dignified, effort "consists in giving the sense of duration, of the lapse and accumulation of time." In dialogue, narrative time slows down and begins to approximate real time. Such a "multiplication of quoted remarks" is an "expedient" that "works exactly to the opposite end, absolutely mini-mising, in regard to time, our impression of lapse and passage" ("London" 1403–4; also see "Balzac" 136). In addition, dialogue silences the author's "supreme" voice that, in its judiciousness, probity, and richness, is essential to the discursive texture of the genre. Even when James admired another author's dialogue—as he did in the case of his friend William Dean Howells—he believed it needed to be "distributed, interspaced with narrative and pictorial matter. [Howells] forgets sometimes to paint, to evoke the conditions and appearances, to build in the subject ... I cannot help thinking that the divinest thing in a valid novel is the compendious, descriptive, pictorial touch, *à la Daudet* ("Howells" 505–6).

Hemingway's prosaics, however, derived from a different genre, the emerging modern short story, which, as did his earlier journalism, placed a premium on discrete events and delimited moments in time. That genre's demands for radical compression, which led to the need for a high degree of suggestiveness and implication, eliminated the thick portrayal of social texture and sense of duration that lay at the heart of the novel of manners. These generic demands enabled Hemingway, perhaps compelled him, to rely on and further compress dialogue, allowing it to assume a hitherto unknown role in fictional composition, even to the point of removing almost completely the narrative commentary and authorial voice without which, James had felt, fiction would cease to be fiction and would cross over into drama. James, of course, could not have anticipated the new genre's heavy reliance on direct speech, and even some of Hemingway's most illustrious contemporaries found his dialogue-laden stories unseemly. Virginia Woolf, for one, criticized him in Jamesian terms in her 1927 review of *Men Without Women*:

> A writer will always be chary of dialogue because dialogue puts the most violent pressure upon the reader's attention. He has to hear, to see, to supply the right tone, and to fill in the background from what the characters say without any help from the author. Therefore, when fictitious people are allowed to speak it must be because they have something so important to say that it stimulates the reader to do rather more than his share of the work of creation. But, although Mr. Hemingway keeps us under the fire of dialogue constantly, his people, half the time, are saying what the author could say much more economically for them. (8)

But Dorothy Parker, herself a gifted storywriter, in reviewing that same volume understood that Hemingway's style was "far more effective" in "the short story than in the novel" (93) and that the modern story genre demanded radically different techniques of construction and representation that empowered readers precisely by giving them a larger role in what Woolf termed "the work of creation."

The clash between Woolf and Parker over the function of dialogue reveals a difference between the views of authors who were primarily novelists, for instance James and Woolf, and those, such as Hemingway, Parker, Elizabeth Bowen, and Eudora Welty, who were completely at home in the modern short story and willing, in their stories, to dispense with the author's "supreme" presence. One traditional notion at odds with the new genre was that dialogue should be limited to illustration. Bowen observes: "Each piece of dialogue *must* be 'something happening.' Dialogue *may* justify its presence by being 'illustrative'—but this secondary use of it must be watched closely, challenged. Illustrativeness can be stretched too far. Like straight description, it then becomes static, a dead weight—halting the movement of the plot" ("Notes" 256). Although Bowen greatly admired James, she felt that his stories, for all their virtuosity, represented a "dead end" in the genre's development that could neither be imitated nor advanced upon (*Faber* 39).

James's dialogue, and that of Edith Wharton—easily the most talented American writers of dialogue before Hemingway—depended upon characters who were highly intelligent, refined, and sensitive to the slightest nuances of words and gestures. Granting both authors this *donnée*, it is nevertheless true that, until Hemingway, no writer was able to write dialogue that demonstrated the rich complexities of the speech of characters who were not particularly bright, cultured, or sensitive. Twain, of course, did vernacular characters justice, especially in first-person narration. The richest, most complex dialogue he ever wrote was for Jim in *Huck Finn*, and this he did with such subtlety that a century of criticism mistook that character's shrewdly manipulative minstrel performance for mere minstrel caricature (see Lamb, "America" 480–83). But although Jim and Huck may not be refined, they are assuredly intelligent and sensitive. As for the dialogue of such later writers as Frank Norris, Gertrude Stein, and Sinclair Lewis, it continued to play a limited role and, with regard to the speeches of common characters, was often condescending.

The Jamesian novel of manners was written for a pre-Freudian audience and treated the romantic egoist within a fully developed social world. Consequently, it focused on the consciousnesses of characters capable of rich perception, feeling, and self-awareness. Dialogue was akin to a game of chess, played by sophisticated characters highly skilled and inordinately clever. Although a great deal of miscommunication occurred, much communication took place too. The Hemingway short story, on the other hand, portrays transient modern individuals cut loose from their social moorings. His characters, no less capable of feeling, are much less articulate, sophisticated, versed in the strategies of speech, and consciously self-aware. But their conversations are every bit as rich as those of James's characters because, however limited their consciousnesses may be, they possess the same complex unconscious motivations as any human characters.

It *should* go without saying that one need not be a highly developed, self-aware, social creature to be worthy of consideration, either in literature or in life. Yet, from the start—with Lee Wilson Dodd's comments on Hemingway's "narrow" attention to "certain sorts of people" with "oddly limited minds, interests, and patterns of behavior" (323); Wyndham Lewis's vicious characterization in *Men Without Art* of Hemingway as a "dumb ox" whose characters are dull-witted and bovine; and D. S. Savage's nearly obscene assessment of Hemingway's art as representing "the *proletarianization* of literature; the adaptation of the technical artistic conscience to the sub-average human consciousness" (14–15)—Hemingway's detractors have invariably based their attacks on his *donnée*: his semi-articulate characters and their class-bound cultural limitations. Such sentiments are, of course, deplorable, and one would expect today's multicultural and putatively class-sensitive critics to denounce them as, at the very least, elitist. But literary criticism has always had an ambivalent attitude toward the uneducated classes, defending them in principle but finding itself viscerally repelled by fiction that features such characters not as a type of "noble savage" or "untutored folk democrat" but from the inside in all of their awkwardness and crudity. Hemingway—cosmopolitan, quadralingual, bookish, and intellectual though he was—did not turn from such characters. In finding ways to allow them to speak, the writer who once half-jokingly referred to himself as "the Henry James of the People" (*Letters* 556), fashioned new techniques that brought their voices fully into the pages of fiction.[2]

What, then, were Hemingway's technical accomplishments in the writing of dialogue? They can be summed up in three phrases: minimum speech with maximum meaning; the elevation of banality into art; and the blurring of distinctions between the genres of drama and fiction. To achieve these goals, he removed or subtilized the controlling presence of the author's voice and incorporated into dialogue the techniques of his non-dialogue prose: indirection, juxtaposition as a means of having meaning derive from proximity, irony, omission, repetition, the objective correlative, and referential ambiguity. In doing so, he met the challenge of writing modern dialogue: representing the dynamics of real-life speech. After Hemingway, writers would have the option of making dialogue illustrative or constructive, and of having their characters show themselves in ways hitherto only revealed by other methods.

In a valuable series of observations about craft, published in 1945 in the aftermath of modernist fiction's heyday, Elizabeth Bowen cut to the crux of why writing modern dialogue is so difficult. Staking a position diametrically opposite to that of James, she observes that dialogue must imitate certain "realistic qualities": "Spontaneity. Artless or hit-or-miss arrival at words used. Ambiguity (speaker not sure, himself, what he means). Effect of choking (as in engine): more to be said than can come through. Irrelevance. Allusiveness. Erraticness: unpredictable course. Repercussion." But behind the "mask of these faked realistic qualities," it must be "pointed, intentional, relevant. It must crystallize situation. It must express character. It must advance plot." It must, in other words, be truly verisimilar—*seemingly* real but not an actual transcription of reality itself. "Speech," Bowen goes on to say, "is what the characters *do to each other*"; aside from a few extreme physical acts, it is "the most vigorous and visible inter-action of which characters ... are capable." Consequently, speech "crystallizes relationships. It *should*, ideally, so be effective as to make analysis or explanation of the relationships between the characters unnecessary" ("Notes" 255). Although dialogue is generally ineffective for purposes of exposition, for conveying necessary information (what invariably occurs at the beginning of a play, which it takes all of the considerable artifice of the theater subsequently to overcome), it can express present relationships and, by implication, their past as well. But this requires great talent; dialogue must imply subtly, suggestively, and never through direct statement. Usually, the *way* characters say something is more important than *what* they say.

Bowen further observes that each sentence spoken by a character must display either "calculation" or "involuntary self-revelation." Great dialogue, I would add, displays both, for in fiction, as in life, it is virtually impossible not to be, to some degree, self-revelatory when speaking. Generally, she states, characters should "be under rather than over articulate," and what they "*intend* to say should be more evident, more striking (because of its greater inner importance to the plot) than what they arrive at *saying*" ("Notes" 256). Robie Macauley and George Lanning agree, noting that "speech, as a way of characterization, moves forward by means of partial concealment, partial exposure" because what characters say may be the result of inner conflictedness, or they may be saying what they think the other person wishes to hear (78). In speech, they may become aware of their own confusion, or something the other person does might make them modify their original intention. They may become even more confused and end up saying the opposite of what they wished to say. In short, all of the myriad complexities that inhere in real-life dialogue inhere as well in fictional dialogue, the one great difference being that in fiction there is an author who exercises some control over what is being expressed (or incompletely expressed). Dialogue therefore demonstrates not only communication but also its limits.

In Hemingway's earliest mature stories we see him still in thrall to, but starting to pull away from, the pre-modern practice of dialogue. In "Out of Season," written in April 1923, a foreign couple's fishing guide tries to persuade them to purchase some wine as they leave the village:

> Peduzzi stopped in front of a store with the window full of bottles and brought his empty grappa bottle from an inside pocket of his old military coat. "A little to drink, some marsala for

the Signora, something, something to drink." He gestured with the bottle. It was a wonderful day. "Marsala, you like marsala, Signorina? A little marsala?"

The wife stood sullenly. "You'll have to play up to this," she said. "I can't understand a word he says. He's drunk, isn't he?"

The young gentleman appeared not to hear Peduzzi. He was thinking, what in hell makes him say marsala? That's what Max Beerbohm drinks.

"Geld," Peduzzi said finally, taking hold of the young gentleman's sleeve. "Lire." He smiled, reluctant to press the subject but needing to bring the young gentleman into action. (*Stories* 174)

This dialogue is quite effective, but in a Jamesian manner. Peduzzi and the wife are well characterized by their speeches; he pathetically attempts to ingratiate himself in order to obtain all that he can in return for his services, and she is contemptuous, classist, impatient, and possibly xenophobic. Peduzzi's importunity, nicely captured by his repetition of *marsala*, begins with him feigning concern for the wife's enjoyment and quickly degenerates into a frantic plea for money in whatever language will communicate this successfully to the husband. But Hemingway does not yet trust the dialogue to be constructive on its own. As James would have done, he uses an adverb to characterize the wife's attitude and subsequent speech ("sullenly"); instead of allowing the husband's silence to speak, he takes the opportunity to delve into that character's consciousness; and he didactically explains Peduzzi's strategy after the final appeal.

For nine months after completing "Out of Season," Hemingway was beset by family responsibilities and had little time to write except for the *in our time* vignettes and his newspaper dispatches, but he continued making mental notes for future stories. Returning to Paris in January 1924, he embarked upon a remarkable period of creativity that would lead, in the next three years, to the publication of two of the finest story collections in literature and his first major novel. In the first of these stories, "Indian Camp," completed in February, he left behind the poorly written speech of the deleted opening (*Nick Adams Stories* 13–15; see Lamb, "Dialogue" 455–56) and unveiled his new art of constructive dialogue.

After successfully performing an emergency Caesarian with fishing equipment on an Indian woman who delivers a boy, Nick Adams' father discovers that her husband, confined to the upper bunk with a foot injury, has cut his throat. Preoccupied before the operation, in which he thoughtlessly had Nick assist, and exhilarated in its aftermath, he is sobered upon realizing that his child has witnessed the dead man. He leaves his brother George in the shanty and removes Nick. In the story's final dialogue, spoken as Nick and his father return to the rowboat, the author disappears completely, even eliminating identification tags, as pure dialogue advances the plot to its conclusion:

> It was just beginning to be daylight when they walked along the logging road back toward the lake.
>
> "I'm terribly sorry I brought you along, Nickie," said his father, all his post-operative exhilaration gone. "It was an awful mess to put you through."

[Q1]   "Do ladies always have such a hard time having babies?" Nick asked.

[A1]   "No, that was very, very exceptional."

[Q2]   "Why did he kill himself, Daddy?"

[A2]   "I don't know, Nick. He couldn't stand things, I guess."

[Q3]   "Do many men kill themselves, Daddy?"

[A3]   "Not very many, Nick."

[Q4]   "Do many women?"

[A4]   "Hardly ever."

[Q5]   "Don't they ever?"

[A5]   "Oh, yes. They do sometimes."

[Q6]   "Daddy?"

[A6]   "Yes."

[Q7]   "Where did Uncle George go?"

[A7]   "He'll turn up all right."

[Q8]   "Is dying hard, Daddy?"

[A8]   "No, I think it's pretty easy, Nick. It all depends." (*Stories* 94–95)

The opening sentence efficiently locates the action following a narrative ellipsis. The word *daylight* is a literal descriptor that also resonates as a figurative comment on Dr. Adams, who is just beginning to see the light. The suicide has deflated his earlier illusion of power, forcing him to accept things beyond his control. Now aware of his son's needs and his parental responsibilities, in his first speech the doctor admits his mistake. His use of the diminutive *Nickie* suggests that he is concerned with Nick's anxieties (he used the same diminutive in the deleted opening after his frightened child summoned him), but he also betrays his own feelings of guilt. His apology is not for Nick's having seen the dead Indian (which could not have been anticipated) nor for his thoughtlessness in having Nick attend the horrific operation (his most irresponsible act). Instead, he apologizes for having brought Nick to the Indian camp rather than leaving him alone in the woods (a necessary decision), which undercuts the apology by passing over his truly unconscionable act. What he had previously termed a "little affair" (the operation), he now calls an "awful mess"—an understatement that covers everything Nick has witnessed (including his father's paternal inadequacies) and, by its euphemistic nature, continues to diminish the apology. The phrase about his "post-operative exhilaration" being gone is superfluous and inappropriate in this story internally focalized through Nick, and should have been deleted. The last phrase of his statement shows Dr. Adams looking at these events from Nick's perspective ("to put you through") in order to console him, but his shame is manifest in his use of an inert construction; a more direct admission of culpability would have been: "I put you through an awful mess." By his need to assuage his own guilt, then, the doctor's apology is involuntarily self-revelatory; he is still absorbed in his own needs, not his child's.

If the doctor's initial speech is revealing, the ensuing eight questions and answers are a marvel of indirection, miscommunication, suggestiveness, and compression. Nick has conflated all the events he has witnessed and therefore asks about the operation, but by the end of the passage it is clear that what he really wants to know about is the probability of death (either his father's or his own). His father, however, is obsessed with the suicide and so, for all his newfound sensitivity toward his son and Nick's careful attention to his father, the two characters miscommunicate throughout the conversation.

Nick's first question ("Do ladies always have such a hard time having babies?") elicits a somewhat detached response from his father, whose thoughts are elsewhere. Dr. Adams can draw upon his medical knowledge to answer the question; the repetition of *very* and the understated *exceptional* give the impression of a considered, dispassionate reply. Nick's second question, however, directly presents the mystery at the heart of the story: "Why did he kill himself, Daddy?" The use of *Daddy*, which Nick said earlier when frightened by the woman's screams, suggests the anxiety beneath his outwardly calm demeanor. (In the story's opening scene, when Nick was calm, he called him *Dad*.) His father does not notice Nick's anxiety and he cannot, in any case, satisfactorily answer the question. His profession has equipped him for medical queries, not psychological ones. He answers honestly—he does not know. But he also senses that this is not enough to satisfy his son, so he follows with a strategically vague explanation ("He couldn't stand things, I guess."). This reply is evasive yet suggestively self-revelatory. He consciously means to say that the Indian was emotionally unable to go on living, but he employs an idiom with the word *stand*, reminding the reader of the Indian's injured foot which prevented him from joining the other Indian men outside the shanty and forced him to be a silent witness to his wife's ordeal. The Indian father's injury led to his humiliation and helplessness, and unconsciously functions in Dr. Adams' speech as a self-reflexive indication of the helplessness the story's other father now feels.

When Nick asks about the suicide, the dialogue takes a notable turn. The Indian's suicide revealed that Nick's father was not omnipotent. Now, he must confess that neither is he omniscient. The words "I don't know," coming from so proud a man who has just performed so expertly under extreme conditions, resonate with the doctor's deep sense of confusion, guilt, and deflation. From this point on, Nick focuses on death and suicide, asking questions that cannot be answered or that his father does not wish to address. Dr. Adams's inability to answer these questions and the shock he feels over what has happened force him back into the self-absorption he displayed in the shanty. But although his answers are brief and perfunctory, they have an oddly calming effect on Nick, relieving his anxiety. The characters miscommunicate but, ironically, this failure produces a successful result.

With a child's curiosity and unerring ability to ask precisely the questions that an adult wishes to avoid, Nick pursues his interrogation. When he catches his father in an inattentive reply ("Hardly ever."), he immediately issues a follow-up question ("Don't they ever?") that reveals his dissatisfaction. Other times, he jumps from one question to another, catching his distracted father off guard. His father's preoccupation can be glimpsed in the laconic, vague nature of his replies ("Not very many"; "Hardly ever"; "They do sometimes"; "He'll turn up"; "It all depends"). He answers Nick's questions, but just barely, making no effort to address the obvious anxieties lying beneath them. The sixth reply is particularly revealing. Nick says "Daddy?" just to get his attention and Dr. Adams replies "Yes." The absence of a question mark indicates that his father's inflection is declarative rather than interrogative; he acknowledges Nick's speech but remains lost in his own thoughts. When Nick then asks about Uncle George, a subject his father is especially not interested in, the reply is again unspecific ("He'll turn up all right."). The phrase "all right" resonates with the two times the expression was previously used: Nick's response to his father's post-operative inquiry about how Nick liked being an intern and a sarcastic remark George made after the operation about Dr. Adams being a "great man, all right" (*Stories* 93, 94). Nick's "all right" was intended to satisfy his father but revealed his lack of enthusiasm. George's use both intended and revealed his resentment of his brother. Here, Dr. Adams wishes to satisfy his son, but he unconsciously reveals both his own lack of enthusiasm for answering any more questions and his resentment toward George, whose earlier sarcasm anticipated the doctor's present feelings of inadequacy.

Nick is too young to comprehend death and can only feel it as absence. His first glimpse of death was the Indian father's withdrawal from life. Therefore, the anxieties he expresses in this passage concern absent fathers. The four questions he asks ending with "Daddy?" (2, 3, 6, and 8) make manifest the subject of these anxieties (including his sixth question, which is intended to bring his mentally absent father back into the conversation). In his second question, he asks why the Indian baby's father killed himself and receives an uncomforting but honest reply. What he really wants to know, however, is whether he is safe from suffering the same fate as the Indian baby; that is, will his father kill himself too? He continues his inquiry circuitously. His next two questions, about the frequency of male and female suicide, are unconsciously self-referential—he wants to know about his own father and mother—and the responses are comforting. But the real point of the last three questions is revealed only in their juxtaposition. The sixth question is about Nick's sense of his own father's mental absence; the seventh question is about Uncle George's physical absence, foreshadowed by his brief disappearance during the first boat trip across the lake and here serving as a displacement of Nick's anxiety over his own father's mortality; and the eighth question ("Is dying hard, Daddy?"), read in the above context, is about the *probability* of Nick's father's death. Ironically, his father solipsistically assumes the question to be, in light of his own concerns, about whether the act of dying is difficult to face, and his answer is unintentionally chilling: "it's pretty easy." Even more ironically, however, the words that confirm Nick's anxieties about his father's mortality do not matter, for, as the doctor says, it all "depends."

The story concludes with an objective correlative that further illuminates this dialogue. What mortality "depends" on is revealed in the final two paragraphs:

> [1] They were seated in the boat, Nick in the stern, his father rowing. [2] The sun was coming up over the hills. [3] A bass jumped, making a circle in the water. [4] Nick trailed his hand in the water. [5] It felt warm in the sharp chill of the morning.
>
> [1a] In the early morning on the lake sitting in the stern of the boat with his father rowing, [1b] he felt quite sure that he would never die. (*Stories* 95)

During the opening boat trip, Nick sat in the stern with his father's arm around him while an Indian rowed. Here Nick again sits in the stern but his father is rowing and in control. His father's physical presence is strong enough for Hemingway to omit it and know that the reader will feel it: the sight of him pulling the oars, the sound (and perhaps smoke) of his breath as he rows, the steady surges of the boat along the water (as in the description of the first boat trip). That pervasive presence counteracts both Nick's experiential sense of absence and his father's words about dying being easy; consequently, Nick no longer countenances the idea that his father could ever cease to be. In this way, his father's tangible physical actions are far more comforting than his vague words. These implied but omitted actions enable Nick to dismiss considerations of death and suicide, and resume his state of youthful innocence.

The other sensory impressions of the paragraph, abundantly suggestive and not omitted, are also comforting, unlike those of the initial trip. The scene is vibrant with life. The sun is just coming up, signaling the start of a new day and marking the end of the previous night's horrors. Nature is animated and, in a positive metaphor of birth, a bass emerges from the water; life appears from nowhere. The word *hand*, by now, has developed a good deal of symbolic significance. Earlier, his father's hands had been carefully scrubbed, but during the operation they were covered in blood and later his hand came away from the upper bunk "wet" with the Indian father's blood. The lake water cleans Nick's hand and also links him to the impressions of life going on around him. The water feels warm in the sharp morning chill, suggesting that this scene feels warm in the sharp chill of what has gone before. In the midst of all this palpable being, it is impossible for Nick to imagine nonbeing.

The form of the paragraph underscores its meaning, with five short sentences that slow down the reader's pace as he or she takes in the living sensations that impress themselves upon Nick. The paragraph scans as iambic and anapestic, mimicking the motion of the boat as it crosses the lake. The only double stresses, either spondees or else iambs followed by trochees or dactyls, are: "boat, Nick"; "up over"; "bass jumped"; "Nick trailed"; "felt warm"; and "sharp chill." The first double-stress is mitigated by the comma; the second underscores the appearance of the sun and new day; the third contributes to the surprise of the fish's sudden appearance and links it to the emergence of the sun; the fourth prosodically links Nick to the thematics established by the "new" sun and the "newly emerged" fish; and the final two double-stresses juxtapose the contrasting sensations of warmth and cold, heightening the effect of the former in a wonderfully tactile image of life.

In the first part of the final paragraph, Hemingway employs what I've termed *recapitulation with variation* as he gathers up the scattered impressions from the preceding paragraph and restates them in a continuous manner to convey their literal simultaneity and their processing, in retrospect, in both Nick's and the reader's consciousness. As the images from the previous impressionistically presented paragraph are processed or integrated within the mind, they are repeated as variations (e.g., "the sun coming up" above the "water" becomes "the early morning on the lake"). The phrase, "his father rowing," is repeated exactly, emphasizing Nick's focus on his father's hands, which are the engines of the action sequences throughout the story, and further linking the final two paragraphs.

Five years after composing "Indian Camp," Hemingway wrote fellow writer Owen Wister: "I know . . . how damned much I try always to do the thing by three cushion shots rather than by words or direct statement. But maybe we must have the direct statement too" (*Letters* 301). So far, these two paragraphs have been three-cushion shots, impressionistically conveying Nick's state of mind. But they also prepare us for the direct statement comprising the second part of the final sentence. This statement functions not as an explanation, but as an articulation and further confirmation of what has already been implied. It expresses Nick's feeling that the Indian camp is not his world. His is the world depicted in this scene in which his father is in control and Nick is free from responsibility, where the sun comes up and fish jump and the water feels warm in the morning chill. This bountiful natural world denies the reality of the dark and bloody Indian camp with its silent Indians, dying fathers, and screaming mothers. Immersed in this world, it is altogether believable that Nick would have "felt quite sure" (the three consecutively stressed syllables emphasizing the certainty of his feeling) "that he would never die" (the iambic float-off ending).

The sentence is more than an affirmation, however. The first part, an objective correlative of Nick's sense of immortality, placed in juxtaposition with the earlier speech in which Uncle George's absence served as a signifier of death ("Where did Uncle George go?"), does indeed triumph over it, yet ambiguities and ironies compound. If the antecedent to the final "he" is Nick's father, a possibility that Hemingway purposely leaves open, then all the miscommunication between the two and his father's disquieting responses have inadvertently comforted Nick. On the other hand, if the antecedent is Nick, the much more likely possibility, then another irony is created by the disjunction between Nick's sense of his own immortality and the reader's knowledge that it is otherwise. Moreover, it is the final turn in the screw of the previous dialogue's indirection, for it means that what Nick was really asking about all along concerned his anxieties about *his own* finitude, not his father's. Therefore, the entire conversation was really about Nick's first encounter with what I term *ontological shock*, the numbing realization of one's own mortality. Indeed, this is what Hemingway omitted from "Indian Camp" when he discarded the original opening—which addressed Nick's fear of death directly—only to treat it at the end of the final version by, characteristically, having Nick deny it. If the visible part of the iceberg is Nick's denial of his own mortality, then the seven-eighths lying beneath the surface of the dialogue is that he must have, at some point during this story, experienced, however fleetingly and inchoately, a recognition of his eventual non-being. Even in his "direct statement," Hemingway operated by three-cushion shots, and all of these matters are compressed into just a few "simple" sentences of enormously suggestive dialogue in which two characters thoroughly miscommunicate in such subtle ways that many critics of the passage, for the past eight decades, have assumed they were communicating clearly.

Hemingway's new dialogue would play a major role in six of his next seven stories, written in March and April 1924. In the first of these, "Cat in the Rain," an American couple is confined by rain to their second-floor hotel room. From their window, the wife observes a cat crouched under a café table, "trying to make herself so compact that she would not be dripped on." The first dialogue ensues:

[W1]   "I'm going down and get that kitty," the American wife said.
[H1]   "I'll do it," her husband offered from the bed.
[W2]   "No, I'll get it. The poor kitty out trying to keep dry under a table."
[DS]   The husband went on reading, lying propped up with the two pillows at the foot of the bed.
[H2]   "Don't get wet," he said. (Stories 167–68)

When critics talk about Hemingway's dialogue, they usually point to such stories as "The Killers" or "Hills Like White Elephants" in which its significance (if not its craft) is unmistakable. But this brief passage seems rather banal, merely a way of getting the story into gear. How is it different from James or from the dialogue in "Out of Season?" Why do I insist on viewing it as innovative?

The passage consists entirely of direct speech with some neutrally depicted actions. Not only is the focalization external, but the author's "supreme voice" is absent. The wife's first speech is subtly revealing. It appears intended to let the husband know why she is leaving the room, but, given his passivity throughout the story in which he never leaves the bed, it suggests much more. The rain has confined them to their room, and he has occupied himself with a book while she looks out the window with nothing to do. The resolve indicated in the words "going down" and "get that kitty" implies the wife's desire for self-assertion that is focused on a specific object and/or a desire to get a reaction from him. The husband's reply seems responsive, but is unconsciously revealing. First, by changing the specifics of her speech—"going down" and "get that kitty" to "I'll do it"—he exposes his actual indifference by making the act abstract, in effect saying "I'll do the thing you want done." The speech is thoughtless in its intention to pacify her (he has probably sensed her restlessness) rather than engage her expressed concern about the cat (or her implied concern about herself). It also ignores that she feels the need to do something herself in order to assert her agency, a need implicit in the specific wording of her original speech. Second, "offered from the bed" further undercuts the sincerity of his reply; he says the words of a caring husband but makes no move to give them substance.

That she senses his disinterest is clear in her reply. "No" appears intended to stop him from usurping her mission, but his actions seem to pose no threat of that happening; since he has not budged, her "no" is either sarcastic or else indicates her alarm at the possibility that he may, however grudgingly, arise. "I'll get it" suggests a great deal. Is it, too, an act of self-assertion, both in its insistence on her own ability to act and in the way she replaces his vague verb *do* with her original specific verb *get*, or is she self-conscious about disturbing his reading and seeming a burden, or both (her need for his attention conflicting with her desire not to irritate him and cause him to retreat even further into his self absorption)? Whichever holds true, her intentions, which I think are unconscious, are clearly revealed in the second part of her speech. Although the "poor kitty" will, by the end of the story, come to symbolize the things, such as a baby, that she wants but cannot have, here she projects onto it her sense of her own situation. The cat and the wife are both confined by forces outside of their control (the rain for the cat, the rain and her marriage for the wife); both are frustrated by the limitations imposed upon them, and both want to assert their agency.

If her second sentence is, however unconsciously, some sort of plea for her husband's attention, he is, to put it in a Hemingwayesque manner, a disappointing audience. The juxtaposition of his reading with her plea makes us sense the poignancy of her marriage. In addition, the entire descriptive sentence [DS] is a wonderful example of Hemingway's technique of sequence displacement, . . . "Propped up" and "reading" is the position he was in during his first speech when he offered to "do it" (which makes that "offer" seem, if possible, even less genuine), and the beautifully subtle "went on reading" indicates that he never looked up from his book when he made that offer, a fact underscored later when he is described as putting the book down (to rest his eyes), reading it again (while she is pouring out her heart to him), looking up at her (when her back is turned and she is expressing concerns about her physical attractiveness), and finally telling her to shut up (after she tells him the things she wants out of life), going back to his book, and ceasing even to listen to her anymore. If the cat and the wife are restless in their confinements, the husband has turned his confinement into repose. His final speech ("Don't get wet") is highly revealing. He again feigns concern for his wife's welfare, he unconsciously acknowledges her identification with the cat (who is the only one trying not to "get wet"), and he demonstrates conclusively that his original offer was half-hearted (his eyes are still on his book). He even issues, again unconsciously, a subtle warning that if she is going to try asserting herself—instead of resting content to be his patient wife—then such assertion carries some risk.

　　... [T]he shift in focalization from the wife to the husband just before the open ending of this story creates the text's ambiguity—we never know whether she receives the specific cat she wanted. But that aesthetically ingenious moment, upon which so much of the richness of the story depends, was set up from the start in this tiny unobtrusive passage of dialogue. Although Hemingway would write many dialogue passages more developed and complex, this sort of passage can be found throughout his stories. In just the stories he wrote in March and April 1924, examples would include the conversations between Nick and Marjorie and between Nick and Bill in "The End of Something," in which calculation and involuntary self-revelation can be found in virtually every speech, and the long conversations between Nick and Bill in "The Three-Day Blow" and between Nick and George in "Cross-Country Snow," in which Hemingway employs lengthy passages of indirection to show how characters discuss something by *not* addressing it. Even when they finally do address what's really on their minds, they do so with such phrases as "I guess so" and "I don't know" and "Sure" and "No" and, of course, just plain silence ("Nick said nothing") in which more meaning is conveyed about what that character is thinking than could be depicted in hundreds of words of speech.

　　With the completion of "The Battler" in March 1925, Hemingway had written the final story for *In Our Time* and two stories that would go into *Men Without Women*. Between "An Alpine Idyll" in April 1926 and "Hills Like White Elephants" in May 1927, he wrote eleven more stories for the new book. In them, he continued to employ the innovative dialogue techniques of *In Our Time*, which he had also used extensively in *The Sun Also Rises*. Dialogue crystallized situation, expressed character, and advanced plot; verisimilitude was achieved by indirection, banality, simplicity of diction, and pervasive miscommunication; and speeches were marked by conscious calculation and involuntary self-revelation.

　　A new technique, repetition, already a significant part of his prose, began to enter his dialogue in four stories completed between April and September 1926. Extending repetition to dialogue mimicked the way people repeat themselves in conversations, which contributes to verisimilitude though it does not advance the plot. An example occurs in "An Alpine Idyll" when the characters refer to their skiing: "'You oughtn't to ever do anything too long.' / 'No. We were up there too long.' / 'Too damn long,' John said. 'It's no good doing a thing too long'" (*Stories* 345). This repetition is mimetic but must be restricted to a brief exchange or else it would interfere with advancing the plot (even though the idea of "doing a thing too long" is relevant to the story's theme). An even more purely mimetic example is in "Today Is Friday," a brief story in the form of a play:

> *2d Soldier*—Why didn't he come down off the cross?
> *Ist Soldier*—He didn't want to come down off the cross. That's not his play.
> *2d Soldier*—Show me a guy that doesn't want to come down off the cross.
> *Ist Soldier*—Aw, hell, you don't know anything about it. Ask George there. Did he want to come down off the cross, George? (*Stories* 357)

These sorts of banal repetitions also run throughout "The Killers," especially in the conversations between the two Chicago gunmen who wait in the diner to kill Ole Andreson. When George, the counterman, asks what they want to eat, the response is: "'I don't know,' one of the men said. 'What do you want to eat, Al?' / 'I don't know,' said Al. 'I don't know what I want to eat'" (*Stories* 279). Here, however, the repetitions also serve to characterize the two men as unimaginative and barely distinguishable from each other; all either can do is parrot the same phrases the other comes up with. After being introduced to Nick, Al's response is: "'Another bright boy,' Al said. 'Ain't he a bright boy, Max?' / 'The town's full of bright boys,' Max said" (*Stories* 280). This is characteristic of conversations between people who spend much time together but have little to say to each other and is not significantly different from the exchanges in "Today Is Friday."

But the repetitions function more complexly when these characters come into conflict with characters whom they do not know. Informed that dinner is not served for another forty minutes, Max orders a chicken dinner and is told by George, "That's the dinner." Max replies: "Everything we want's the dinner, eh? That's the way you work it" (*Stories* 280). Here, the differences between the two characters change the meaning of the repeated word. For George, "dinner" means an order has been placed from the wrong menu. To Max, "dinner" represents something he wants and is being refused; moreover, this refusal becomes a signifier of regulations he resents, making him see George's unwillingness to serve him dinner as a contest of power. George begins to repeat the list of available items—"I can give you ham and eggs, bacon and eggs, liver"—but is interrupted by Al, who says, "I'll take ham and eggs," indicating his desire not to get caught up in this trivial conflict when they have business at hand. Al's decision causes Max to repeat another item from George's list—"Give me bacon and eggs"—parroting Al's words but with the slight individuation of changing "I'll take" to "Give me" and "ham" to "bacon." Hemingway then expands on what he's already conveyed through the gunmen's dialogue: "[Max] was about the same size as Al. Their faces were different, but they were dressed like twins." He follows with another repetition in which a word's meaning changes according to the difference between the speaker's intention and the auditor's understanding: "'Got anything to drink?' Al asked. / 'Silver beer, bevo, ginger-ale,' George said. / 'I mean you got anything to *drink*?'" (*Stories* 280). To George, "drink" means a beverage; to Al it means alcohol.

Most people repeat themselves endlessly when they speak, anxious that their auditors catch every detail and all intended meaning. For Max and Al, this sort of repetition is less the product of their desire to be understood or to have others see them as they wish to be seen than it is a form of insistence that they be obeyed. After George serves Max his meal, the gangster starts harassing him again:

> "What are *you* looking at?" Max looked at George.
> "Nothing."
> "The hell you were. You were looking at me."
> "Maybe the boy meant it for a joke, Max," Al said.
> George laughed.
> "*You* don't have to laugh," Max said to him. "*You* don't have to laugh at all, see?"
> "All right," said George.
> "So he thinks it's all right." Max turned to Al. "He thinks it's all right. That's a good one."
> "Oh, he's a thinker," Al said. (*Stories* 281)

The repetition of the command "*you* don't have to laugh" is an order, whereas the repetition of "he thinks it's all right" is a coded witticism that only Al grasps.

The closer people are, the more they speak to each other in a shorthand that makes their conversation incomprehensible to an outsider (or reader). Edith Wharton observes, "All that is understood between [people] is left out of their talk" in real life. Thus, if characters in fiction "have to tell each other many things that each already knows the other knows," then the only way "to avoid the resulting shock of improbability" would be to water down the dialogue with so many irrelevant commonplaces that the reader would grow bored (*Writing* 74). Wharton's own Jamesian solution was to resort to summary treatment or to interlace her dialogue with narrative, which enabled her to control dialogue through access to the consciousnesses of her characters. Hemingway, however, found a way out of the dilemma that allowed him to rely heavily on dialogue. By repeating phrases, words, sounds, and even cadences, he made his dialogue seem repetitive while the different contexts of these repetitions changed their meanings and enabled the dialogue to advance the story. In Bowen's terms, he created dialogue that *seems* irrelevant while, in fact, remaining perfectly relevant.

For instance, after Al comes up with the witty idea of calling George "bright boy," the two gunmen use this term to refer to George and Nick twenty-eight times over the next five pages. With each repetition, the potential danger to George and the other diner occupants becomes more alarming. They also mock their captives by repeating the boys' phrases back at them. After George asks, "What's it all about?" Max twice asks George what he thinks it's all about, and George replies, "I don't know" and "I wouldn't say." To which, Max responds, "Hey, Al, bright boy says he wouldn't say what he thinks it's all about" (*Stories* 282–83). Before they leave, in response to Al's implied question of whether they should allow their captives to live, Max says, "They're all right" (*Stories* 285). Here, the context changes the meaning of George's previous use of the expression "all right" from "I'll do what you say and not laugh" to Max's "They won't tell anyone about us after we leave." In this manner, Hemingway mimics the repetitiveness of real-life speech while still using it for characterization and to keep the plot moving.

The dialogue repetitions of "The Killers" are foregrounded, but in the last of the four stories written during that six-month span in 1926, Hemingway raised his art to new heights in one of the finest, most complex passages of dialogue he would ever write. In "A Canary for One," completed in September, an American couple returning to Paris from southern France shares a train compartment with an older, xenophobic, obnoxious American lady who is bringing a caged canary to her daughter, whose romance she broke up. Although not revealed until the end of the story, the couple is about to separate. The passage commences with the narrator becoming aware of his "breakfast-less" state and then hearing the American lady speak the words *American* and *husband*. Because these words have relevance for him, his full attention is engaged, and he reports the entire dialogue:

> "Americans make the best husbands," the American lady said to my wife. I was getting down the bags. "American men are the only men in the world to marry."
>
> "How long ago did you leave Vevey?" asked my wife.
>
> "Two years ago this fall. It's her, you know, that I'm taking the canary to."

"Was the man your daughter was in love with a Swiss?"

"Yes," said the American lady. "He was from a very good family in Vevey. He was going to be an engineer. They met there in Vevey. They used to go on long walks together."

"I know Vevey," said my wife. "We were there on our honeymoon."

"Were you really? That must have been lovely. I had no idea, of course, that she'd fall in love with him."

"It was a very lovely place," said my wife.

"Yes," said the American lady. "Isn't it lovely? Where did you stop there?"

"We stayed at the Trois Couronnes," said my wife.

"It's such a fine old hotel," said the American lady.

"Yes," said my wife. "We had a very fine room and in the fall the country was lovely."

"Were you there in the fall?"

"Yes," said my wife.

We were passing three cars that had been in a wreck. They were splintered open and the roofs sagged in.

"Look," I said. "There's been a wreck."

The American lady looked and saw the last car. (*Stories* 340–41)

On the surface, the conversation seems superficial and repetitious—what one might expect from strangers on a train. It's also a model for using indirection in dialogue. First, the conversation appears to be about Vevey and the American lady's daughter, but it's really about the conflicted emotions experienced by the separating couple. Second, the passage observes the Joseph Conrad and Ford Madox Ford "unalterable rule" regarding the rendering of "genuine conversations": "no speech of one character should ever answer the speech that goes before it." As Ford explains, such "is almost invariably the case in real life where few people listen, because they are always preparing their own next speeches" (200–201). This is what produces incremental repetition or stichomythia. But beneath the verisimilar surface there is conscious calculation and unconscious revelation, character is expressed, and plot is advanced (the passage provides the emotional climax to any rereading of the story). The repetition here is not merely verisimilar; even more than in "The Killers," by repeating words in different contexts Hemingway changes their referents. These semic qualities accrue to the repeated words, gathering force each time the word reappears.

The narrator and his wife face forward: he looks out the window toward Paris and the future, his wife looks at the American lady, and the American lady faces the rear of the train and the past. The American lady comments on the exclusive virtue of American husbands in conjunction with the narrator's apparently quotidian act of getting the bags, an act that seems to correspond to her views on the superiority of American husbands but that is given ironic relevance in juxtaposition with what must be the narrator's sense of his action as a step toward the separation of the couple's possessions. When the American lady repeats her observation about American husbands, the wife asks about Vevey, partly to change the painful course of the conversation. Yet, by choosing to divert it with talk of Vevey, she unconsciously betrays her desire to talk about the once happy past. The narcissistic American lady predictably takes the question about Vevey as a cue to talk about her daughter, and the wife goes along. Instead of conversing about the canary that the American lady has just mentioned, however, she is irresistibly drawn to asking about the nature of the broken love affair that resonates, for her, as symbolic of her own impending separation. When the American lady then tells of the Swiss with whom her daughter fell in love, she twice mentions Vevey, causing the narrator's wife, in a moment of weakness and out of a desire to turn from the symbol of her imminent unhappy future to the memory of her happy past, to utter the enormously understated "I know Vevey," revealing that it was the site of her honeymoon. From that moment on, the narrator's wife will try to hold onto Vevey and the past. At the same time, the narrator experiences her attempts, by dwelling on Vevey, to ward off the painful emotions caused by their ever-nearing separation. He, in turn, tries unconsciously to hold onto their married status by using, in his wife's remaining five speeches, the identification tag "said my wife" although these are obviously unnecessary for the purpose of identifying the speaker.

The American lady, who could not care less about the couple's honeymoon, predictably shifts the conversation back to her daughter's love affair, and inadvertently reveals that she feels somewhat defensive, perhaps even guilty, about what she has done. As in a previous dialogue, she uses the phrase "of course" to justify her actions. But the narrator's wife drops even the amenity of talking about the unhappy daughter and continues her spoken reverie on Vevey. Here an extraordinary event occurs. The American lady, who throughout the story has been oblivious to all around her, *realizes* that the narrator's wife wants to talk about Vevey. For the rest of the conversation, she actually focuses on what the wife wants to talk about, asking questions about the honeymoon and responding to the wife's speeches.

Part of the emotional impact of the conversation derives from the fact that if the narrator's wife makes an impression strong enough to pierce the self-absorption and alter the discourse of the American lady, then it must be quite a strong impression indeed. The wife also emerges from her near anonymity in the story to become the center of the scene, a transformation heightened by the drum roll of "said my wife" tags supplied by the narrator. And when the wife's speeches are stitched together, they are emotionally compelling in and of themselves: "I know Vevey. We were there on our honeymoon. It was a very lovely place. We stayed at the Trois Couronnes. Yes. We had a very fine room and in the fall the country was lovely. Yes." It's almost as though Hemingway has taken a piece of Molly Bloom's soliloquy from *Ulysses* and broken it up into half of this dialogue.

When the American lady starts responding to the narrator's wife, she slips into the present tense: "Isn't it lovely?" But in asking about the honeymoon, she returns to the past tense: "Where did you stop there?" The wife unconsciously changes the verb to "stayed" (avoiding the primary meaning of "stopped") and gives the name of the hotel. Hemingway deliberately chooses "Trois Couronnes" for its literary allusiveness; it is the same hotel in which Henry James's "Daisy Miller" takes place. Both stories present American travelers who are robbed of their innocent illusions (although in "Canary" we are presented with the aftermath of the characters' initiation). Trois Couronnes means "three crowns," but both James and Hemingway, with their excellent command of French, probably knew that it also means "three fool's caps." If the narrator, so closely modeled on Hemingway himself, also knows the double-meaning of Trois Couronnes, then perhaps he is aware of how the name ironically reflects on the three inhabitants of the compartment.

As noted, the conversation is manifestly repetitious, investing it with verisimilitude as the women repeat, in various contexts, each other's phrases. The American lady, who seems incapable of meaningful conversation, can only parrot what the narrator's wife says. And the wife, lost in her memories, latches onto phrases used by the American lady that she herself, in the grip of these memories, finds meaningful. As noted, however, the repetition serves a dual purpose, without which the entire passage, however mimetic, would be inert, as beneath the banal surface the repeated words and phrases expand in meaning because of the changing contexts in which they appear.

For instance, the words *fall*, *Vevey*, and *lovely* appear four times and the word *fine* twice. The American lady tells the narrator's wife that she and her daughter left Vevey two years ago "this *fall*." Moments later, responding to the information that the couple had honeymooned in Vevey, she says, "That must have been *lovely*" but follows by saying that she did not know that her daughter would "*fall* in *love* with" the Swiss, changing the original meaning of "fall." The wife agrees that "it was a very *lovely* place," slightly changing the referent of "lovely" from honeymooning in Vevey to Vevey itself. A second implied meaning accrues to Vevey here: it was a place where one could "fall in love." The American lady then agrees with the wife who has just agreed with her but puts her statement in the present tense—"Isn't it *lovely*?"—changing the referent from Vevey past to Vevey present, and calls the Trois Couronnes "a *fine* old hotel." The wife then utters her own recapitulation with variation, gathering the repeated words and phrases to sum up her sense of the conversation: "We had a very *fine* room and in the *fall* the country was *lovely*." In her sentence, the meaning of *fine* changes from "prestigious" (revealing the American lady's values) to "nice" or "lovely" (indicating the wife's values); *fall* once more refers to a season (although it still echoes with the previous sense of "to fall in love"); and *lovely* describes Vevey in the past tense (conflating lovely, fine, falling in love, the room, the countryside, and Vevey—but locating it all in the past). When the American lady then asks if the couple was "there in the *fall*" and the wife replies "Yes," the conversation that began with the wife asking when the American lady left Vevey is brought full circle. Its focus has, by subtle increments, shifted from the American lady and her daughter in the present ("this fall") to the American couple in Vevey in the past. (All emphases in quotations mine.)

The narrator listens carefully, the bags at his feet. Perhaps he, too, is being lured into the past by the circular, mesmerizing conversation (which lacks discordant elements because of the repetitive phrases and the manner in which each speech seems to agree with and flow from the one that precedes it). But then he sees the wrecked train. When the American lady asks if they *were* in Vevey in the fall, his wife says yes, but now they *are* passing three wrecked cars. The narrator, in his second and final speech in the story, calls their attention to the present—"Look"—and announces, "There's been a wreck." Just as in an earlier speech when he used the term *braces* instead of *suspenders* (*Stories* 339), his statement seems commonplace but actually reveals a half-calculated rudeness and resentment: toward the American lady, the dissolution of his marriage, and the painful reliving of the happy past. His statement works a comparable change in focus and tone as Jake's reply to Brett in the final line of *The Sun Also Rises*.

When the narrator points out the wreck—in five syllables totaling a mere twenty letters—his statement serves six functions (a remarkable example of dialogue compression) that bring together several strands of the story in a multilayered objective correlative. First, he indicates the literal wreck that has occurred. Second, the wreck is the physical realization of the fears about a train crash that the American lady has expressed throughout the story. Third, the couple's marriage, which the narrator's wife has been reliving, is a wreck. Fourth, the three people, similar to the three cars they are passing, are wrecks. (Significantly, the narcissistic American lady sees only the "last car," just as she "sees" only herself.) Fifth, the narrator, by his statement, wrecks the women's conversation. Sixth, since that conversation has been a reenactment, of sorts, of their previously happily married state, he has perhaps repeated in the present (especially since the story is based upon the real-life first marriage that Hemingway wrecked) what he had done in the past. Certainly, his speech seems to, in Bowen's words, "crystallize relationships." What he has said is pretty much the equivalent of "Shut the hell up!"

With the writing of "A Canary for One," Hemingway's innovations in constructive dialogue were complete. But the question of how far he could push his new art—to what extent dialogue could carry a whole story—remained. The answer came in May 1927 with "Hills Like White Elephants," a story almost entirely in dialogue. A couple sits outside a bar at a station in Spain waiting for the train to Madrid—and they talk. As opposed to the American lady and the narrator's wife in "A Canary for One," these characters know each other well and thus speak in the sort of shorthand that Wharton observed would make a conversation unintelligible to an outsider. Therefore, the premise of the story forced Hemingway to construct relevance for the reader from what should have seemed nonsense. He made his task even more difficult by omitting the actual subject of their conversation (she is pregnant and he wants her to have an abortion); as countless critics have noted, abortion, pregnancy, and babies are never once mentioned. As if to increase the challenge, he employed external focalization, eschewing access to any character's consciousness; the non-dialogue is completely neutral and, with the exception of two objective correlatives, contributes nothing toward the reader's making sense of the dialogue.

Following a brief description of the setting, we get their first exchange:

> "What should we drink?" the girl asked. She had taken off her
> hat and put it on the table.
> "It's pretty hot," the man said.
> "Let's drink beer." (*Stories* 273)

The woman's first speech gives us a glimpse of a character who lacks a sense of autonomy and looks to her partner to make the decisions. His reply is even more revealing. Although she is perfectly willing to let him make the decisions, whether about drinks or abortions, he needs to believe that she is taking part in the decision-making process even as he prevents her from doing so. Here, he gets her to request the beers he obviously wants merely by making a statement about the weather. Such successful manipulation conveys the dynamics of their relationship in the present and, we may assume, in the past. This first exchange, so easy to overlook, tells us what we need to know about these people; it crystallizes their relationship, expresses their characters, and encapsulates the ensuing plot. It also amply demonstrates

Bowen's other main points about dialogue—it is what characters *do to each other*, and it contains calculation and involuntary self-revelation—all beneath a seemingly banal, spontaneous, and artless surface.

The remainder of the story leading up to their climactic exchange plays out the couple's problems as they discuss, in an extremely veiled and short-hand manner, her pregnancy and their relationship. Much of the conversation is so obscure that it can be comprehended only in light of the entire story. For instance, early on when it's clear that they are having a conflict but not what that conflict is about, she says her *Anis del Toro* "tastes like licorice," and he seems to respond innocuously, "That's the way with everything." She agrees, but adds, "Everything tastes of licorice. Especially all the things you've waited so long for, like absinthe." He is caught short by her statement and can only weakly reply, "Oh, cut it out" (*Stories* 274). To anyone but them, the conversation is about alcohol that tastes like licorice, whereas it's really about her desire to have a baby.

Or is it? Later on, she seems amenable to having the "simple operation," as he terms it, if that will make everything all right between them, by which she means if he will respond to her when she makes such statements as the hills "look like white elephants." Such a response, however, is beyond him—it requires a capacity to see the world through her eyes and not just his own—so he tries to distract her by saying that if she has the operation they will be "fine afterward." At the same time, he undercuts his promises even as he protests his love for her:

> "And if I do it you'll be happy and things will be like they were and you'll love me?"
> "*I love you now.* You know I love you."
> "I know. But if I do it, then it will be nice again if I say things are like white elephants, and you'll like it?"
> "I'll love it. *I love it now* but I just can't think about it. You know how I get when I worry." (*Stories* 275; emphasis mine)

Although he ostensibly says what she wants to hear, the way he says it reveals more than what he says. Not only does he avoid answering her questions, the juxtaposition of "I love you" and "I love it" speaks volumes about his true feelings.

Throughout the story, he cloaks his desires in a "logic" that assaults her language of metaphorically expressed desire. Since he cannot understand her language, she resorts to mimicking his words and phrases ("things will be like they were"), or responding with passive aggressive self-abnegation ("Then I'll do it. Because I don't care about me"), or merely negating his statements ("We can have everything." / "No, we can't." / "We can have the whole world." / "No, we can't." / "We can go everywhere." / "No, we can't. It isn't ours any more." / "It's ours." / "No, it isn't") (*Stories* 275–76). Finally, she requests silence to avoid further verbal battering—"Can't we maybe stop talking?" (*Stories* 276). But he won't shut up.

If she wants respect and understanding even more than she wants the baby, it is equally clear that what he wants is not just for her to have the abortion, but to acknowledge that she *wants* to have it, that is, to feign volition, thus absolving him from responsibility for the actions he demands. His motive is manifest in an utterance halfway through the story that he repeats, in various forms, six more times—"'Well,' the man said, 'if you don't want to you don't have to. I wouldn't have you do it if you didn't want to'" (*Stories* 275). Her responses to these attempts at verbal manipulation range from asking him if *he* wants her to have the operation (making him assume responsibility), to asking whether he'll love her if she does (forcing a concession for agreeing to the abortion), to saying that she'll do it because she doesn't "care about" herself (a passive aggressive counterattack), to requesting that they stop talking about it (avoidance). The only action she will not perform is to allow him to coerce her into pretending that the abortion is her own decision.

The following passage, which begins with the penultimate variation of his trademark utterance (here introduced with particular insistence), takes place after her weary plea that they "maybe stop talking" and is the emotional climax of the story:

[P1] "You've got to realize," he said, "that I don't want you to do
       it [#1] if you don't want to. I'm perfectly willing to go through
       with
       it [#2] if it [#3] means anything to you."
[P2] "Doesn't it [#4] mean anything to you? We could get along."
[P3] "Of course it [#5] does. But I don't want anybody but you. I don't
       want any one else. And I know it's [#6] perfectly simple."
[P4] "Yes, you know it's [#7] perfectly simple."
[P5] "It's [#8] all right for you to say that, but I do know it [#9]."
[P6] "Would you do something for me now?"
[P7] "I'd do anything for you."
[P8] "Would you please please please please please please please stop
       talking?"
[P9] He did not say anything but looked at the bags against the wall of
       the station. There were labels on them from all the hotels where
       they had spent nights.

[P10]   "But I don't want you to," he said, "I don't care anything about
        it [#10]."
[P11]   "I'll scream," the girl said. (*Stories* 277)

The techniques employed in the above passage, so representative of
Hemingway's art of dialogue, should, by now, be manifest. The gender-based
miscommunication in which the man's assertive declarative statements are
parried by the woman's mimicking of him (paragraphs 2 and 4), by her questions (2, 6, 8), and by her urgent request that he stop talking at her (8) that
finally explodes in frustration (11) are typical of their entire conversation.
Equally typical is how he makes a general statement, the content of which
is intended to pacify her ("I'd do anything for you."), that is revealed as a lie
when she subsequently asks for "something" specific (8) and he puts her off
(10). Moreover, he again reveals his hypocrisy through juxtaposition when
he initially employs *perfectly* to modify his willingness to have the baby (1)
and in his next speech uses it to modify the supposed simplicity of having
an abortion (3). That juxtaposition does not go unnoticed, as her mimicry
indicates (4).

The most remarkable aspect of the passage, however, is Hemingway's
full-blown employment of repetition. The repetition of key words such as *want*
and *perfectly* and polysyllabic words that have syllables in common (*anything,
anybody, any one, something*) creates a powerful verisimilitude, but the changing contexts of these words keep advancing the plot. More extraordinary
are the various uses of the referentially ambiguous pronoun *it* in achieving
these dual purposes of dialogue. *It* (an example of Carlos Baker's "hovering
subject") is used ten times but the antecedent/referent continually changes.
The first *it* refers to having the abortion, the second to having the baby, and
the third through fifth either to having the baby or to the baby itself. The
sixth *it* again refers to having the abortion; the seventh *it* refers to having the
abortion or, perhaps, to her sense of their entire situation; the eighth *it* is an
expletive with no antecedent; and the ninth *it* refers to the "knowledge" that
having an abortion is simple. These uses of *it* not only mirror the shorthand
manner by which people refer to matters they both understand (or think they
understand), "it" also creates the ironic ambiguity that makes for relevance. By
subsuming such incompatible antecedents within one pronoun, Hemingway
demonstrates how, in dialogue, communication can become impossible.

After the woman's emotional request for the man to stop talking (paragraph 8), Hemingway allows himself two brief sentences of non-dialogue that
aptly sum up the man's real attitude toward his mate. But he does not access
the man's consciousness through a direct statement; instead, he employs an

objective correlative with the man providing the camera angle. Looking at
the bags with the hotel labels, which function as a symbol of his desire to
make the woman into a purely sexual object, leaving him unencumbered by
the responsibilities of love and family (and mutual respect), the man tries one
last time his verbally violent sentence (in a truncated form) in order to coerce
her into "choosing" the abortion of her own "free will" (paragraph 10). In the
sentence he uses the word *care*, which he had previously used in insisting that
he "cared" about her. Here, he says that he doesn't care about "it," which in its
tenth and final incarnation conflates the abortion, the baby, the entire conversation, and (in juxtaposition with her as a mere sexual object in the objective
correlative of paragraph 9) the unsubjugated, non-sexual part of the woman's
self. Her reply, and ours? "I'll scream." Then, we have one final irony—"'I'd
better take the bags over to the other side of the station,' the man said" (*Stories*
277). Yes, by now, a very good place for that particular objective correlative!
There is also one final moment of possible triumph as she smiles at him in
the knowledge that she has not relinquished her last small shred of autonomy.
With her concluding speech—"'I feel fine,' she said. 'There's nothing wrong
with me. I feel fine'" (*Stories* 278)—Hemingway leaves his talking couple to
an ambiguous fate, all the more uncertain because we do not know, in this
seeded closed ending, whether to attribute any significance to his taking the
bags to the "other side" of the station, and brings his dialogue experiment to
a close.[3]

NOTES

1. Even as late as 1996, when I published a less developed version of this
chapter in *Twentieth Century Literature*, there existed only one sustained scholarly
analysis of Hemingway's art of dialogue (a chapter in Sheldon Norman Grebstein's
Hemingway's Craft, published in 1973). Critics had commented upon his dialogue
endlessly, but no one had fully analyzed how it works, addressed all of the principles
that lie behind it, or located it in the evolution of fictional dialogue or in the development of the modern short story.

2. The poet John Ciardi observes: "What counts . . . as I see it, is the way in
which the GIs of World War II lived and died with Hemingway dialogue in their
mouths. . . . Their language was not out of Hemingway but out of themselves. Yet
it justified his power as nothing else could. Hemingway had taken their emotions
to war, and had expressed war and loss and the necessary reticence so truly that he
evolved their language before they got to it" (32).

3. For an excellent complementary reading that explores how the characters'
miscommunication derives from gender-based linguistic, ontological, and episte-
mological differences, see Pamela Smiley. For an insightful reading that locates the
story in the context of Hemingway's courtship of Pauline Pfeiffer and concludes that
the man gradually comes to understand and acquiesce in his lover's point of view, see
Hilary K. Justice. Although I have a much more cynical view of the male character,
Justice's biographical argument is extremely interesting.

Works Cited

Baker, Carlos. *Hemingway: The Writer as Artist* (1952). Revised 4th edition, Princeton, NJ: Princeton UP, 1972.

Bowen, Elizabeth. "The Faber Book of Short Stories" (1936). In *Collected Impressions*. New York: Knopf, 1950. 38–46.

———. "Notes on Writing a Novel" (1945). In *Collected Impressions*. New York: Knopf, 1950. 249–63.

Ciardi, John. "The Language of an Age." *Saturday Review* 44 (29 July 1961): 32.

Dodd, Lee Wilson. "Simple Annals of the Callous." Review of *Men Without Women* by Ernest Hemingway. *Saturday Review of Literature* 4 (19 November 1927): 322–23.

Ehrenburg, Ilya. "The World Weighs a Writer's Influence: USSR." *Saturday Review* 44 (29 July 1961): 20.

Ford, Ford Madox. *Joseph Conrad: A Personal Remembrance*. Boston: Little, Brown, 1924.

Grebstein, Sheldon Norman. *Hemingway's Craft*. Carbondale: Southern Illinois UP, 1973.

Hemingway, Ernest. *Ernest Hemingway: Selected Letters, 1917–1961*. Ed. Carlos Baker. New York: Scribner's, 1981.

———. *The Nick Adams Stories*. Ed. Philip Young. New York: Scribner's, 1972.

———. *The Short Stories of Ernest Hemingway*. New York: Scribner's, 1954.

———. *The Sun Also Rises* (1926). New York: Scribner's, 1954.

James, Henry. "The Lesson of Balzac" (1905). In *Henry James: Literary Criticism: French Writers, Other European Writers, The Prefaces to the New York Edition*. Ed. Leon Edel. New York: Library of America, 1984. 115–39.

———. "London Notes" (1897). In *Henry James: Literary Criticism: Essays on Literature, American Writers, English Writers*. Ed. Leon Edel. New York: Library of America, 1984. 1387–1413.

———. *The Portrait of a Lady* (1881). In *Henry James: Novels 1881–1886*. Ed. William T. Stafford. New York: The Library of America, 1985. 191–800.

———. Preface to *The Awkward Age* (1908). In *Henry James: Literary Criticism: French Writers, Other European Writers, The Prefaces to the New York Edition*. Ed. Leon Edel. New York: Library of America, 1984. 1120–37.

———. "William Dean Howells" (1886). In *Henry James: Literary Criticism: Essays on Literature, American Writers, English Writers*. Ed. Leon Edel. New York: Library of America, 1984. 497–506.

Jones, Gavin. *Strange Talk: The Politics of Dialect Literature in Gilded Age America*. Berkeley: U of California P, 1999.

Justice, Hilary K. "'Well, well, well': Cross-Gendered Autobiography and the Manuscript of 'Hills Like White Elephants.'" *The Hemingway Review* 18.1 (1998): 17–32.

Lamb, Robert Paul. "'America Can Break Your Heart': On the Significance of Mark Twain." In Robert Paul Lamb and G. R. Thompson, eds. *A Companion to American Fiction, 1865–1914*. Malden, MA and Oxford: Blackwell Publishing, 2005. 468–98.

———. "Hemingway and the Creation of Twentieth-Century Dialogue." *Twentieth Century Literature*. 42.4 (1996): 453–80.

Lewis, Wyndham. *Men Without Art*. London: Cassell, 1934.

Macauley, Robie, and George Lanning. *Technique in Fiction*. 2nd ed. New York: St. Martin's, 1987.

Parker, Dorothy. "A Book of Great Short Stories." Review of *Men Without Women* by Ernest Hemingway. *The New Yorker* 3 (29 October 1927): 92–94.

Powell, Anthony. *Messengers of Day*. Vol. 2 of *To Keep the Ball Rolling: The Memoirs of Anthony Powell*. New York: Holt, Rinehart, 1978.

Pryce-Jones, Alan. "The World Weighs a Writer's Influence: England." *Saturday Review* 44 (29 July 1961): 21.

Reynolds, Michael S. *Hemingway: The Paris Years*. Oxford: Blackwell, 1989.

Savage, D. S. "Ernest Hemingway." In *Focus Two*. Eds. B. Rajan and Andrew Pearse. London: Dennis Dobson, 1946. 7–27.

Smiley, Pamela. "Gender-Linked Miscommunication in 'Hills Like White Elephants.'" *The Hemingway Review* 8.1 (1988): 2–12.

Twain, Mark. "Fenimore Cooper's Literary Offences" (1895). *Mark Twain: Collected Tales, Sketches, Speeches, & Essays 1891–1910*. Ed. Louis J. Budd. New York: Library of America, 1992. 180–92.

Welty, Eudora. *The Eye of the Story: Selected Essays and Reviews*. New York: Vintage, 1979.

Wharton, Edith. *The Writing of Fiction* (1925). New York: Octagon Books, 1966.

Woolf, Virginia. "An Essay in Criticism." Review of *Men Without Women* by Ernest Hemingway. *New York Herald Tribune Books* 9 (9 October 1927): 1, 8.

NORMAN FRIEDMAN

Harry or Ernest? The Unresolved Ambiguity in "The Snows of Kilimanjaro"

Interpretations of this story, generally acknowledged to be one of Hemingway's best, tend to run the gamut from seeing Harry as a failed writer who is simply failing again, to regarding him at least as finally performing his craft and dying honest, to claiming that he wins through to a spiritual victory. A similar ambiguity seems to plague the views of Harry's wife, Helen, where she is customarily seen as the rich bitch, destructive to the male, somewhat as if she were the wife in "The Short Happy Life of Francis Macomber," Hemingway's other famous African tale. A third issue is what, precisely, is the function—or functions—of Harry's italicized reminiscences, the materials of which, as Hemingway claimed, could have been used for many other stories?

While any successful literary work can and should be interpreted on different levels and in various ways, I am not deconstructionist enough to be content with *opposing* views of the same work without at least attempting to explain the causes of such diversity. I shall be trying out, then, alternative hypotheses.

It is generally acknowledged that this story represents not only a technical advance in Hemingway's fictional art, in that it deals less with "action" and more with feeling, but also a parallel growth in vision, in that it questions on a very fundamental level his ambivalence over the relative weight he should

From *Creative and Critical Approaches to the Short Story*, edited by Noel Harold Kaylor Jr., pp. 359–73. Copyright © 1997 by The Edwin Mellen Press.

be giving to "life" as opposed to "art." Let us look first, though, at the story's structure itself, which consists of three distinct layers: Harry's present conversations with Helen as he lies dying on his cot from gangrene, his present interior monologues when she's absent, and his italicized recalls of his past. In the unfolding sequence of the story's chronological development, these elements are alternated, with the italicized sections expanding and then contracting, as a number of critics have noted.

I

The story begins in the heat of the afternoon. Helen is sitting by Harry as he lies on his cot, his leg having become gangrenous. His behavior is psychologically defensive, although it is practically conscious: he quarrels with her, as he says, because it makes the time pass, but underneath that is his attempt to put the blame on her, now that it is too late to redeem his writing career, for his having let it slip through his fingers—"Your bloody money," he says. Beneath that is an even deeper defensive rationalization: that he has been saving things "to write until he knew enough to write them well."[1] Then there is the defensive system itself: if you detach yourself, things won't hurt you, and lying to a woman you love works better than the truth.

It is at this point, tired out, that he withdraws into his mind and engages in the first of his italicized recalls—scenes of war, snowy mountains and skiing, playing cards, etc. Several purposes are being served here. First of all, these events represent, as he himself says, things he's been saving to write about but now will not be able to. They represent, in the second place, the normal response of a person who feels himself dying—that is, to review one's life. Third, and even more significantly, they represent a course of self-psychoanalysis, as they lead him, in his growing ability to face difficult memories, toward his upcoming acknowledgement of his own complicity in his failure. Fourth, they represent, in his very act of remembering them, a resurrection of his ability to write, because as he himself says later, he feels he's actually "writing" these reminiscences. Fifth, they offer proof that Hemingway himself, as the *writer* of this writer's reminiscences, and in his self-proclaimed prodigality in condensing the material for many stories into one, has not lost *his* will to write. Finally, in their actual contents, offering scenes of violence and peace, plus recurring images of snow and mountains, they provide a subtext reinforcing the surface "action" of the story itself.

There is, then, a boxes-within-boxes structure here, with the author writing about an author who has lost his will to write and yet who is regaining that will in the very act of thinking of what he hasn't written about. But, of course, it is too late to *do* anything about it for Harry—he even asks Helen at one point if she can take dictation!—and so Hemingway kills him off while at the same time offering proof of his own continuing artistic growth in that very act. In Kenneth Burke's terms, he is scapegoating his own protagonist and having him die for his—Hemingway's—sins, thereby ridding himself of them. But there is, as I hope to show, some difficulty in making it work.

When Harry turns again to speak to Helen, he asks her about *their* past—"Where did we stay in Paris?" But he's still in his defensive-attack mode, and he hurts her again. She replies, justifiably, "If you have to go away . . . is it absolutely necessary to kill off everything you leave behind?" He replies, "It's trying to kill to keep yourself alive, I imagine." Then he slips into "the familiar lie he made his bread and butter by," and he tells her he loves her. But then he calls her a bitch, saying, "I don't like to leave things behind."

II

It is evening, and he falls asleep. She's gone to kill a piece of meat for supper. Upon awakening, he engages in an extended rumination in the present, wherein he begins coming to the cathartic realization that he has no one to blame for his failure but himself. In the process, he exempts Helen from blame and acknowledges his own defensive rationalization that he allowed himself to mingle with the rich in order to be able to write about them some day—"that you were really not of them but a spy in their country. . . ." "But he would never do it, because each day of not writing . . . dulled his ability and softened his will to work. . . ." So he had gone on this safari to start again, to "get back into training" and "work the fat off his soul." But now it was ending thus badly, and he knows "he must not turn like some snake biting itself because its back was broken. It wasn't this woman's fault." "He had destroyed his talent himself. Why should he blame this woman because she kept him well. . . . What was his talent anyway? It was a talent all right but instead of using it, he had traded on it. It was never what he had done, but always what he could do."

There are two controversial issues to take up at this point. One is the question of whether Harry was *ever*, in fact, a very good or serious writer in the first place, and therefore whether his "self-knowledge" here is simply another rationalization. All this talk about how good he used to be, or, how good he could have become, or how much talent he has wasted might be nothing but more self-deception: if he was such a good writer, why would he have let it all slip away in the first place? It would make very little sense, however, if he were just a hack, for it would be a much less interesting and effective story if it were to be taken merely as a non-writer's dying lament for his non-existent talent. And several factors mitigate against that interpretation: one is his ability now to be honest about himself and about Helen (see below), and the other is found in the substance and quality of his memories—the memories he has been saving to write about—for clearly Hemingway has invested all his skill in rendering them—in style, tone, feeling, and imagery, they are in fact like prose poems.

The other question is whether Helen is simply one more rich bitch, a Margot Macomber, another example of Hemingway's misogyny and inability to portray a real living woman sympathetically. We have learned recently that his attitude toward women is much more complex than it originally appeared, but I would argue on the evidence in this story alone that Hemingway was quite capable of portraying a woman sympathetically as a real person. To see her as less than that is to fall into the trap of judging her in terms of her bitter and self-justifying husband's initial evaluation and behavior. But as we have already seen, and will investigate further, his feelings are in the process of evolving.

It is during this particular stage of his ruminations, beginning with "Now she came in sight," that he thinks about *her* past, what *she* has been through, and how she came to be attracted to him. "She was a damned nice woman," he thinks, "very pleasant and appreciative and ... never made scenes." He speaks more cordially to her this time, and he feels "the return of acquiescence in this life of pleasant surrender. She *was* very good to him. He had been cruel and unjust in the afternoon. She was a fine woman, marvelous really." That he has seen her as singing the Sirens' Song or himself as a Lotos-Eater was his own doing.

III

"And just then it occurred to him that he was going to die," and he thinks he did well to stop quarrelling. She goes in to bathe. "He had never quarrelled with this woman, while with the women he loved he had quarrelled so much they had finally, always, with the corrosion of the quarrelling, killed what they had together. He had loved too much, demanded too much, and he wore it all out." This leads naturally to the ensuing italicized section where he recalls his first real love and how he had lost her. There follow more memories of war and of Paris afterwards, and of how a letter from his first wife was noticed by his then wife, "*and that was the end of the beginning of that.*" He hadn't written about that either, but he always thought he would finally. Harry is clearly moving toward taking increased responsibility for himself, just as Hemingway is in exposing his own failings in the person of his protagonist, and not waiting until *his* last moment to write about them. There is a difference, however, as we shall see later, between exposing one's failings and *indulging* in them.

Helen returns from her bath and offers him hot broth. He knows he is going to die tonight and feels the second of those approaches of death. He feels increased urgency in his desire to write of these things before it's too late—perhaps he could telescope "it all into one paragraph." And there follows the third and central italicized section, the longest of the five, where he recalls his childhood in the woods and how his grandfather's cabin burned down, melting the guns; more post-war memories of fishing in the Black Forest; and of the poor section of Paris where he began his writing career.

There follows a brief return to the present scene—talking with his wife—and he feels relieved for the moment of the approach of death.

His fourth batch of memories concerns itself with stories he had meant to write about his experiences on the ranch, especially of the time when "*the half-wit chore boy*" shot the "*old bastard from the Forks*" who had beaten him. "*He knew at least twenty good stories from out there and he had never written one. Why?*" This passage is linked to the ensuing return to the present scene with his wife by his saying, "You tell them why." She replies, "Why what, dear?" And he says, "Why nothing."

IV

There follows the famous rumination in which Harry thinks condescendingly of "poor Julian," originally "Scott" [Fitzgerald], and his "romantic awe" of the rich. Hemingway, of course, has been criticized for this gratuitous cruelty to his ostensible friend and colleague, which also shows up again in *A Moveable Feast*. But let us see if anything can be said in favor of this section before we conclude that it represents an artistic—as well as a personal—failing.

First of all, this is Harry and not Ernest, and Harry is a part of Ernest that Hemingway is distancing and correcting. Second, Harry by his own account has permitted *himself* to be held in thrall by the rich, as we have noted above. "But in yourself, you said that you would write about these people; about the very rich; that you were really not of them but a spy in their country; that you would leave it and write of it and for once it would be written by someone who knew what he was writing of. But he would never do it, because each day of not writing, of comfort, of being that which he despised, dulled his ability and softened his will to work so that, finally, he did not work at all."

Harry now thinks that he would never write about Helen, if he lived, "Nor about any of them. The rich were dull and they drank too much, or they played too much backgammon. They were dull and repetitious." Then he recalls how Julian "had started a story once that began, 'The rich are very different from you and me ["The Rich Boy"].' And how someone had said to Julian, Yes, they have more money. But that was not humorous to Julian. He thought they were a special glamorous race and when he found they weren't it wrecked him just as much as any other thing that wrecked him." Harry, on the other hand, "had been contemptuous of those who wrecked. You did not have to like it because you understood it. He could beat anything, he thought, because no thing could hurt him if he did not care."

This may seem strange, as he has previously himself ruled out such an attitude as a defensive rationalization: "He had sold vitality, in one form or another, all his life and when your affections are not too involved you give much better value for the money." My sense of what's going on here is that Harry is facing the increasing certainty of his own imminent death, and that he is trying to steel himself against the fear: "All right. Now he would not care for death. One thing he had always dreaded was the pain. He could stand pain as well as any man, until it went on too long, and wore him out, but here he had something that had hurt frightfully and just when he had felt it breaking him, the pain had stopped." The final italicized passage, the shortest of all, consists of a recall of how Williamson, an Allied officer, "*had been hit by a stick bomb someone in a German patrol had thrown as he was coming in through the wire that night and, screaming, had begged every one to kill him.*"

In the third place, therefore, I feel that Harry's attitude here toward Julian and the rich is conditioned by what he is experiencing in this present moment—that is, his ultimate terror of dying. He is reverting, in other words, to an even deeper defensive rationalization than the previous one where he had told himself that he was consorting with the rich in order to be able to write about them from the inside. At this moment he is projecting onto them his own boredom—as he thinks during the ensuing conversation with his wife, "I'm getting bored with dying as with everything else, he thought." We have something of a paradox here, then, in which it is suggested that boredom in the face of death is more terrible than terror itself. This is his rationalization: "Still this now, that he had, was very easy; and if it was no worse as it went on there was nothing to worry about."

Fourth, it is clear, of course, that Hemingway himself *did* write about the rich, not only here and in "The Short Happy Life of Francis Macomber," but also in *To Have and Have Not* (1937), and that he had, therefore, a continuing struggle with them. When Harry says, "He had been contemptuous of those who wrecked," as Julian was wrecked, he has now forgotten what he had told himself previously: "He had destroyed his talent himself. . . . He had traded it for security, for comfort too, there was no denying that, and for what else? He did not know." Perhaps to placate his mother, as Hemingway felt the need to, because she disapproved of his choice of a career?

On the other hand, perhaps Hemingway is suggesting that, although Harry *has* sold himself out to the rich, he has not done so because of *romanticizing* them, as with Julian, but rather because of the release they offered from the more rigorous inner demands of his craft and art. Harry has victimized himself not so much out of glamorizing the rich as of seeking the life of ease they offered. "Yes, they have more money," then, becomes even more ominous a remark than "The very rich are different from you and me."

The trouble with Harry, we begin to realize as the story evolves, is not so much that a life of ease has corrupted his will to write as that his will to write—if not his talent—was too weak in the first place. Recall: "It was never what he had done, but always what he could do. And he had chosen to make his living with something else instead of a pen or pencil." The phallic joke points up the irony of his bitter self-awareness—he has not, in fact, been a writer at all, and all those italicized memories of the wonderful and difficult experiences he has been saving up to write about are going to be lost not merely because of his approaching death—they have been lost all along. Harry has been making his living as a gigolo: "It was strange, too, wasn't it, that when he fell in love with another woman, that woman should always have more money than the last one?"

We are constrained to conclude, then, that the hard self-knowledge he has been struggling toward is now, as he approaches his final moments, proving to be too difficult to sustain, thereby reinforcing our original impression of him as a self-serving, self-justifying opportunist who is lashing out at the one nearest to him in a vain effort to take the blame away from himself, where it belongs: "he would rather be in better company," he thinks of her now, forgetting what he had told himself before, that "She was a damned nice woman too ... because she was very pleasant and appreciative and because she never made scenes." This reversion will certainly affect how we are supposed to understand his final fantasy.

V

As they talk now for what will be their last time together, he urges her to turn in, and their final exchange concerns his sensing death's presence once again:

> "You know the only thing I've never lost is curiosity," he said to her.
> "You've never lost anything. You're the most complete man I've ever known."
> "Christ," he said. "How little a woman knows. What is that? Your intuition?"

Perhaps here he is reclaiming once again a bit of the projection by acknowledging his own incompleteness, that—except for curiosity—he *has* lost everything. But at the same time he is revealing once again his own misogyny in condescending to her about it; and this, in the face of his own previous admission of the play-acting he has engaged in in order to "please" his rich wives, simply will not wash. How is a woman supposed to "know" a man if his "talent" is to sell "vitality," and who believes that when his affections are not involved, he gives better value for the money?

Death has now come to claim him at last, while she, unknowing, has gone to sleep. During the interval before the actual moment of his death and her awakening in the middle of the night to find his corpse, he has this two-page fantasy. "It was morning and had been morning for some time and he heard the plane." Upon first reading one cannot be sure that this indeed is a fantasy. Before this passage, he feels this weight upon his chest, and he cannot speak to tell them "to make it go away," crouching heavily, "so he could not breathe." "And then, while they lifted the cot, suddenly it was all right and the weight went from his chest." We could, then, believe that the plane is indeed coming, and so we read this two-page passage as if it were real. Compie in fact says we'll have to stop at Arusha to refuel, and Harry is watching the shifting terrain below as they rise and soar.

A shift occurs, however, before the end, "And then instead of going on to Arusha they turned left, he evidently figured that they had the gas. . . ." Then, after seeing a cloud of locusts and going through a thick rainstorm, "Compie turned his head and grinned and pointed and there, ahead, all he could see, as wide as all the world, great, high, and unbelievably white in the sun, was the square top of Kilimanjaro. And then he knew that there was where he was going." Which refers us back, of course, to the epigraph at the head of the story, where we are informed that the mountain is called "*the House of God*" by the Masai and that "there is the dried and frozen carcass of a leopard" near the western summit. "No one has explained what the leopard was seeking at that altitude."

There is a tendency to read Harry's dying fantasy here as if it were intended to represent a symbolic regaining of his artistic integrity through his difficult course of self-examination up to this point. The leopard, after all, was "aspiring" after *something*, going up the difficult mountain, and its having died in the process merely represents the heroic difficulty of its quest. Just so is Harry dying after scaling *his* mountain of self-recognition. Hemingway's prose itself becomes lyrical, ecstatic almost, and indeed, many have noticed that it is a favorite Hemingway theme that physical defeat can represent a moral victory as, for example, in *For Whom the Bell Tolls* and *The Old Man and the Sea*.

Further, there is some reason in favor of an hypothesis which would see the action of this story as forming a tragic plot, in the Sophoclean / Aristotelian / Shakespearean sense: a man of noble aspirations suffers defeat because of a moral flaw, discovering the truth about himself only after it is too late to remedy the situation and avoid the catastrophe, thereby arousing pity and fear in the audience, and leading to a catharsis of these emotions. Thus, we may recall, in *Hamlet*, Horatio's eulogy after the hero's self-sought death: Goodnight, sweet prince; a flight of angels sing thee to thy rest. Hamlet has caught himself up in the coils of his *own* tragic flaw—his fear of committing himself to the assigned task of revenging his father's death—and his death is both a way of accomplishing that revenge and of paying for his delay. Harry's flaw is literally his failure properly to care for that scratch on his leg, which of course symbolizes his failure properly to care for his talent as a writer. So *his* flight is also intended to be eulogistic, consolatory, a moral victory in the face of physical defeat.

VI

But there are several difficulties with this "moral victory" interpretation. One is the unfortunate resurgence of Harry's habit of projecting, just before his last reminiscence: his churlish remarks about Julian and the rich fly directly in the face of his previous moments of self-awareness, as for example: "The one experience that he had never had he was not going to spoil now. He probably would. You spoiled everything. But perhaps he wouldn't." We can no longer argue that the churlish Harry is not Ernest, for Harry *himself*, and not just Ernest, had come to this better place *before* needing to put down "Julian."

And then, as we have noticed, he returns to his habit of condescending to and patronizing his wife: "he would rather be in better company."

A third difficulty is that the story does not *end* with Harry's "flight" to the top of the mountain. It ends, rather, with Helen's horrified awakening to the sound of the hyena's whimpering in the night and seeing Harry's leg hanging "down alongside the cot." She calls for their African guide and repeats her husband's name. "There was no answer and she could not hear him breathing." It is the hyena who gets the last word—which, however, she does not hear for the beating of her heart.

We could hypothesize, then, as others have suggested, that what the leopard was seeking at that height was *food*—in the form of mountain goats, say—and that he just didn't make it, just as Harry has been seeking nourishment by scaling the heights of the wealthy and not making it either. And we may recall that Catherine, in *A Farewell to Arms*, also dies while having a child among some snowy mountains.

The problem, however, is that we can't be sure whether Hemingway *intended* to have Harry revert back to his pre-enlightened state just before his death, or whether he was unaware that he had embroiled himself in an artistic incongruity.

It would seem that the latter is our best candidate for a working hypothesis, for the irreducible fact is that he had originally called Julian "Scott." Clearly he had difficulty here in sustaining that essential distance between Harry and Ernest upon which the meaning, integrity, and success of the story depends. He simply could not resist the temptation to reach through the frame of the fiction to give a friend and colleague a swat: did it not occur to him, even *before* Scott complained, that if he said "Scott," then he'd have to call Harry "Ernest"? This is not merely a moral failing, it is an artistic impossibility, for he is changing one part without adjusting the other to match. He even wrote (in 1951) later in one of his letters, "Poor Scott; and didn't he know that the man in 'The Snows of Kilimanjaro' would have spoken of him, or thought of him, exactly as he, Scott, would have mentioned actual things, cars and places?"[2]

But this is obviously a self-serving rationalization, for "actual things, cars and places" are one thing, and naming names is quite another. Even after "Scott" becomes "Julian," however, the conceited boasting—"He had been contemptuous of those who wrecked"—does credit neither to Harry nor Ernest. Nor does it cohere with the previous gains in self-awareness Harry had been making before this—namely, that *he also* had "wrecked" his career as well as his very life. He has therefore not earned the right to criticize Julian, no more than Hemingway had earned the right to criticize Fitzgerald—did not he too suffer from alcoholism, not to mention doubts about his masculinity, inordinate needs for love and approval, etc.?

VII

What do we come up with, on the other hand, if we assume that Hemingway knew what he was doing, and that he intended Harry to be morally and psychologically strong enough to fight his way through to self-knowledge in the face of death, but not strong enough to sustain it to the very end? If Hemingway is here symbolically killing off that weak part of himself, we could say that he gives it as much credit as is probable, but not more than probability can bear. Harry's flight to the snow-topped peak of Kilimanjaro is a wish-fulfillment fantasy of reaching God's House, and he is given at the end what he was not able to give himself while alive. But this does not in any way reward or redeem him: it would have been simply too sentimental to have had him finally become morally and spiritually strong in his last few hours as a result of having to face up to his imminent death. He went as far as he could, like the leopard, and then fell back and froze.

VIII

The truth hovers tantalizingly somewhere among these various possibilities, like the peak of Kilimanjaro among the clouds, and Hemingway's own career tends to bear out this ambiguity. Serious and dedicated artist in the mornings, then soldier, sportsman, celebrity, drinker, and lover of wealthy women the rest of the time, he played a dangerous and ambiguous game with his life and career. He *was* Harry, as well as Ernest, and he apparently *dared* himself to be both. But it would seem that the latter—Harry—won out over the former—Ernest—in the end, for his knock-about career landed him in one too many plane crashes, and he died by his own hand in despair over his vanishing ability to focus his mind on his writing—which was, after all, his basic *raison d'être*, and which gave him permission to be a playboy in the first place, somewhat in the fashion of Harry himself, so that he could know about the rich and thus be able to write about them, a rationalization if there ever was one for self-indulgence and which is precisely what this story purported to be about in the first place.

Although there can be no doubt over the severity of Hemingway's medical problems at the end, I cannot help but conclude that his daring to split his life in this way was what finally did him in. I am not the first to point out the prominence of his counterphobic defense system, deliberately forcing himself to face what most he feared. But of course to face it externally is in the long run no help: putting oneself and one's life continually on the line, literally and physically, repeatedly and compulsively, finally cannot quench that inner terror of being swallowed by the disapproving and devouring mother and abandoned by the remote and self-destroying father. And if it results in recurring physical injury, as in Hemingway's case, it can in fact put an end to the quest altogether—and not merely psychologically.

A writer does not need, of course, to knock about the world seeking material for his stories and novels. The dilemmas and dramas of human existence are just as palpable in the drawing-rooms of Henry James as they are on the battlefield or in the jungle, although they may be more stark in the latter. Nevertheless, one assumes that Homer was a bard rather than a soldier or voyager; and as Hemingway himself well knew, Stephen Crane wrote brilliantly about war before he had ever seen one. Hemingway's need to prove himself as a man as well as a writer stemmed from a deeper source than his professional need for vivid and dramatic material. One suspects that his excessive maleness, in combination with the androgynous tendencies which have only lately come to light, reveal a person deeply troubled in his sexuality and feelings of gender-identity.

My task here, however, is to clarify the formal problems of this story rather than to analyze its author's psychology, and I need only as much of the latter as helps to illuminate the former. I conclude that this story resists a unified hypothesis, and I hope I have shown how and why. Although D.H. Lawrence once claimed that one heals one's sickness in one's books, and

Fitzgerald himself said he was wiser in his books than in his life, it is problematic indeed that one can conduct one's own psychotherapy successfully by oneself. It is becoming clearer of late, for example, that Freud himself could not really do it. It is nevertheless a bold and risky thing to attempt, especially if it is combined with authentic artistic genius, and for *that* attempt it would seem that Hemingway's courage was strong enough, if not to resolve his dilemma, at least to bring him face to face with it.

NOTES

1. Malcolm Cowley, ed., *The Viking Portable Hemingway* (New York: The Viking Press, 1949) 601–627. All "Snows of Kilimanjaro" quotations are from this source.

2. Carlos Baker, ed., *Ernest Hemingway: Selected Letters 1917–1961* (New York: Scribner's, 1981) 716.

SUSAN F. BEEGEL
Santiago and the Eternal Feminine:
Gendering La Mar *in* The Old Man and the Sea

"Hemingway is always less embarrassing when he is not attempting to deal with women," Leslie A. Fiedler writes, with some smugness, of *The Old Man and the Sea*, "and he returns with relief (with what we as readers at least feel as relief) to that 'safe' American Romance of the boy and the old man" ("Adolescence" 108). Like Fiedler, most critics of this novella overlook the fact that *The Old Man and the Sea* has a powerful feminine persona in a title role. Hemingway tells us that Santiago "always thought of the sea as *la mar* which is what people call her in Spanish when they love her. Sometimes those who love her say bad things of her but they are always said as though she were a woman" (29). If the novella is an "American Romance," it is not the love story of Santiago and Manolin but of the old man and the sea, conjoined in the title like Hero and Leander, Troilus and Cressida, Antony and Cleopatra, Tristan and Isolde. Given the nature of the sea in Hemingway's novella, this is not a "safe" romance at all but a story about the tragic love of mortal man for capricious goddess.

I propose a reading of *The Old Man and the Sea* that abandons the anthropocentric critical practice of relegating nature to the role of setting—of thinking like the novella's young fishermen, who consider the sea to be "a place" rather than a living being (30). When we recognize that the sea, as the novella's title suggests, is a protagonist on an equal footing with Santiago, we

From *Hemingway and Women: Female Critics and the Female Voice*, edited by Lawrence R. Broer and Gloria Holland, pp. 131–56, 305–07. Copyright © 2002 by the University of Alabama Press.

109

see how Hemingway—using a rich tapestry of images drawn from mythology, folklore, religion, marine natural history, and literature—genders the sea as feminine throughout the text, thereby raising key questions about the right relationship of man and nature.[1] Although one strand of ecofeminist thought argues that men characteristically gender nature as female to justify treating the land in a dominating, exploitative way (virgin land), while expecting unending forgiveness (Mother Earth), Hemingway argues that the true sin is masculinizing nature, treating nature as an enemy or contestant to be met in combat. Examining the role played by the feminine sea in this story may reveal that *The Old Man and the Sea* has a stronger ecological ethic than previously supposed.

Santiago genders the sea early in the novella as he rows out to fish in the early morning darkness. He begins by "feeling sorry for the birds, especially the small delicate dark terns that were always flying and looking and almost never finding" (29). Then he wonders, "Why did they make birds so delicate and fine as those sea swallows when the ocean can be so cruel? She is kind and very beautiful. But she can be so cruel and it comes so suddenly." This is the moment when we learn that Santiago "always thought of the sea as *la mar*, which is what people call her in Spanish when they love her." We learn further that

> [T]he old man always thought of her as feminine and as something that gave or withheld great favours, and if she did wild or wicked things, it was because she could not help them. The moon affects her as it does a woman, he thought. (30)

These few sentences propose a complex persona for the sea that resonates throughout the novella. I want to begin by examining how they suggest the sea's connection to a spiritual and biological principle of the Eternal Feminine. The sea's kindness, beauty, and generosity—the zenith of the natural cycle involving fecundity, copulation, birth, and nurture—offer important suggestions about right relationship to nature. Next, I want to look at the sin of masculinizing the sea instead of honoring her feminine nature, then examine the "bad things" said about the sea as though she were a woman—that she is cruel, wild, and wicked, and represents the nadir of the natural cycle—the inexorability of the death and decomposition that nourishes life. Throughout, I want to refer not only to published criticism on *The Old Man and the Sea* but also to the voices of those women students who seem less culturally conditioned than men to accept this as a story of contest and who are more likely to question the novella's violence. Finally, I will consider how gendering the sea relates to the tragedy of Santiago and its redemptive message.

Those, like Santiago, who gender what is supremely dangerous in nature as feminine (hurricanes, for instance, were traditionally called by women's names before the National Hurricane Center decided this folkloric practice was "sexist") and especially as maternal (the Tibetan name for Everest is Jomolungma, Mother Goddess of the World) do so in part as a form of appeasement. They hope if they approach with love, understanding, and respect, nature will treat them with feminine gentleness and especially with the unconditional love of a mother. Walt Whitman provides an example in "As I Ebbed with the Ocean of Life" that illuminates Santiago's professions of love for *la mar*:

> Ebb, ocean of life, (the flow will return,)
> Cease not your moaning you fierce old mother,
> Endlessly cry for your castaways, but fear not, deny not me,
> Rustle not up so hoarse and angry against my feet as I touch you
> or gather from you.
> I mean tenderly by you and all,
> I gather for myself. (186)

Santiago's hope that the sea will not rise up angry against him as he gathers for himself explains in part his need to gender the "cruel" sea as feminine.

Santiago begins his consideration of *la mar* from a pagan or "primitive" viewpoint. The words "why did *they* make" imply his belief in a pantheon of gods responsible for natural creation. At once kind and beautiful, cruel and capricious, the sea is goddess and member of that pantheon—"they" know this "she"; "they" should have considered "her" cruelty when they made terns. Associated with the creative and destructive forces in nature, the sea in this novella represents the Eternal Feminine. She might remind us of a figure from Greek or Roman mythology—Tethys, wife of Oceanus and daughter of Uranus and Gaia, or Aphrodite, daughter of Zeus and Dione. Santiago, however, knows her as "*la mar*."

The novella also draws from Catholic imagery in representing the sea as the Eternal Feminine. A devotional picture of the Virgin of Cobre, the patroness of Cuba, hangs next to an image of the Sacred Heart of Jesus on the wall of Santiago's shack.[2] The Virgin is a feminine icon, relic of his dead wife (16). During his agon at sea, he promises to make a pilgrimage to the Virgin of Cobre's shrine if he should catch his fish, and the prayers that he offers are "Hail Marys," which he finds "easier to say" than "Our Fathers" (65). She too is a sea goddess. Santiago acknowledges this when he prays to her for a great favor—"the death of this fish" (65). Bickford Sylvester recounts the Cuban legend of how this small statue of the Virgin, now enshrined in a sanctuary at Cobre, arrived from the sea. She was "floating on a wooden board off the coast . . . in 1628, when . . . found by two Indians and a Creole in a rowboat" ("Cuban Context" 252).

The Virgin Mother of Christ is most familiar to us in her medieval roles as Mater Dolorosa and mediatrix: kind and beautiful, meek and mild, sorrowing for the suffering of man, compassionately interceding for him, offering clemency "at the hour of our death," in the words of the Ave. But mariologists remind us that she is also the descendant of the pagan Magna Mater and Eternal Feminine (Katainen) and of Old Testament figures including Eve and the bride of the erotic "Song of Songs" (Johnson). Her biblical foremothers are tricksters Tamar and Ruth, the prostitute Rahab, and the adulteress Bathsheba—brave and holy women, to be sure, but scarcely meek and mild (Schroer). Mary functions "as a bridge between cultures and traditions" (Johnson), linking both paganism and Judaism to Christianity. Ben Stoltzfus notes that "the effect of the christological imagery" in *The Old Man and the Sea* "is essentially non–Christian," that the novel is less "Christian parable" than "pagan poem," and this is certainly true of the Virgin of Cobre (42–43).

Insofar as she represents the Eternal Feminine and *la mar*, the Virgin of Cobre's origins reside deep in humanity's primitive past. In *The Log from the Sea of Cortez*,[3] John Steinbeck and Edward F. Ricketts suggest how the Virgin may be more pagan than Christian as they describe the Virgin of Loreto. Patroness of a Mexican fishing village on the Sea of Cortez, she is a sister to Hemingway's Virgin of Cobre:

> This Lady, of plaster and wood and paint, is one of the strong ecological factors of the town of Loreto, and not to know her and her strength is to fail to know Loreto. One could not ignore a granite monolith in the path of the waves. Such a rock, breaking the rushing waters, would have an effect on animal distribution radiating in circles like a dropped stone in a pool. So has this plaster Lady a powerful effect on the deep black water of the human spirit. She may disappear, and her name be lost, as the Magna Mater, as Isis have disappeared. But something very like her will take her place, and the longings which created her will find somewhere in the world a similar altar on which to pour their force. No matter what her name is, Artemis or Venus, or a girl behind a Woolworth counter dimly remembered, she is as eternal as our species, and we will continue to manufacture her as long as we survive. (207–08)

In the *la mar* passage, Santiago continues to gender the sea in a pagan vein when he considers that "The moon affects her as it does a woman" (30).

Now he invokes the ancient personification of the moon as a feminine principle in nature, the monthly lunar changes affecting both the tides of the sea and woman's cycle of ovulation and fecundity, her provision of "the nutriment, the catamenia, or menstrual blood" (Merchant 13, 18–19), the nourishing matrix from which life grows. "Moon and sea and tide are one," write Steinbeck and Ricketts, and:

> The imprint [of tidal forces] is in us and in Sparky and in the ship's master, in the palolo worm, in mussel worms, in chitons, and in the menstrual cycle of women. The imprint lies heavily on our dreams and on the delicate threads of our nerves. . . . (37, 39)

The disciplines of oceanography and marine biology both supply a scientific basis for Santiago's mythologizing the sea-as-matrix, a Mother Goddess obeying the cycles of the moon, with "changing woman" her acolyte. In *The Sea Around Us*,[4] Rachel Carson explains in a chapter titled "Mother Sea" how all life evolved from the sea and how the development of the human embryo recapitulates this evolutionary history.

> Fish, amphibian, and reptile, warm-blooded bird and mammal—each of us carries in our veins a salty stream in which the elements sodium, potassium, and calcium are combined in almost the same proportions as sea water. . . . Our lime-hardened skeletons are a heritage from the calcium-rich ocean of Cambrian time. Even the protoplasm that streams within each cell of our bodies has the chemical structure impressed upon all living matter when the first simple creatures were brought forth in the ancient sea. And as life itself began in the sea, so each of us begins his individual life within his mother's womb, and in the stages of his embryonic development repeats the steps by which his race evolved, from gill-breathing inhabitants of a water world to creatures able to live on land. (*The Sea Around Us* 28–29)

Carson postulates that man's love for and desire to return to "mother sea," his mythologizing and gendering of the sea as female, springs from his evolutionary history and longing for "a world that, in the deepest part of his subconscious mind, he ha[s] never wholly forgotten" (29).

Santiago knows the maternal, womblike space the fishermen call "the great well," a sudden deep hole teeming with life, where the current stirs a nutrient upwelling and brings "all the wandering fish" to feed on "shrimp and bait fish and sometimes schools of squid" (28). He also experiences the sea-as-matrix when he looks at plankton and feels happy because it means fish:

The water was a dark blue now, so dark that it was almost purple. As he looked down into it he saw the red sifting of the plankton in the dark water and the strange light the sun made now. He watched his lines to see them go straight down out of sight into the water and he was happy to see so much plankton because it meant fish. (35)

"Plankton," Thor Heyerdahl explains in *Kon-Tiki*,[5] "is a general name for thousands of species of visible and invisible small organisms which drift about near the surface of the sea. Some are plants (phyto-plankton), while others are loose fish ova and tiny living creatures (zoo-plankton)" (138). Where there is plankton, Steinbeck and Ricketts write, the sea "swarms with life." Plankton water is "tuna water—life water. It is complete from plankton to gray porpoises" (54). "These little animals, in their incalculable numbers, are probably the base food supply of the world"—their disappearance would "eliminate every living thing in the sea" if not "all life on the globe" (256).

Hemingway's sparing lines hint at all of this when Santiago experiences the plankton as a "red sifting" in the water (35). It's a "strange light" that makes translucent zooplankton and greenish phytoplankton appear red. But this coloring aligns the plankton with all of the blood of life spilled in the sea throughout the novella, and especially with the nutritive blood of the womb. Heyerdahl calls it "plankton porridge . . . the squashy mess . . . magic gruel" (140). From it, Mother Sea brings forth life.

The sea, Herman Melville reminds us in *Moby-Dick*, has its "submarine bridal-chambers" as well as its nurseries (400), and of this, Santiago is well aware. To him, "a great island of Sargasso weed that heaved and swung in the light sea" looks "as though the ocean were making love with something under a blanket" (72). In the night, two porpoises come around his boat, and Santiago "could tell the difference between the blowing noise the male made and the sighing blow of the female." He identifies with and values the porpoises for their mated love: "They are good. . . . They play and make jokes and love one another. They are our brothers . . ." (48). Later, he dreams of "a vast school of porpoises that stretched for eight or ten miles and it was in the time of their mating and they would leap high in the air and return into the same hole they had made when they had leaped" (81).

Asked in class how Hemingway's seemingly simple and objective prose could achieve such poetic quality in *The Old Man and the Sea*, a woman student gave this explanation: "It's the difference between a man taking a photograph of a woman and a man taking a photograph of a woman he loves." Throughout the novella, the images selected to represent *la mar* establish that she is indeed "very beautiful," and that Santiago is a lover, engaged in what

Terry Tempest Williams has called an "erotics of place," a "pagan" and "primal affair" (84). The sea itself is sublimely beautiful, with its deep blue waters and shafts of sunlight, as is the sky with its canyons of clouds. All of the sea's creatures except the *galano* sharks are beautiful, even the mako and the poisonous jelly fish, and some are exceptionally so, like the dorado that takes Santiago's bait from beneath the erotically heaving blanket of Sargasso weed: "He saw it first when it jumped in the air, true gold in the last of the sun and bending and flapping wildly in the air" (72).

Always the prose seeks what Hemingway called "the action that makes the emotion" ("Monologue" 219), and the emotion is love: "In the dark the old man could feel the morning coming and as he rowed he heard the trembling sound as the flying fish left the water and the hissing that their stiff wings made as they soared away in the darkness" (29). Or, "as the old man watched, a small tuna rose in the air, turned and dropped head first into the water. The tuna shone silver in the sun and after he had dropped back into the water another and another rose and they were jumping in all directions, churning the water and leaping in long jumps after the bait" (38). "Listen to Hemingway write!" responds another woman student. "Gorgeous!" (Gensler). Most "gorgeous" of all is the giant marlin that is the sea's great gift to Santiago:

> The line rose slowly and steadily and then the surface of the ocean bulged ahead of the boat and the fish came out. He came out unendingly and water poured from his sides. He was bright in the sun and his head and back were dark purple and in the sun the stripes on his sides showed wide and a light lavender. (62)

Although *The Old Man and the Sea* may seem to be about "men without women," the figure of a man *wedded* to a feminine sea is omnipresent in our culture, from ancient myths of Venus rising from the foam of the sea to be given as bride to Vulcan, to a contemporary rock ballad such as E. Lurie's "Brandy," where a sailor tells his human lover, "You're a fine girl. What a good wife you would be. But my life, my lover, my lady is the sea." Santiago is no exception. He is a widower and feels his loss—"[T]here had been a tinted photograph of his wife on the wall but he had taken it down because it made him too lonely to see it" (16)—and his loss gives him empathy and compassion for the marlin. "The saddest thing [he] ever saw with them" was the reaction of a male to the capture of his mate. "He was beautiful, the old man remembered, and he had stayed" (50). But now the beauty of the sea assuages Santiago's loneliness for his flesh-and-blood wife: "[H]e looked ahead and saw a flight of wild ducks etching themselves against the sky over the water, then etching again and he knew no man was ever alone on the sea" (61).

In the course of the story, Santiago becomes wedded to the marlin. His angling uses the language of seduction: "'Yes', he said. 'Yes.'" (41). "Come on ... Aren't they lovely? Eat them good now and then there is the tuna. Hard and cold and lovely. Don't be shy, fish" (42). "Then he felt the gentle touch on the line and he was happy" (43). Even after the marlin is firmly hooked and Santiago's ordeal begins, his developing sense of connectedness with the fish is expressed in language from the sacrament of marriage: "Now we are joined together" (50) and "Fish ... I'll stay with you until I am dead" (52).

This sense of the sea-as-wife is not incompatible with Santiago's calling the marlin his "brother." Porpoises and flying fish of both sexes are Santiago's "brothers," too (48), and the word "brother" is neither gender-specific nor used only of humans in Hemingway's work. In "The Last Good Country," Nick's sister Littless looks like a "small wild animal" (SS [The Short Stories of Ernest Hemingway] 101), and wants to be both his "brother" (95) and his "wife" (104). In The Garden of Eden, Catherine Bourne tells David that he is "my good lovely husband and my brother too" (29), and David comes to understand that the elephant also is his "brother" (197).

Brothers are children of the same mother, living together in an implied state of equality and fraternity, depending on one another for mutual support. In To Have and Have Not Captain Willie says, of the human community at sea, "Most everybody goes in boats calls each other brother" (83). In The Old Man and the Sea, that marine community expands to include sea creatures. The man o' war bird is "a great help" to Santiago in locating fish (38), and Santiago in his turn aids the exhausted migrating warbler, "Take a good rest, small bird" (55). Hemingway's signature use of the word "brother" reflects longing for an Eden where men and women, husbands and wives, as well as birds, beasts, and fish might live together on such terms. Such an Eden would bring male and female principles, as well as man and nature, into harmony and balance.

How then may Santiago ethically "live on the sea and kill [his] true brothers" (75)? To render sea creatures as children of the same mother raises vital questions about right relationship to nature. Hunter-philosopher Ted Kerasote proposes some answers. "Hunting," he writes, should be a "disciplined, mindful, sacred activity. . . . hav[ing] much to do with kindness, compassion, and sympathy for those other species with whom we share the web of life. . . . based on the pre-Christian belief that other life-forms, indeed the very plants and earth and air themselves, are invested with soul and spirit" (191). Here we recognize the "primitive" Santiago who fishes with unmatched physical and mental discipline and with prayers, the Santiago who hits the landed tuna on the head "for kindness" (42), who begs the female marlin's pardon and butchers her promptly (50), and who understands that the great marlin not only is his "brother," but suffers as Santiago himself suffers (92). In his introduction to *Atlantic Game Fishing*, Hemingway writes that "Anglers have a way of . . . forgetting that the fish has a hook in his mouth, his gullet, or his belly, and is driven to the extremes of panic at which he runs, leaps, and pulls to get away until he dies" (qtd. in Farrington II). Santiago never forgets the "fish's agony" (93).

Ethical killing, Kerasote tells us, is not for "the cruel delight that comes at another's demise," but for "the celebratory joy inherent in well-performed hunting that produces a gift of food" (190). The blood of life may only be spilled to nourish life. Here we recognize the Santiago who sacramentally partakes of the flesh of every fish he kills—dolphin, tuna, marlin, and even tiny shrimp from the floating blanket of Sargasso weed. This is the Santiago who seeks a fish to feed "many people," and who hopes to repay his indebtedness to his human community with "the belly meat of a big fish" (20). He is drawn in part from Hemingway's Cuban boat-handler, Carlos Gutiérrez, who unlike the trophy-hunting sport fishermen always calls the marlin "the bread of my children," relating it to the staff of life—and the continuity of life: "Oh look at the bread of my children! Joseph and Mary look at the bread of my children jump! There it goes the bread of my children! He'll never stop the bread the bread the bread of my children!" (Hemingway, "On the Blue Water" 242). "Everything kills everything else in some way" as Santiago observes (106), and is ethical so long as the killing is followed by eating, the act of communion, of sharing the blood of life.

Aldo Leopold writes that all ecological ethics "rest upon a single premise: that the individual is a member of a community with interdependent parts. His instincts prompt him to compete for his place in the community, but his ethics prompt him also to co-operate" (239). Glen A. Love feels that *The Old Man and the Sea* lacks a fully developed ecological ethic, because Santiago perceives some creatures of the sea, such as sharks and poisonous jellyfish, as "enemies." Hemingway, Love argues, does not understand that all of the sea's creatures "are members of a community which man is not privileged to exterminate for real or assumed self-benefits" (208). Yet Love's is an environmental sensibility that places man outside of the food web, forgetting, as Leopold does not, that survival demands an ethic that includes the necessity of competition as well as of cooperation.

Santiago, as a subsistence fisherman, knows that he is part of the web of life. His community is truly "the great sea with our friends and our enemies" (120). He loves to see big sea turtles eating the jellyfish, and then he in turn eats the eggs of the turtles that eat the jellyfish in order to be strong "for the truly big fish" he himself hunts (36–37).[6] Others do not like the taste, but Santiago drinks "a cup of shark liver oil each day from the big drum in the shack where the fishermen keep their gear" to sharpen his eyesight (37). Indeed, Santiago's eyes, "the same color as the sea ... cheerful and unde-feated" emblematize that the sea and its creatures are the well-spring of his own life—"with his eyes closed there was no life in his face" (10, 19). He understands that the lives of his "enemies" too are part of the "celebratory gift," part of his fisherman's communion with life.

A woman student who does not accept the primitive hunter's commu-nion of blood, the pagan appreciation of the intimate proximity of life and death, objects to Santiago's slaying of the marlin in gendered terms:

> Ultimately, while I pity Santiago and mourn his defeat, I can't relate to his struggle. I do not share his need to defeat the marlin, or his desire for conquest. This type of battle is common to Hemingway, I've come across the same one in *Islands in the Stream* and I know he's restaged it with bulls and matadors in other books. What I wonder is what form these epic battles would take if Hemingway had been a woman. How would she describe childbirth? Imagine, these arduous, protracted ordeals produce nothing but dead fish, but what magic, what power would be imparted to a two-day struggle to produce a screaming new human being? (Betancourt)

In one sense, *The Old Man and the Sea* may already fulfill this student's wish for a Hemingway who places the male values of strength and endurance in the service of the Eternal Feminine, of bringing forth rather than taking life. To *la mar*, Santiago owes his disciple, the boy Manolin who is more to him than a son. Santiago has no child by his mortal wife, but has delivered Manolin from the sea in a violent birthing. "How old was I when you first took me in a boat?" the boy asks Santiago, in the manner of a child asking a parent for the legend of his birth. "Five and you were nearly killed when I brought the fish in too green and he nearly tore the boat to pieces. Can you remember?" (12). Manolin responds:

> I can remember the tail slapping and banging and the thwart breaking and the noise of clubbing. I can remember you throwing me into the bow where the wet coiled lines were and feeling the whole boat shiver and the noise of you clubbing him like chopping a tree down and the sweet blood smell all over me. (12)

Fish and boy are elided here, as man-midwife Santiago forcibly extracts the flapping, struggling fish from the sea and throws the child slicked in "sweet blood" into the bow. "Can you really remember that or did I just tell you?" asks Santiago. Manolin insists that he can, but the scene is so primal that readers may share Santiago's doubt, wondering whether the boy remembers it any more than he would remember the scene of his birth.

In an essay titled "Forceps" that is in part a history of masculine involvement in obstetrics, Hemingway's doctor father writes that for centuries men were not permitted to attend or witness normal births. "Men midwives," he mourns, "were not allowed at confinements . . . except in cases where an extraction by *force* [his emphasis] of a dead fetus was required." He celebrates the eventual inclusion of men in the process of normal birthing: "to help and share the responsibility" of the "sacred trust" (C. Hemingway 3). In the "birthing" scene from *The Old Man and the Sea*, where Santiago acts as a man-midwife, we do see how his great strength and heroism might serve the cause of life.

On the positive side of the ledger, then, Santiago's gendering the sea as *la mar* underlies this novella's strong ecological ethic. To gender the sea as female or as a mother goddess implies reciprocal obligation. The man who approaches nature as his lover, wife, or mother, expecting "great favours" and kindness, must also, as Whitman phrases it, "mean tenderly" by her. The concept of the sea as a feminine, living being ought to serve, as Carolyn Merchant has pointed out on behalf of the earth, "as a cultural constraint restricting the actions of human beings. One does not readily slay a mother, dig into her entrails . . . or mutilate her body. . . . As long as the earth [is] considered to be alive and sensitive, it could be considered a breach of human ethical behavior to carry out destructive acts against it" (3).

There is no more potent example in American literature of a book that genders the sea as masculine than Herman Melville's *Moby-Dick*, celebrating its centennial the year Hemingway composed *The Old Man and the Sea*.[7] "To and fro in the deeps, far down in the bottomless blue," Melville writes, "rushed mighty leviathans, sword-fish, and sharks, and these were the strong, troubled, murderous thinkings of the masculine sea" (543). No character more obviously treats the sea as masculine contestant and enemy than Captain Ahab, or is more closely associated with man's self-destructive technological assault on nature: "Swerve me? The path to my fixed purpose is laid with iron rails, whereon my soul is grooved to run. Over unsounded gorges, through the rifled hearts of mountains, under torrents' beds, unerringly I rush! Naught's an obstacle, naught's an angle to the iron way!" (172)

Santiago seems to uphold an ecological ethic diametrically opposed to Ahab's "iron way" when he recognizes that those who gender the sea as masculine treat the sea more violently than those who think of her as *la mar*:

Some of the younger fishermen, those who used buoys as floats for
their lines and had motorboats, bought when the shark livers had

brought much money, spoke of her as *el mar* which is masculine.
They spoke of her as a contestant or a place or even an enemy. (30)

These two sentences are dense with environmental history. Aligned with
technology, Santiago's young fishermen are not only the workaday descen-
dants of Captain Ahab, they are the ancestors of today's long-liners. Dr.
Perry W. Gilbert, a shark expert familiar with the Cuban fishing village of
Cojimar where Hemingway based *The Old Man and the Sea*, explains the
fishing rig described above:

> Fishermen put out from Cojimar in their small boats, only eighteen
> to twenty-four feet over all, and head for the deep water.... Two
> men comprise the crew, and their boat carries ten to fifteen floating
> fishing rigs of three hooks each ... The hooks of one set hang at
> different intervals in the water, usually at twenty, fifty, and eighty
> fathoms.... The wooden buoys, spaced forty to fifty feet apart, are
> joined to each other by a three-quarter inch manila rope, attached
> at one end to a square wooden float bearing the name of the boat
> ... and a four foot mast carrying a lantern and flag.... After the
> sets are all placed and the lanterns lit, they are patrolled until dawn.
> At daybreak the catch of dolphin, marlin, broadbill, and sharks is
> removed, and if the weather is fair, a set may be rebaited.... The
> "Old Man," of course, did not have this set. His lines were off his
> boat or in his hands. (qtd. in Farrington 28–30)

The young fishermen fish not so much for the "celebratory gift of food,"
Gilbert tells us, but for the "shark factory" mentioned at the beginning of *The
Old Man and the Sea* (11), an industry processing their catch for the Oriental
soup fin trade, for an Ocean Leather Company in New Jersey converting shark
skin to wallets, belts, and shoes, and for the vitamin A in shark liver oil (in
Farrington 30–31). Their motorboats are the fruits of war. "Shark livers had
brought much money" during World War II, when German submarines in the
North Atlantic cut off the Grand Banks and the world supply of cod liver oil
for pharmaceuticals (R. Ellis 45); the Cojimar shark factory would remain prof-
itable until 1958, when vitamin A was synthesized (Gilbert in Farrington 31).

Santiago sees in the young fishermen the death of his way of life, the
end of putting to sea in small boats powered by oar and sail, of locating fish
only with his own intimate knowledge of the sea and her creatures, and of
catching them with the unaided strength of his body. In part, *The Old Man
and the Sea* is Hemingway's elegy for the subsistence fisherman, and perhaps,
as when Santiago wonders what it would be like to spot fish from airplanes

(71), or to have a radio in the boat that would bring him the "baseball," but distract him from "thinking much" about the sea (105), a prophesy of things to come. Mary Hemingway recalled:

> Our habit was to anchor *Pilar* in the little bay of Cojimar. . . . The town's population was almost entirely fishermen who went out as Santiago did in those days with their skiffs and were carried by the Gulf Stream, which flows from west to east across the northern part of Cuba's coast. They would then put their baits down and drift. . . . When they had their fish, or when the day was finished . . . they'd stick up their sails and come sailing back against the Gulf Stream, the wind being stronger than the current. . . . Before we left, the fishermen . . . were able to add outboard motors to their boats. (qtd. in Bruccoli, "Interview" 193)

Neither Santiago nor Hemingway could predict the modern fleet of Atlantic swordboats—long-liners assisted by global positioning systems, weather fax, down temperature indicators, Doppler radar, color sounders, video plotters, radiofrequency beeper buoys, and hydraulic haulbacks for lines twenty-five to forty miles long, indiscriminately cleansing the sea of sword-fish, sharks, sea turtles, tuna, and other deep oceanic fish (Greenlaw 137). Nor could they predict a generation whose most successful fishermen would be "fishing gear engineers and electronics wizards," ignoring birds and clouds to "study data and base decisions on statistics" (Greenlaw 137–38).

But Santiago does know that the fishermen of the future will follow the "el mar" ethos of treating the sea as a masculine enemy or contestant. Con-temporary swordboat captain Linda Greenlaw, ironically a woman, bears him out when she describes her work as "Man vs. Nature." She uses words like "warrior," "relentless beast," "fight," "monstrous sword," "war," "forces," and "combat" to describe a losing contest with a commodified "$2,000 fish," and then, when the line snaps and the swordfish gets loose, leaps to the rail with her men to give the animal, perceived as "gloating" in "victory," the phallic upraised finger, and to scream "Fuck you" until her throat is raw (Green-law 173–75). If Carolyn Merchant is correct that gendering nature as female and as the mother-of-life acts as a cultural constraint against destructive acts, then the converse appears to be true, that gendering the sea as a masculine opponent enables destructive and violent behavior. Since the first swordfish took bait on an American longline in 1961, Santiago's "young fishermen" have swept the Atlantic of 75 percent of its bluefin tuna and 70 percent of its breeding-age swordfish (Safina, Chivers), carrying us ever closer to the "fish-less desert" of Santiago's nightmare (2).

Santiago rejects those who masculinize the sea. But against his view of Mother Sea as a beautiful, kindly, and generous feminine provider—a belief that in many respects does temper his behavior toward her—he sets an opposing view of feminine nature as cruel and chaotic—spawning poisonous creatures, sudden storms, and hurricanes. Although early in the novella Hemingway tells us that Santiago "no longer dreamed of storms, nor of women, nor of great occurrences, nor of great fish, nor fights, nor contests of strength, nor of his wife," *The Old Man and the Sea* is a dream of all such things, and here we learn that Santiago includes the feminine principles of "women" and "wife" with "storms" and "great fish," natural things that might be fought or engaged in "contests of strength" (25). As Merchant points out, such views of nature as a disorderly female force call forth the male need for rationalistic or mechanistic power over her (127).

Critic Gerry Brenner labels the *la mar* passage "a litany of sexist aggressions" in part for Santiago's "metaphoric equation" of woman and the sea "as dependent on the moon or some power over which she has no control" (*Story* 84). However, the point of Santiago's "and if she did wild or wicked things it was because she could not help them," may be that women and the sea are not *under* control, but *beyond* control. Carson writes that man may approach "mother sea only on her terms. . . . He cannot control or change the ocean as . . . he has subdued and plundered the continents" (*Sea Around Us* 29–30). When Santiago thinks "the moon affects her as it does a woman," he betrays male fear of female power, of the menstruous or monstrous woman, whose wildness and wickedness challenges his rationalism and control, and whose cruelty provokes his attempts at dominance. In *The Garden of Eden*, Catherine Bourne (who needs to "go up to the room" because "I'm a god damned woman"), speaks for menstruous woman, and perhaps for *la mar*, when she overrides David's effort to silence and control her: "Why should I hold it down? You want a girl, don't you? Don't you want everything that goes with it? Scenes, hysteria, false accusations, temperament, isn't that it?" (70).

Santiago believes that, in his great love for and understanding of *la mar*, he has accepted "everything that goes with" her femininity. He knows the months of the "sudden bad weather," and is not afraid to be out of sight of land in hurricane season, because he "can see the signs of [a hurricane] for days ahead" in the sky (61). He endures the painful sting of a ray hidden in the sand, and of the Portuguese man o' war jellyfish he genders as female and calls "Agua mala [evil water]" and "You whore." Although the jellyfish strike "like a whiplash," he loves to walk on them on the beach after a storm and "hear them pop when he step[s] on them with the horny soles of his feet" (82). While Brenner finds Santiago's "vilification of the jellyfish" the novella's most "blatant" example of "hostility or contempt towards things female" (82),

Katharine T. Jobes believes the old man's epithet—"You whore"—is familiar, affectionate, a reflection of Santiago's "intimate at-homeness in nature" (16).

Yet despite Santiago's apparent acceptance of the sea's wild and wicked nature, ultimately he sins against her, and she bitches him. Gendering the sea as feminine does not resolve the problem of man's violence toward nature, but raises even more disturbing questions about right relationship than gendering the sea as *el mar*. Our culture generally accepts male-on-male violence—such as the cock-fighting and arm-wrestling in *Old Man*—provided it conforms to the rituals of warfare, chivalry, or sportsmanship. We perceive such violence as the "natural" outcome of male competition for territory and sexual preroga-tive, although neither instinct bodes well when directed against nature. Con-versely, male-on-female violence is taboo, "unnatural" because the biological purpose of male-female relations is procreation, not competition.

As Melvin Backman has noted, *Death in the Afternoon* provides an inter-pretive key to the problem of sin in *The Old Man and the Sea*: "[W]hen a man is still in rebellion against death he has pleasure in taking to himself one of the Godlike attributes; that of giving it. . . . These things are done in pride and pride, of course, is a Christian sin and a pagan virtue . . ." (233). The old man is surely in rebellion against death. His eighty-four days without a fish, the mockery of the young fishermen, the pity of the older fishermen, the charity of his village, the role reversal that sees his much-loved apprentice Manolin taking care of him ("You'll not fish without eating while I'm alive" [19]), and perhaps most of all the loss of Manolin, forced by his parents into a "luckier" boat, conspire to make Santiago feel his proximity to death. These things send him out to sea, beyond all other fishermen, to seek "a big one" (30), and the struggle with the marlin becomes in part a struggle with the "treachery of one's own body" (62), with his spells of faintness and blurred vision, with his cramped hand: "Pull, hands. . . . Hold up, legs. Last for me, head. Last for me" (91). Santiago's rebellion against death draws him first into sin, and then into an orgy of violence against the sea he loves.

In Christian iconography, both the sea and the Eternal Feminine are associated with death and resurrection. *The Book of Common Prayer* makes of the ocean a vast graveyard, and, strangely for a Christian text, feminizes the sea: "We therefore commit his body to the deep, to be turned into cor-ruption, looking for the resurrection of the body, when the Sea shall give up *her* dead" (my emphasis, 552). The Virgin of Cobre places Santiago in this cycle of death and resurrection. Opus Dei scholar Dwight Duncan opines: "Christianity is the celebration of Christ as a man, one of us. So it is natural to approach it through the perspective of the mother. Mary is the guarantor of Christ's manhood" (Kennelly). Phrased somewhat differently, this means that the Virgin is the guarantor of Christ's suffering and death—and Santiago's.

As his mortal progenitor, the Mother makes Christ subject—as all humanity is subject—to the immutable laws of biological nature.

Santiago kills the marlin with the most masculine of weapons, the harpoon, driving it deep into the fish's heart, the organ of love and the seat of life:

> The old man dropped the line and put his foot on it and lifted the harpoon as high as he could and drove it down with all his strength, and more strength he had just summoned, into the fish's side just behind the great chest fin that rose high in the air to the altitude of the man's chest. He felt the iron go in and he leaned on it and drove it further and then pushed all his weight after it.
>
> Then the fish came alive, with his death in him, and rose high out of the water showing all his great length and width and all his power and his beauty. (93–94)

Three times Hemingway tells us that the old man's target was the heart: "I must try for the heart" (91); "the sea was discoloring with the red of the blood from his heart" (94); "I think I felt his heart. . . . When I pushed on the harpoon shaft the second time" (95).

The heart of the marlin recalls the Sacred Heart of Jesus, the other devotional icon that hangs on the wall of Santiago's shack next to the Virgin of Cobre (16). That heart symbolizes the love and suffering of Christ, and his sacrifice—his death that man might live. By suggesting that the marlin too might have a sacred heart, Hemingway asks us to contemplate the passion of the natural cycle, or, as Kerasote puts it, to "fac[e] up to this basic and poignant condition of biological life on this planet—people, animals, and plants as fated cohorts, as both dependents and donors of life" (191). Hemingway invites us to understand that the marlin, in the words of Santiago's "Hail Mary," is the "fruit of the womb" of the Eternal Feminine (65). Coming "alive with his death in him," the marlin conjoins the principles of life and death implicit both in natural cycles and in the iconography of resurrection that arises from them. Santiago sees the eye of the dead fish looking "as detached as mirrors in a periscope or as a saint in a procession" (96), suggesting that the marlin should remind us of our own mortality, and our own mortality should remind us to have compassion for all living things.

Santiago's harpoon, probing the sacred heart, probes again the essential question of male-on-female violence, of right relationship of man and nature. When may man ethically kill the thing he loves? "If you love him, it is not a sin to kill him," Santiago thinks of the great marlin. "Or is it more?" (105). Santiago cannot bear to pursue the question—"You think too much, old man"—he tells himself, but the text would seem to argue "more." Too late, he recognizes that "You did not kill him to keep alive and to sell for food," the only allowable answers, "You killed him for pride and because you are a fisherman" (105). Despite knowing that the marlin is "two feet longer than the skiff" and cannot be landed (63), despite believing that it is "unjust" and that he is doing it to show the marlin "what a man can do and what a man endures" (66), despite feeling that "there is no one worthy of eating him from the manner of his behaviour and his great dignity" (75), the old man proceeds to kill the marlin anyway. When sharks attack the fish, as Santiago knows they must, his tragedy will be to recognize that he was wrong: "'Half fish,' he said. 'Fish that you were. I am sorry that I went out too far. I ruined us both'" (115).

Sylvester has argued that Santiago's "slaying of the marlin and his responsibility for its mutilation are sins," but "tragic precisely because they are a necessary result of his behavior as a champion of his species" ("Extended Vision" 136). Sylvester sees "opposition to nature as paradoxically necessary to vitality in the natural field" ("Extended Vision" 132), and perhaps it's true that a man "born to be a fisherman as the fish was born to be a fish" (105) could not conceive, as Hemingway himself could conceive, of releasing a marlin and "giv[ing] him his life back" (G. Hemingway 73). Perhaps a man who fishes for his living cannot say, as young David Hudson says in *Islands in the Stream* about a marlin that escapes him after a gruelling fight: "I loved him so much when I saw him coming up that I couldn't stand it. . . . All I wanted was to see him closer. . . . Now I don't give a shit I lost him. . . . I don't care about records. I just thought I did. I'm glad that he's all right" (143). Yet if Sylvester's concept of "necessary sin" is correct, then the text violates Santiago's own philosophy—that it is wrong to gender the sea as *el mar* and to treat it as a contestant or enemy. A woman student proposes instead that Santiago's sin is both unnecessary and the direct result of the "masculine" thinking he himself has deplored:

> The code of manhood that gives Santiago the strength for his battle and even the reason to begin it is completely foreign to me. He doesn't *have* to do this—a fisherman can make a living on the tuna and dolphin that Santiago uses only for bait and sustenance. . . . When Santiago says he has not caught a fish in eighty-seven [*sic*] days, he does not mean fish, he means Krakens, sea monsters. The bravery involved in just wresting a living from the sea is nothing . . . Santiago has to be a saint and fight dragons. . . . I guess what it comes down to is greatness. . . . Killing a 1500 lb. Marlin puts him on the same level with the magnificent fish, giving him a power as great as the ocean's. There is nothing about this that's hard to

understand; a man wishes to be strong and so he tests himself
against the strongest thing he can find. (Betancourt)

Nature's punishment for the harpoon in the heart is swift and inexo-
rable. The heart pumps the blood of the stricken fish into the sea—"First it
was dark as a shoal in the blue water that was more than a mile deep. Then it
spread like a cloud" (94). The heart's blood summons the first shark, a mako,
and Santiago recognizes the consequences of his own actions: "The shark was
not an accident. He had come up from deep down in the water as the dark
cloud of blood had settled and dispersed in the mile deep sea" (100). Indeed,
the mako almost seems like the marlin's avenging ghost: "His back was as
blue as a sword fish's and his belly was silver and his hide was smooth and
handsome. He was built like a sword fish except for his huge jaws" (100). Like
the marlin too, the mako is "beautiful and noble" (106). His teeth "shaped like
a man's fingers when they are crisped like claws" (100–101), recall Santiago's
left hand cramped "tight as the gripped claws of an eagle" (63). The mako
comes as a grim reminder that marlin, shark, and man—all predators—are
brothers, children of the same mother.

Yet "the shadow of sharks is the shadow of death," as Peter Matthiessen has observed (5), and when Santiago sees the mako, he curses the
mother—"*Dentuso*, he thought, bad luck to your mother" (101)—and who
is the Mother of Sharks if not *la mar*? Santiago assaults the shadow of
death "without hope but with resolution and complete malignancy" (102).
He harpoons the mako with a precision so reminiscent of the bullfight,
one wonders whether Hemingway knew that the ancient Hawaiians built
marine arenas in shallow water, where men armed with shark-tooth dag-
gers fought sharks to honor Kama-Hoa-Lii, the shark god (Cousteau 205).
Harpooning the mako, Santiago sins a second time, and explicitly partakes
of the matador's sin from *Death in the Afternoon*. "You enjoyed killing the
dentuso, he thought" (105), and this is both the Christian sin of pride in
taking pleasure in the Godlike attribute of giving death, and the pagan sin
identified by Kerasote, of taking "cruel delight" in another's demise (109).
Again Santiago's sin sends a blood message of life wrongfully taken into the
sea: "Now my fish bleeds again," he thinks after the dead mako sinks with
his harpoon, "and there will be others" (103). Santiago's rebellion against
death, which has, from the start of the novella, underlain his quest for the
marlin, now assumes crisis proportions.

Sharks begin to arrive in numbers, and they are a different species—not
the "beautiful and noble" mako, *Isurus oxyrinchus*, that like the marlin preys
on tuna and dolphin (Bigelow 23–25), but *galanos*, probably oceanic whitetip
sharks, *Carcharhinus longimanus*, but certainly—and significantly—members

of the family *Carcharinidae*,[8] commonly known as the "Requiem sharks" (R. Ellis 130). These sharks are not only biologically apt (whitetips are well-known to whalemen and big game fishermen for feeding on their kills, and notorious for attacks on victims of shipwrecks and air disasters), but for a marine naturalist like Hemingway they also allude to the introit of the Roman Catholic mass for the dead. Santiago truly vilifies the *galanos* as

> hateful sharks, bad smelling, scavengers as well as killers, and when they were hungry they would bite at an oar or the rudder of a boat. It was these sharks that would cut the turtles' legs and flippers off when the turtles were asleep on the surface, and they would hit a man in the water, if they were hungry, even if the man had no smell of fish blood nor of fish slime on him. (108)

Rising from the sea as from the grave, their evil smell a reminder that the body is destined "to be turned into corruption," the scavenging *galanos* are the ultimate reminder of death as the reabsorption of the individual into the matrix of life. When Santiago sees them, he makes "a noise such as a man might make, involuntarily, feeling the nail go through his hands and into the wood" (107). "Old men should burn and rave at close of day," Dylan Thomas writes (942), and Santiago does indeed rage against the dying of the light, stabbing, hacking, and clubbing at the sharks with everything he has, although he knows that the fight is "useless" (118). "'Fight them,' he said. 'I'll fight them until I die'" (115). Like the mako, the *galanos* too are sent by the mother, and Santiago seems to perceive himself as sending a message of defiance to her when he says to a shark he has killed: "Go on, *galano*. Slide down a mile deep. Go see your friend, or maybe it's your mother" (109).

The "evil" of the shark, emblematizing the inexorability of suffering and death in nature, has long constituted a theological problem, calling into question the benevolent intentions of God toward man, and suggesting instead cruelty and indifference. "Queequeg no care what god made him shark," pronounces Melville's savage, "wedder Fejee god or Nantucket god; but de god wat made shark must be one dam Ingin" (310). Even a marine ecologist such as Philippe Cousteau, who recognizes that it is risible to "qualif[y] one animal as 'good' and another as 'bad'" (133), can write of the same oceanic whitetip shark that Santiago finds hateful:

> [O]ne of the most formidable of the deep-sea sharks, a great *longimanus*.... this species is absolutely hideous. His yellow-brown color is not uniform, but streaked with irregular markings resembling a bad job of military camouflage.... He swims in a jerky,

irregular manner, swinging his shortened, broad snout from side to side. His tiny eyes are hard and cruel-looking. (89)

Cousteau also recognizes that his fear of sharks is related to his fear of an indifferent, inhuman creator: "The shark moves through my universe like a marionette whose strings are controlled by someone other than the power manipulating mine" (70).

The Old Man and the Sea suggests, through its twice-repeated reference to the "mother" of sharks, that "de god wat made shark" must be one damn woman—cruel, wild, wicked, irrational, beyond control. Santiago's battle with the sharks, his rage and rebellion against *la mar*, is his most Melvillean moment. Like Ahab, Santiago seems to say:

> I now know thee . . . and I now know thy right worship is defiance. To neither love nor reverence wilt thou be kind; and e'en for hate thou canst but kill; and all are killed. . . . I now own thy speech-less, placeless power; but to the last gasp of my earthquake life will dispute its unconditional mastery in me. In the midst of the personified impersonal, a personality stands here. (512)

Santiago puts it more simply, spitting blood coughed up from his chest into the sea when the last of the shark pack leaves the ruined marlin, saying "Eat that, *galanos*, and make a dream you've killed a man" (119). The life that burns in him, the will to survive, is the source of his proud individualism and refusal to submit tamely to annihilation. Ahab proclaims "[O]f thy fire thou madest me, and like a true child of fire, I breathe it back" (512).

Ahab's defiance of a masculine god places him outside of nature and against nature, a crime for which he will be executed with a hempen cord of whale line around the neck. Santiago's defiance of the feminine "mother of sharks" places him inside nature and outside of nature. Like the turtle whose heart beats "for hours after he has been cut up and butchered" (37), like the great marlin who comes "alive, with his death in him" (94), and especially like the shark who is dead but "would not accept it" (102), Santiago is a true child of *la mar*. Her law proclaims that "all are killed," but her law also proclaims that all—turtle, marlin, shark, and man—will dispute their deaths. The sea punishes Santiago for the wrongful deaths of marlin and mako, but for the final battle with the sharks—for breathing back the fire of life—she forgives him.

When the battle with the sharks is finally and irretrievably lost, Santiago achieves a kind of serenity born of acceptance that Ahab never knows. Ahab neither repents nor relents—"for hate's sake I spit my last breath at thee"

(574–75). Santiago does both, apologizing to the marlin and acknowledging that he has been "beaten now finally" by the sharks (119). This the old man experiences as a lightening, a release from a great burden:

> He settled the sack around his shoulders and put the skiff on her course. He sailed lightly now and he had no thoughts nor any feelings of any kind. He was past everything now. . . . In the night sharks hit the carcass. . . . The old man paid no attention to them and did not pay attention to anything except steering. He only noticed how lightly and how well the skiff sailed now there was no great weight beside her. (119)

Eric Waggoner reads this passage as a restoration of harmony, citing the *Tao-te Ching*: "Return is the movement of the Way; / yielding is the function of the way" (102). Waggoner's Taoist perspective prompts us to understand that by yielding to the sea, by accepting his place in nature, "[Santiago] can re-place himself in the balance of his fishing life and sail his skiff 'well'" (102). Still more important, however, is the end of Santiago's rebellion against death, and the beginning of his acquiescence.

Now Santiago is "inside the current," and the text restores him to his original love and reverence for the sea with all her vagaries and caprices. In this key passage, *la mar* is aligned not with an enemy wind that sends great storms, but with the friendly wind that carries an exhausted fisherman lightly home. The sea is associated not with the cruelty of a watery grave and its scavenging sharks, but with bed, where a tired man may find rest:

> The wind is our friend, anyway, he thought. Then he added, sometimes. And the great sea with our friends and enemies. And bed, he thought. Bed is my friend. Just bed, he thought. Bed will be a great thing. It is easy when you are beaten, he thought. I never knew how easy it was. (120)

Now, in Whitmanian rather than Melvillean fashion, Santiago hears the word up from feminine rather than masculine waves, the word of "the sweetest song and all songs," the word "out of the cradle endlessly rocking," the word whispered by the sea—death (184).

Santiago's acquiescence is not Christian. Earlier, Santiago has confessed that he is "not religious" (64); there is no hint that he believes in resurrection. But if he believes in the sea as both friend and enemy, cradle and grave, life and death, and accepts her cycles, then he may partake in the "natural" consolation of Ecclesiastes slightly revised—"One generation passeth away and

another generation cometh: but the [sea] abideth forever" (1.6). The pagan—
and the naturalist—both draw spiritual comfort from material immortality
in the Eternal Feminine. As Carson puts it in *Under the Sea Wind*: "[I]n the
sea, nothing is lost. One dies, another lives, as the precious elements of life are
passed on and on in endless chains" (105).[9]

A text that masculinized the sea might end with Santiago "destroyed but
not defeated" (103), the existential hero with the trophy of his pyrrhic victory,
"the great fish . . . now just garbage waiting to go out with the tide" (126). But
The Old Man and the Sea ends instead not only with Santiago's acceptance of
death as natural as sleep—but with the cycle of life turning upwards once
more. Hemingway reunites Santiago with Manolin, the boy who is more-
than-son to him, the child of Santiago's man-midwifery, delivered from the
sea. Theirs is what Claire Rosenfeld calls a "spiritual kinship" (43); the sea as
wife-and-mother joins them as father-and-son. Manolin cares tenderly for
the old man, allowing him to sleep undisturbed, bringing him coffee, food,
newspapers, and a clean shirt, and making cheerful talk about the future.
When Santiago cannot see him, the boy weeps for the old man's ordeal and
shows his understanding: he weeps for Santiago's suffering when he sees the
bloody stigmata of the rope on the old man's hands (122), he weeps for the
ruin of the great fish when he sees the skeleton lashed to the skiff (122), and
he weeps for his mentor's heartbreak and imminent death after Santiago tells
him that "something in his chest [feels] broken" (125).

Manolin will carry Santiago's legacy forward, insuring the continuity of
life in the face of destruction. The boy asks for and receives the spear of the
great marlin from his mentor (124), a gift that represents not only Santiago's
greatness as a fisherman, but the dignity and courage and beauty of the fish
himself and the lesson of his loss. The spear is also a gift from the sea that
binds man and boy and fish together, a true family heirloom, and a pagan
devotional icon. Having received the bequest of the spear, Manolin promises
in his turn to leave the boats of the young fishermen where his other "family" has placed him, to follow Santiago for "I still have much to learn" (125).
If Santiago is dying, then Manolin's discipleship may be more metaphorical
than literal, but the passage of the marlin's spear to him affirms the continu-
ation of Santiago's values, the perpetuation of a line of fishermen who gender
the sea as *la mar* because they love her. That Manolin is a worthy heir, we
know. From the beginning of the text, when he tells Santiago—"If I cannot
fish with you, I would like to serve in some way" (12)—this filial boy has met
the test of love as defined by the priest in *A Farewell to Arms*: "When you love
you wish to do things for. You wish to sacrifice for. You wish to serve." (72).
We expect Manolin to honor both Santiago and the sea by fishing in the
disciplined, mindful, sacred way.

Making his bequest, accomplishing this transition, brings Santiago final serenity and this text full circle. We leave him asleep, the boy keeping vigil beside him, dreaming the recurrent dream of lions that has been with him from the beginning of the story (25, 127). The dream lions, we know, come to a long yellow beach to play like young cats in the dusk, and Santiago "love[s] them as he love[s] the boy" (25). "Why are the lions the main thing that is left?" (66), Santiago has wondered, and we may wonder too. Perhaps his dream of innocent predators, allied with the boy and the continuity of life, carries him to a Peaceable Kingdom, an Eden unspoiled by sin where men no longer need to "live on the sea and kill our true brothers" (75), to a place where viewing nature as a contestant or an enemy is no longer possible, and love alone remains.

NOTES

1. This essay will refer to works Hemingway read (*Moby-Dick*, the poetry of Whitman, Thor Heyerdahl's *Kon-Tiki*) before composing *The Old Man and the Sea*, as well as books that he may have read during its composition (Carson's *The Sea Around Us* and *Under the Sea Wind*, Steinbeck and Ricketts's *The Log from the Sea of Cortez*). Hemingway drafted his novella in January and February 1951 (Baker, *Life* 489–90) but did not publish the story until 1 September 1952, in a single installment of *Life* magazine. The long lag between the initial composition of the story and its publication has interesting implications for understanding how Hemingway's reading might have influenced *The Old Man and the Sea* and its ecological ethics. During this period, Hemingway was reading Carson, Steinbeck, and Ricketts and was probably rereading *Moby-Dick*, celebrating its centennial year in 1951. The John F. Kennedy Library holds two typescripts of *The Old Man and the Sea* with corrections in ink; however, Mary Hemingway recalled that her husband "did the whole thing by hand and then I typed it" (qtd. in Bruccoli 191). No longhand draft of *The Old Man and the Sea* has yet been located, making a study of Hemingway's possible revisions based on his 1951 reading impossible.

2. When Hemingway won the Nobel Prize, in part for his achievement in *The Old Man and the Sea*, he gave his medal to the Virgin of Cobre, to be kept in her sanctuary at Santiago de Cuba (Baker, *Life* 528).

3. Originally published in 1941 as *Sea of Cortez: A Leisurely Journal of Travel and Research*, this book was reissued in 1951 as *The Log from the Sea of Cortez*, with its scientific apparatus (an appendix including a phyletic catalogue on the marine animals of the Panamic faunal province) removed.

4. Hemingway owned a copy of the 1951 edition (Brasch and Sigman).

5. Hemingway owned a copy of *Kon-Tiki*, a nonfiction bestseller of 1950, the year before he wrote *The Old Man and the Sea* (Brasch and Sigman).

6. Santiago also admires the loggerheads because they are "strange in their lovemaking" (36), and in *To Have and Have Not*, Hemingway refers to the widely held belief that loggerheads copulate for three days—"Do they really do it three days? Coot for three days?" Marie asks Harry (113). For this reason, the loggerhead eggs that Santiago eats to "give himself strength" (37) are considered an aphrodisiac

(Dennis), and some of this folklore may resonate in his three-day battle with the fish.

Hemingway's description of the loggerhead turtle eating jellyfish with its eyes closed is probably drawn from Thomas Barbour's *A Naturalist in Cuba*, a book in Hemingway's library (Brasch and Sigman). Barbour writes:

> I saw an enormous loggerhead ease up to a Portuguese man-of-war, close its eyes, and nip at the beast. Physalia is well provided with stinging cells and its tentacles are dangerous things to touch. It was amusing to see the old turtle close his eyes as he made his dab at the jellyfish. I have no doubt that the membranes surrounding his eyeballs were the only place where the stinging cells of the siphonophore's arms would have been effective. All other regions were protected by heavy armor. (76)

7. Malcolm Cowley notes that when *The Old Man and the Sea* was published, it was widely referred to as "the poor man's *Moby-Dick*" ("Hemingway's Novel" 106).

8. In Caribbean Spanish, the word *galano*, when applied to an animal, simply means having a dappled or mottled skin (Mandel, e-mail to Beegel). Hence, the Cuban common name for this shark helps with identification. Shark expert Dr. Perry Gilbert notes that near the village of Cojimar a "grande Galano" may be a bull shark (in Farrington 32), or *Carcharhinus leucas*. However, this species, which can inhabit fresh and brackish water as well as saltwater, is never found far from land (R. Ellis 139) and hence cannot be Santiago's deepwater *galano*. Miriam B. Mandel located among Hemingway's papers a 1936 list of commercially valuable fish published by the Cuban secretary of agriculture giving for a *galano* the scientific name of *Charcharias limbatus* (*Reading Hemingway* 352), probably an error for *Carcharhinus limbatus*. But the characteristic black-tipped fins of *C. limbatus* (R. Ellis 302) mean it cannot be Santiago's *galano*, which has "white-tipped wide pectoral fins" (107). Mandel's correspondence with Dr. José I. Castro, senior research scientist of the National Marine Fisheries Service, Miami Branch, identifies the *galano* as the oceanic whitetip, *Carcharhinus longimanus* (*Reading Hemingway* 352, 522). In my opinion, this is the only identification that satisfactorily covers the shark's deepwater habitat, mottled skin, white-tipped fins, aggressive scavenging behavior, and notoriety as a man-eater.

9. Rachel Carson first published *Under the Sea Wind* in 1941. The book was republished in April 1952, when it joined *The Sea Around Us* on the *New York Times* bestseller list (Lear 226). Hemingway owned a copy of the 1952 edition (Brasch and Sigman).

WORKS CITED

Backman, Melvin. "Hemingway: The Matador and the Crucified." *Modern Fiction Studies* 1 (1955): 2–11.

Baker, Carlos. *Ernest Hemingway: A Life Story*. New York: Scribner's, 1969.

Barbour, Thomas. *A Naturalist in Cuba*. Boston: Little, 1945.

Betancourt, Cecilia. "Reaction Paper: El Viejo y La Mar." Unpublished essay, 1997.

Bigelow, Henry B., and William C. Schroeder. *Fishes of the Gulf of Maine*. Fishery Bulletin of the Fish and Wildlife Service. Washington DC: GPO, 1953.

The Book of Common Prayer and Administration of the Sacraments. 1662. Cambridge: Cambridge UP, 1968.

Brasch, James, and Joseph Sigman, comps. *Hemingway's Library: A Composite Record.* New York: Garland, 1981.

Brenner, Gerry. *The Old Man and the Sea: Story of a Common Man.* New York: Twayne, 1991.

Bruccoli, Matthew. "Interview with Mary Welsh Hemingway." *Conversations with Writers.* Detroit: Gale, 1977. 180–91.

Carson, Rachel. *The Sea Around Us.* 1951. New York: Mentor, 1989.

Cousteau, Jacques-Yves, and Philippe Cousteau. *The Shark: Splendid Savage of the Sea.* Trans. Francis Price. Garden City, NY: Doubleday, 1970.

Cowley, Malcolm. "Hemingway's Novel Has the Rich Simplicity of a Classic." Rev. of *The Old Man and the Sea. New York Herald Tribune Book Review* 7 Sept. 1952. Rpt. in *Twentieth Century Interpretations of "The Old Man and the Sea."* Ed. Katherine T. Jobes. Englewood Cliffs, NJ: Prentice Hall, 1968. 106–08.

Ellis, Richard. *The Book of Sharks.* New York: Grosset, 1975.

Farrington, S. Kip. *Fishing with Hemingway and Glassell.* New York: David McKay, 1971.

Fiedler, Leslie A. "Adolescence and Maturity in the American Novel." *An End to Innocence: Essays on Culture and Politics.* Boston: Beacon, 1955. Rpt. in *Twentieth Century Interpretations* of *The Old Man and the Sea.* Ed. Katherine T. Jobes. Englewood Cliffs, NJ: Prentice Hall, 1968. 108.

———. *Love and Death in the American Novel.* New York: Stein, 1982.

Gensler, Mindy. "Response Paper: *The Old Man and the Sea.*" Unpublished essay, 1997.

Greenlaw, Linda. *The Hungry Ocean: A Swordboat Captain's Journey.* New York: Hyperion, 1999.

Hemingway, Clarence Edmonds. "Forceps." Unpublished essay, 1913. Archives of the Ernest Hemingway Foundation of Oak Park, Illinois.

Hemingway, Ernest. *Death in the Afternoon.* 1932. New York: Scribner's, 1960.

———. *A Farewell to Arms.* 1929. New York: Scribner's, 1957.

———. *The Garden of Eden.* New York: Scribner's, 1986.

———. "Hemingway's Introduction to Atlantic Game Fishing." Farrington. *Fishing with Hemingway and Glassell.* New York: David McKay, 1971. 9–14.

———. "Monologue to the Maestro: A High Seas Letter." *Esquire* Oct. 1935. Rpt. in *By-Line.* Ed. William White. New York: Scribner's, 1967, 213–20.

———. "On the Blue Water: A Gulf Stream Letter." *Esquire* Apr. 1936. Rpt. in *By-Line.* Ed. William White. New York: Scribner's, 1967, 236–44.

———. "On Writing." *The Nick Adams Stories.* New York: Bantam, 1973, 213–20.

———. *The Old Man and the Sea.* New York: Scribner's, 1952.

———. *The Old Man and the Sea.* Mss. Hemingway Collection. John F. Kennedy Library, Boston.

———. *To Have and Have Not.* New York: Scribner's, 1937.

Heyerdahl, Thor. *Kon-Tiki: Across the Pacific by Raft.* Trans. F. H. Lyon. Chicago: Rand McNally, 1950.

Johnson, Elizabeth A. Rev. of *Mary Through the Centuries: Her Place in the History of Culture. Theological Studies* 58 (1997): 372–74. Infotrac Search Bank. Article A19540892.

Katainen, V. Louise. Rev. of *Mary Through the Centuries: Her Place in History. National Forum* Winter 1998: 44–46. Infotrac Search Bank. Article A53644242.

Kennedy, J. Gerald. *Imagining Paris: Exile, Writing, and American Identity.* New Haven: Yale UP, 1993.

Kennelly, Eleanor. "Rediscovering the Madonna: Virtue as an Icon for the Ages." *Insight on the News* 23 Jan. 1995: 26–28. Infotrac Search Bank. Article A16679524.

Kerasote, Ted. "A Talk about Ethics." *Heart of Home: People, Wildlife, Place.* New York: Villard, 1997. 179–92.

Lear, Linda. *Rachel Carson: Witness for Nature.* New York: Holt, 1997.

Love, Glen A. "Hemingway's Indian Virtues: An Ecological Reconsideration." *Western American Literature* 22 (1987): 202–13.

Lurie, E. "Brandy (You're a Fine Girl)." Perf. Looking Glass. Rec. Sony Music Entertainment, 1972.

Mandel, Miriam B. E-mail to Susan Beegel. 6 June 1999.

———. *Reading Hemingway: The Facts in the Fictions.* Metuchen, NJ: Scarecrow, 1995.

Matthiessen, Peter. *Blue Meridian: The Search for the Great White Shark.* New York: Random, 1971.

Melville, Herman. *Moby-Dick; or, The Whale.* 1851. Berkeley: U of California P, 1979.

Merchant, Carolyn. *The Death of Nature: Women, Ecology and the Scientific Revolution.* San Francisco: Harper, 1983.

Schroer, Silvia. "Mary's Foremothers." *National Catholic Reporter* 25 Dec. 1992: 3. Infotrac Searchbank. Article A1332397.

Steinbeck, John, and Edward F. Ricketts. *The Log from the Sea of Cortez.* 1951. New York: Penguin, 1986.

Stoltzfus, Ben. *Gide and Hemingway: Rebels Against God.* Port Washington, NY: Kennikat, 1978.

Sylvester, Bickford. "The Cuban Context of *The Old Man and the Sea.*" *Cambridge Companion to Hemingway.* Ed. Scott Donaldson. Cambridge: Cambridge UP, 1996. 243–68.

———. "Hemingway's Extended Vision: *The Old Man and the Sea.*" *PMLA* (Mar. 1966): 130–38.

Thomas, Dylan. "Do Not Go Gentle Into That Good Night." *The New Oxford Book of English Verse.* Ed. Helen Gardner. New York: Oxford UP, 1972. 942.

Waggoner, Eric. "Inside the Current: A Taoist Reading of *The Old Man and the Sea.*" *Hemingway Review* 17.2 (1998): 88–104.

Williams, Terry Tempest. *An Unspoken Hunger: Stories from the Field.* New York: Pantheon, 1994. 81–87.

DAVID SAVOLA

"A Very Sinister Book":
The Sun Also Rises *as Critique of Pastoral*

"See that horse-cab? Going to have that horse-cab stuffed for you
for Christmas. Going to give all my friends stuffed animals. I'm a
nature-writer."

—Bill in *The Sun Also Rises*

Although Hemingway's work has begun to attract the attention of ecocritics, the most widely taught and frequently analyzed work of the entire
Hemingway canon, the 1926 novel *The Sun Also Rises*, has yet to receive
detailed ecocritical analysis.[1] What little attention the book has attracted
has been dismissive. Glen A. Love, a founding member of the Association
for the Study of Literature and Environment and a pioneer in environmen-
tally-concerned criticism, presents the novel as a test case of the narrowly
anthropocentric vision of much literary scholarship. Love says,

> [W]e must . . . recognize . . . our discipline's limited humanistic
> vision, our narrowly anthropocentric view of what is consequential
> in life. . . . The challenge that faces us in these terms is to outgrow
> our notion that human beings are so special that the earth exists
> for our comfort and disposal alone. . . . While critical interpretation
> . . . tends to regard ego-consciousness as the supreme evidence of
> literary and critical achievement, it is eco-consciousness which is

From *The Hemingway Review* 26, no. 1 (Fall 2006): 25–46. Copyright © 2006 by the Ernest
Hemingway Foundation.

a particular contribution . . . of nature-writing, and of many other ignored forms and works passed over because they do not seem to correspond to anthropocentric—let alone modernist and post-modernist—assumptions and methodologies. In such a climate of opinion, for example, Hemingway's *The Sun Also Rises*, which is little concerned with ecological considerations, is widely taught in college classes, while his *The Old Man and the Sea*, which engages such issues profoundly, is not. ("Revaluing Nature" 230)

Despite Love's objections, *The Sun Also Rises* is profoundly concerned with ecological considerations, as the passage of Ecclesiastes echoed in its title would suggest. The novel presents the main characters as aimless, displaced persons without a secure sense of meaning or value and suggests that the characters could find that meaning and value in cultivating a more intimate connection with the natural environment. The novel criticizes conventional depictions of nature, and calls for a literature that offers a more complex picture of the connection between humanity and the natural world.

The Sun Also Rises has been so frequently treated as a novel of the Lost Generation that this approach has become something of a critical cliché. Yet Hemingway described the novel as less about the life of postwar expatriates than about the rhythms of nature as an expression of eternity. "The point of the book to me was that the earth abideth forever—having a great deal of fondness and admiration for the earth and not a hell of a lot for my genera-tion," Hemingway remarked in a 1926 letter to Maxwell Perkins. "I didn't mean the book to be a hollow or bitter satire but a damn tragedy with the earth abiding forever as the hero" (*SL* 229). We have not paid enough atten-tion to this statement, or to the ecocentric implications of the novel's title.

Hemingway is noted as a writer concerned with truth in representation. Suzanne Clark claims, "the true reporting of experience, of the active life carefully observed—that was a moral basis for writing itself that Heming-way translated into the literary tradition" (56). This concern is reflected in numerous statements Hemingway made about writing at various points in his career, perhaps most forcefully in *Green Hills of Africa*, where he says "I cannot read other naturalists unless they are being extremely accurate and not literary" (21).[2] This concern with truth in art is one of the central concerns of *The Sun Also Rises*. Frederic Svoboda, in his study of the novel's develop-ment through various manuscript versions, says that Hemingway "hoped to write a new sort of prose that would derive from the language and facts of real life" (12). Svoboda quotes Hemingway from an early notebook version: "none of the significant things [in the novel] are going to have any literary signs marking them. You have to figure them out for yourself" (12). Svoboda demonstrates that accurate representation is one of the fundamental principles on which the novel is built. Hemingway, Svoboda says, "was very much opposed to an artificially imposed conventional structure. He was seeking to remove the conventional frameworks interposed between the reader and the reality that is represented in a work of art" (12).

A concern with truth in representation is evident in the views of Jake Barnes, who is impatient with people who rely on conventional ways of seeing. At a news conference Jake distinguishes reporters who ask questions "to hear themselves talk" from those who ask because they "wanted to know the answers" (*SAR* 44). Jake criticizes Robert Cohn for letting literary convention dictate his opinions. Jake reports that Cohn thinks he can solve his problems by running to South America and that he does not like Paris. Cohn "got the first idea out of a book," Jake says, "and I suppose the second came out of a book too" (20). Jake's narration suggests that he connects truthfulness with a degree of self-reflectivity, an awareness of the limitations built into any mode of discourse. "I mistrust all frank and simple people," Jake says, "especially when their stories hold together" (12). The novel's concern with truthfulness in representation is reflected in its careful use of allusion.

Although criticism has recognized much of Hemingway's use of allusion in *The Sun Also Rises*, one important allusion which remains unacknowledged is Hemingway's extensive reference to pastoral throughout the novel.[3] The novel has the use of pastoral convention built into its very structure. *The Sun Also Rises* is not only "a damned tragedy with the earth abiding forever as the hero," as the author claimed, but is also a critique of pastoral. The novel tests the pastoral vision, acknowledges its enduring attraction, and interrogates its limitations.

The novel invokes the central elements of pastoral convention: the presentation of city life as complex and of city people as corrupt, the presentation of rural life (and of nature) as somehow more "real" and more simple than life in the city, and the presentation of rural folk as more honest, direct, and virtuous than city dwellers. Invoked as well are the pattern of retreat and return and a nostalgic vision of a lost Golden Age. In addition to these familiar conventions of pastoral, Hemingway has built into the novel extensive allusions to the *Idylls* of Theocritus and the *Eclogues* of Virgil, the two works most central to the establishment of the pastoral mode.

As Glen Love notes,

> Literary pastoral traditionally posits a natural world, a green world, to which sophisticated urbanites withdraw in search of the lessons of simplicity which only nature can teach. There, amid sylvan groves and meadows and rural characters—idealized images of

country existence—the sophisticates attain a critical vision of the good, simple life, a vision which will presumably sustain them as they return at the end to the great world on the horizon. ("Revaluing Nature" 231)

The novel follows this pattern of retreat and return: the central characters leave cosmopolitan Paris and travel to the rural countryside of northern Spain to attend a fiesta, then return to the city.

The novel's most direct reference to pastoral is sharply critical, and woven into Jake's harshly disparaging portrait of Robert Cohn. Jake resents Cohn because Cohn reminds Jake of the most unflattering aspects of himself. Cohn falls in love with Brett, and then follows her around like a lost puppy. Jake similarly follows Brett, often at the expense of his own personal dignity, spends sleepless nights on the verge of tears over their hopeless relationship, and even offers to pay for Brett's divorce so that she can marry Mike. Jake seems to be conscious of his similarity to Cohn. He says, "Somehow I feel I have not shown Robert Cohn clearly. The reason is that until he fell in love with Brett I never heard him make one remark that would, in any way, detach him from other people" (*SAR* 52). In Jake's mind, Cohn's love for Brett becomes his defining quality. Yet Jake seeks to suppress any qualities he shares with Cohn.[4] This is evident in his critique of Cohn's taste in literature:

> He had been reading W.H. Hudson. That sounds like an innocent occupation, but Cohn had read and reread "The Purple Land." "The Purple Land" is a very sinister book if read too late in life. It recounts splendid imaginary amorous adventures of a perfect English gentleman in an intensely romantic land, the scenery of which is very well described. For a man to take it at thirty-four as a guide-book to what life holds is about as safe as it would be for a man of the same age to enter Wall Street direct from a French convent, equipped with a complete set of the more practical Alger books. Cohn, I believe, took every word of "The Purple Land" as literally as though it had been an R.G. Dun report. (17)

This "very sinister book" is a pastoral novel. It tells the story of an Englishman, Richard Lamb, who, living in Uruguay circa 1870, marries a local woman against her father's wishes, and travels through the countryside seeking a living. After several "amorous adventures" Lamb returns to rescue his lady fair from her disapproving father. Throughout his adventures, Lamb is secure in the superiority he feels as an Englishman traveling among the South American peasants, whom he characterizes as "simple-minded pastoral people" (87) living in "the one spot on the wide earth where the golden age still lingered . . . this sweet Arcadia" (80). Certainly *The Purple Land* is pastoral at its most sentimental, and this seems to be the reason Hemingway calls such attention to it.[5] The novel inspires Cohn to escape his unhappy life in Paris by fleeing to South America. Jake tries to dissuade Cohn. "Going to another country doesn't make any difference. I've tried all that. You can't get away from yourself by moving from one place to another" (*SAR* 19).

Cohn is attracted to the pastoral convention of retreat. Terry Gifford notes that pastoral involves "some form of retreat and return, the fundamental pastoral movement, either within the text, or in the sense that the pastoral retreat 'returned' some insights relevant to the urban audience" (2). Although Jake is critical of Cohn for succumbing to the pastoral influence of *The Purple Land*, he engages in a similar pastoral retreat. Each summer Jake, the sophisticated expatriate, goes on a vacation to Pamplona to attend the fiesta of San Fermín. This trip is for him a restorative, a flight from the confusion and sorrow of urban life into pastoral simplicity.[6] When Jake and his friend, the humor writer Bill Gorton, travel to Spain, Jake views the landscape in pastoral terms. As their car approaches the Spanish border, Jake's description emphasizes the land's pastoral qualities:

> We started off up the street and out of the town. We passed some lovely gardens and had a good look back at the town, and then we were out in the country, green and rolling, and the road climbing all the time. We passed lots of Basques with oxen, or cattle, hauling carts along the road, and nice farm-houses, low roofs, and all white-plastered. In the Basque country the land all looks very rich and green and the houses and villages look well-off and clean. (*SAR* 97)

The details Jake emphasizes tie the Spanish countryside to the Arcadia of pastoral.

As Terry Gifford notes, Virgil's "Arcadia is significantly an alpine region that is cut off on all sides by other high mountains. It was the perfect location for a poetic paradise, a literary construct of a past Golden Age" (20). The Basque country of the Pyrenees is described in just such terms. Riding atop a double-decker bus, Jake and Bill are treated to a wonderful view of the country.

> After a while we came out of the mountains, and there were trees along both sides of the road, and a stream and ripe fields of grain, and the road went on, very white and straight ahead, and then lifted to a little rise, and off on the left was a hill with an old castle, with

buildings close around it and a field of grain going right up to the walls and shifting in the wind. . . . Then we crossed a wide plain, and there was a big river off on the right shining in the sun from between the line of trees, and away off you could see the plateau of Pamplona rising out of the plain. . . . In back of the plateau were the mountains, and every way you looked there were other mountains, and ahead the road stretched out white across the plain going toward Pamplona. (*SAR* 99)

Pamplona, then, is described as an isolated town cut off by surrounding mountains. It is also made a location of nostalgia, linked with a pre-modern Golden Age. At the Spanish frontier Jake sees "an old man with long, sunburned hair and beard, and clothes that looked as if they were made of gunny-sacking, [and he] came striding up to the bridge. He was carrying a long staff, and he had a kid slung on his back, tied by the four legs, the head hanging down" (98). This goatherd seems to have stepped out of the distant past, or out of the *Idylls* of Theocritus. Significantly, the old man is turned back at the border by customs officials because he lacks an important trapping of modern life: a passport.

The Basque peasants Jake and Bill meet on their journey are idealized as the simple, generous shepherds of pastoral. The Basques gladly share their wine with the two Americans, teaching them to drink from leather winebags, and are wonderfully generous, polite, and friendly. "These Basques are swell people," Bill says (*SAR* 110). When they stop at a roadside *posada* for a drink priced at forty centimes, Jake says "I gave the woman fifty centimes to make a tip, and she gave me back the copper piece, thinking I had misunderstood the price" (112). Clearly, among these people, Jake is no longer in Paris, where "everything was on a clear economic basis. . . . [In France] no one makes things complicated by becoming your friend for any obscure reason. If you want people to like you you have only to spend a little money" (237). Emphasizing a distinction between city and country is a hallmark of pastoral.

The scene in which Bill and Jake rest after fishing and engage in lunchtime banter recalls classical pastoral in several ways. The scene has a number of connections to the *Idylls* of Theocritus and the *Eclogues* of Virgil. Walking from the inn in Burguete to the Irati River, they pass through a pastoral landscape. Bill and Jake walk through fields that were "rolling and grassy and the grass was short from the sheep grazing. The cattle were up in the hills. We heard their bells in the woods" (*SAR* 121). In the first *Idyll* of Theocritus, Thrysis and his friend the Goatherd take their rest at noon alongside a waterfall that runs from a flowing spring. Bill and Jake rest at noon on a riverbank where water tumbles over a dam. Jake chills their wine in a spring "so cold my hand and wrist felt numbed" as he lowers the bottles into the water (123). This is also in keeping with the conventions of classical pastoral. In the fifth *Eclogue* of Virgil, the shepherd Menalcus offers to "make the banquet glad with much wine" (278), just as Bill and Jake do. A passage of Virgil could describe Bill and Jake's pastoral excursion: "Here are chill springs, here soft meadows, O Lycoris: here the woodland: here with wasting time I too at thy side would waste away" (*Eclogue* X 291). The pastoral convention of *otium*, or leisure, is evident in this scene.

The witty banter with which Bill entertains Jake, beginning at breakfast at the inn, and continuing during their streamside lunch, is analogous to the song with which the shepherd Thyrsis entertains his friend the Goatherd in the *Idylls*. Thyrsis is renowned for his singing; Bill is a successful writer of humor, and the badinage he performs for Jake, full of "Irony and Pity" and mocking topical references, is his stock in trade (*SAR* 118). "He had been going splendidly," Jake says. "But he stopped. I was afraid he thought he had hurt me with that crack about being impotent. I wanted to start him again" (120). Jake enjoys Bill's speech just as much as the Goatherd of the *Idylls* enjoys Thyrsis' song.

The Goatherd of Theocritus' *Idylls* offers his friend Thyrsis a prize for his song, a wooden cup decorated with an image of a woman:

> [O]n the inside [of the cup] a woman is fashioned, some masterpiece of the
> Gods' manufacture, outfitted with robe and diadem. By her
> Side are two men with elaborate hair-dos, disputing in speech, one
> After another, but none of their dialog touches her deeply,
> Rather, she gazes on one of them one moment, absently smiling,
> Then, in an instant she casts her attention again to the other. (4)

The woman depicted here could be Brett Ashley. The diadem indicates the woman is an aristocrat, like Lady Brett. Waiting for Brett in Pamplona, Cohn gets a haircut, irritating Jake by indulging in "all that barbering" for Brett's sake (*SAR* 105). Mike, the man Brett is supposed to marry, also indulges in a fair bit of barbering, and "disputes in speech" with Cohn. He asks Cohn "why do you follow Brett around like a poor bloody steer? Don't you know you're not wanted?" and tells Cohn "What if Brett did sleep with you? She's slept with lots of better people than you" (146). And, while her various lovers dispute, Brett "gazes on one of them one moment," then "casts her attention again to the other." These allusions clearly link the novel to the *Idylls* of Theocritus.

Thyrsis' song, in the first *Idyll*, finds some echoes in Bill's conversation with Jake. Thyrsis sings of Daphnis, traditionally regarded as the original shepherd-poet of pastoral. James Sambrook explains, "Theocritus makes Daphnis a chaste shepherd who has angered Aphrodite, because he has boasted that he could overcome sexual love, but now he is overcome by love, and is dying" (Sambrook 3). This is quite analogous to Jake's position; unable to consummate his love for Brett, he is trying to overcome sexual love. Thyrsis sings, as Daphnis lies dying of lovesickness: "Hermes came first from the mountain and said to him, 'Daphnis, my good friend, / Tell me now, who is tormenting you? Whom are you so much in love with?'" (5). Similarly, Bill asks Jake, "What about this Brett business? . . . Were you ever in love with her?" Jake answers, "On and off for a hell of a long time." Bill seems to realize that this is a touchy subject for Jake, and apologizes for prying. Jake tells him, "I don't give a damn anymore . . . Only I'd a hell of a lot rather not talk about it" (*SAR* 128). The novel clearly links Jake's situation to that of Daphnis.

The song of Thyrsis finds another echo in Bill's conversation with Jake. Bill, in the midst of his witty disquisition, touches on another sore subject:

> "You're an expatriate. You've lost touch with the soil. You get precious. Fake European standards have ruined you. You drink yourself to death. You become obsessed by sex. You spend all your time talking, not working. . . . You don't work. One group claims women support you. Another group claims you're impotent." (*SAR* 120)

This recalls a portion of Thyrsis' song:

> Then came Priapus
> Saying, "Unfortunate Daphnis—but why are you wasting away?
> . . . .
> 'Cowherd,' you used to be called, but are now rather more like a goatherd,
> One of those goatherds who, when he observes how the she-goats are getting
> Stuffed, deliquesces in tears because he cannot be such a he-goat." (5)

The scene from *The Sun Also Rises* echoes speeches given by Priapus and Hermes in the *Idylls*. Significantly, each of these gods was frequently depicted with an erect phallus, precisely the body part Jake has lost in the war. The novel's echoes of pastoral underlie Jake's need to escape the sorrows he associates with his urban life, and yet show how he is constantly reminded of the main sources of his sorrow: his love for Brett, his rivalry with Cohn, and the genital wound that prevents consummation.[7]

The fishing scene, particularly with its air of *otium*, seems a pause, a reprieve from the emotional tension of the rest of the novel. The scene seems a testament to the continuing appeal of pastoral, in its presentation of a close and friendly relation between humanity and the natural world. But the humorous tone suggests an intention of undercutting or parodying familiar pastoral conventions. Terry Gifford notes that Virgil designed his Arcadia not only as a mountainous location separated from the surrounding countryside by other high mountains (like Pamplona), but also as "a literary construct of a past Golden Age in which to retreat by linguistic idealization" (20). When the highly artificial language of pastoral verse is transplanted into a realistic prose narrative, this linguistic artifice becomes comic, much as the inflated language and idealized characterizations of chivalric romance are made comic when Cervantes transplants them into a realistic narrative like *Don Quixote*. In this sense, Bill's humorous language in the fishing scene is an example of just this sort of linguistic idealization.

Other elements which critique and subvert the pastoral elements of the novel introduce the comic tone of the fishing scene. In contrast to the simple, generous, hospitable peasants of pastoral (such as the Basques in this narrative), the lady who keeps the inn at Burguete is tightfisted and inhospitable. When she tells Jake the price of the room, she is so ashamed of the inflated price that she cannot look him in the eye. The landlady mollifies Jake by telling him that wine is included in the price of the room, but is so stingy as to peek in to count the empty bottles they accumulate. Jake's description of the room in which they stay also seems to undercut the pastoral vision in this portion of the narrative. The room is decorated with "one panel of rabbits, dead, one of pheasants, also dead, and one panel of dead ducks" (*SAR* 116). These portraits of dead game animals recall Bill's earlier comment when he (drunk) and Jake (sober) walk by a taxidermist's shop in Paris. Bill tries to get Jake to buy a stuffed dog. Jake sensibly demurs. Bill comments, "See that horse-cab? Going to have that horse-cab stuffed for you for Christmas. Going to give all my friends stuffed animals. I'm a nature-writer" (79–80). Such scenes critique pastoral as a dead form, one so entrenched in artifice and convention that it fails to communicate one of the salient qualities of the natural environment: its organic vitality. To present an accurate and responsible picture of the natural world, a work of literature must create an impression of teeming masses of interconnecting, interdependent life forces. Instead, Jake and Bill confront stuffed animals and pictures of dead ducks.[8]

The fishing scene, in which the central characters are happiest and most at peace, is acutely self-reflexive. The scene is laden with allusion and introduced by other elements which question and complicate conventional depictions of the natural world. Bill parodies William Cullen Bryant's "A Forest Hymn" (1815), a poem rife with the sentiments of natural theology. Bryant's poem begins "The groves were God's first temples." "Let no man be ashamed to kneel in the great out-of-doors," Bill says. "Remember, the woods were God's first temples" (*SAR* 127). He also pillories the creationist sentiments of William Jennings Bryan, the fundamentalist minister and sometime presidential candidate who assisted the prosecution in the Scopes Monkey Trial of 1925, in which a high school biology teacher was charged with the crime of teaching Darwin's theory of evolution. "Let us not doubt, brother," Bill says. "Let us not pry into the holy mysteries of the hencoop with simian fingers" (127). Both Bryant and Bryan follow a naively anthropocentric vision of the relationship between humanity and the natural world, and Bill and Jake take great delight in puncturing this illusion.[9] In calling attention to the artificiality of these "frank and simple" constructions of the relationship between people and nature, the novel admits a more complex understanding of this relationship.

Hemingway's inclusion of elements which undercut and call into question the pastoral dream of escape mark the difference between *The Sun Also Rises* and *The Purple Land*, as well as the difference between two versions of pastoral. The Hudson novel, which, Jake claims, Cohn wishes to use as "a guide book to what life holds," is a simple fable of escape (17). *The Purple Land* accepts without question the pastoral dream, and even preaches it as a sort of moral lesson. *The Sun Also Rises* uses pastoral materials, but in a much more critical and self-conscious manner.

The difference between these two types of pastoral is analogous to the distinction Leo Marx makes between sentimental and complex pastoral. The sentimental pastoral espouses a naïve dream of escape from the difficulties of civilization into rural simplicity. The complex pastorals, Marx says,

> do not finally permit us to come away with anything like the simple, affirmative attitude we adopt toward pleasing rural scenery. In one way or another, if only by virtue of the unmistakable sophistication with which they are composed, these works manage to qualify, or call into question, or bring irony to bear against the illusion of peace and harmony in a green pasture. (25)

By placing such extensive allusions to pastoral in the novel, Hemingway is able to explore the attractions of the pastoral vision, and at the same time acknowledge how it conventionalizes our relationship to the natural world.

Marx identifies the complex pastoral by its inclusion of a device which he terms the counterforce—an image, symbol, or event which intrudes on the scene, abruptly puncturing the quiet, idyllic dream. The steamboat that looms out of the night to smash Huck and Jim's raft is one prime example. The locomotive whistle that pierces the quiet of Walden Pond is another. Marx says that for most American writers of complex pastorals the counterforce that upsets the quiet of the pastoral dream has typically been some element of technology—the machine smashing into the garden. In *The Sun Also Rises*, the counterforce is more internal than external. Jake himself will spoil his own pastoral escape, as the novel's attention to the *corrida* makes manifest.

Although Jake criticizes Cohn for desiring a pastoral retreat, the retreat he himself attempts is a failure. Jake finds, on his pastoral retreat, that he cannot "get away from [himself]" by going to some imagined Arcadia. Everywhere he turns, he is reminded of his sexual incapacity and his doomed love for Brett. As Glen Love observes, the pastoral retreat is supposed to offer urban sophisticates "a critical vision of the good, simple life, a vision which will presumably sustain them as they return at the end to the great world on the horizon" ("Revaluing Nature" 231). "Yes," one can imagine Jake saying in response, "isn't it pretty to think so?" (*SAR* 251).

Jake ends up polluting the thing he values most about the "good, simple life" he seeks in Pamplona. Jake places enormous value on his membership in the exclusive coterie of the *corrida*. He particularly values his friendship with Montoya, the owner of a hotel frequented by only the most serious and worthy of matadors. Jake says of Montoya,

> He always smiled as though bull-fighting were a very special secret between the two of us; a rather shocking but really very deep secret that we knew about. He always smiled as though there were something lewd about the secret to outsiders, but that it was something that we understood. It would not do to expose it to people who would not understand. (136)

The outsiders, the people who would not understand, are the members of the urban culture Jake has left behind in Paris and in America. By contrast, the bullfighting aficionados make Jake feel exceptional, set apart from the foreigners with whom he travels. Jake tells us

> It amused them very much that I should be an American. Somehow it was taken for granted than an American could not have *afición*. He might simulate it or confuse it with excitement, but he could not really have it. When they saw that I had *afición*, and there was no password, no set questions that could bring it out, rather it was a sort of oral *spiritual examination* with the questions always a little

on the defensive and never apparent, there was this same embarrassed putting the hand on the shoulder, or a *"buen hombre."* (137;
my emphasis)

Jake's membership in this group is an important part of his pastoral retreat
from his urban life because it sets him apart from the other members of
the Left Bank bohemian community. The reference to the "oral spiritual
examination" suggests the enormous cultural importance of the *corrida*.
"Bullfighting is not a sport," Hemingway explains in a 1923 article for the
Toronto Star, "It is a tragedy" (*DT* 344). It is a religious ritual, an enactment
of a pre-Christian blood sacrifice, and the matador is the priest who enacts
the ritual.

In this supposed pastoral retreat, foreigners are regarded as a corrupt-
ing influence, and the priest, the matador, must be protected from them. This
becomes evident when Montoya approaches Jake to ask his advice on a delicate matter. After Jake meets the promising young matador Pedro Romero,
Montoya looks to Jake to help protect the young matador from corruption.
Montoya comes to confide in Jake, explaining that the American ambassador has sent a message inviting Romero to a party at the Grand Hotel. Jake
tells Montoya "Don't give Romero the message." Immediately, Montoya is
relieved. He sees that Jake understands the priest must be protected. "People
take a boy like that," Montoya says, "they don't know what he's worth. They
don't know what he means. Any foreigner can flatter him. They start this
Grand Hotel business and in one year they're through. . . . He ought to stay
with his own people. He shouldn't mix in that stuff" (*SAR* 176). Jake values
the trust Montoya has placed in him. It confirms his membership in the
exclusive club of aficionados and his cherished identity as *"buen hombre,"* setting him apart from his fellow foreigners.

However deeply Jake values his membership in the order of aficionados,
Jake betrays the trust Montoya places in him. Romero joins Jake in the hotel
dining room, sitting at a table filled with foreigners. Montoya "came into the
room. He started to smile at me, then he saw Pedro Romero with a big glass
of cognac in his hand, sitting laughing between me and a woman with bare
shoulders, at a table full of drunks. He did not even nod" (*SAR* 180). Jake
takes this betrayal of trust even further when he arranges a sexual liaison
between Brett and Romero. This causes Jake to lose much of what remains of
his self-respect, and destroys his membership in the order of *aficionados*. After
Romero leaves the café with this foreign woman, Jake is aware of how deeply
he has offended the brotherhood of the *corrida*. He reports, "the hard-eyed
people at the bull-fighter table watched me go. It was not pleasant" (191). This
experience punctures the idyllic dream Jake sought in coming to Pamplona.

His own presence has polluted the pure and simple nature he expected to find, and offended the local people whose esteem he valued so highly.

This puncturing of Jake's pastoral dream is one aspect of the "counterforce" to pastoral offered in the novel. Marx notes a common element in the work of Fitzgerald, Frost, Nathaniel West, and Hemingway. "Again and again," says Marx,

> they invoke the image of a green landscape—a terrain either wild or, if cultivated, rural—as a symbolic repository of meaning or value. But at the same time they acknowledge the power of a counterforce, a machine or some other symbol of the forces which have stripped the old ideal of most, if not all, of its meaning. Complex pastoralism, to put it another way, acknowledges the reality of history. (363)

In acknowledging the affect the foreign visitors have upon this supposed Arcadia, the novel offers a much more complex vision than that offered in *The Purple Land*. In Hudson's novel, the central character, Lamb, is confident his presence will have no lasting effect on the Arcadia he travels through. As Lamb departs the remote back country he says

> Farewell, beautiful land of sunshine and storm, of virtue and of crime; may the invaders of the future fare on your soil like those of the past and leave you in the end to your own devices . . . may the blight of our superior civilization never fall on your wild flowers, or the yoke of progress be laid on your herdsmen. (371)

In Marx's terms, *The Purple Land* ignores the reality of history, unlike *The Sun Also Rises*. In so doing, the novel exhibits a concern for ecological responsibility quite absent from Hudson's tale.

Love's contention that *The Sun Also Rises* is little concerned with ecological issues is linked to a recent tendency to disregard the significance of the novel's title. Peter L. Hays, for instance, dismisses altogether the idea that the title has any important thematic significance. "There is the novel's title," Hays says, "from Ecclesiastes 1:4–7, but, Hemingway's comment about 'the earth abiding forever' notwithstanding that particular passage has less direct significance for the novel than such titles as *A Farewell to Arms*, *For Whom the Bell Tolls*, or *The Old Man and the Sea* for the novels they head. Few critics any longer see 'the earth abiding forever' as the hero of the novel" (16). Kurt J. Krueger makes a similar claim. He says, "despite Hemingway's insistence that the point of *The Sun Also Rises* is 'that the earth abideth forever' . . . there are scant explicit references in the novel to the permanence of the earth or to the efficacious effects of nature on its observers" (340).[10] But to reject the title's significance is to accept the novel as a mere portrait of the lost generation, and to overlook any serious social critique the novel may offer.

Wallace Stegner, in his famous "Wilderness Letter" (1960), offers a generalization about American literature that applies quite directly to *The Sun Also Rises*. Stegner sees a pronounced bitterness in American culture, a bitterness that has increased since the closing of the frontier in 1890:

> Literature [is] a reflection, indirect but profoundly true, of our national consciousness. And our literature . . . is sick, embittered, losing its mind, losing its faith. Our novelists are the declared enemies of their society. There has hardly been a serious or important novel in this century that did not repudiate in part or in whole American technological culture for its commercialism, its vulgarity, and the way in which it has dirtied a clean continent and a clean dream. (149)

Certainly *The Sun Also Rises* depicts embittered characters who have lost their faith. But that loss of faith is balanced against the eternal cycles of nature, just as the novel's two epigraphs balance Gertrude Stein's remark, "you are all a lost generation," against the passage of Ecclesiastes that gives the novel its title:

> One generation passeth away, and another generation cometh; but the earth abideth forever . . . The sun also ariseth and the sun goeth down, and hasteth to his place where he arose . . . the wind goeth toward the south, and turneth about unto the north; it whirleth about continually, and the wind returneth again according to his circuits. . . . All the rivers run into the sea; yet the sea is not full; unto the place from whence the rivers come, thither they return again. (Ecclesiastes 1.4–7)

Here we have a powerful rebuke against the vanity of anthropocentrism, portraying the struggles of individual humans, even of entire generations of humanity, as tiny, fleeting, minuscule occurrences when measured against the indomitable rhythms of nature. What has brought Jake, Cohn, Brett and company to such a sorry pass is the fact that their perspective has become too narrow, too exclusively attached to human concerns. As Bill jokingly tells Jake, "you've lost touch with the soil. Fake European standards have ruined you" (*SAR* 120). If they were to cultivate a greater sense of attachment to the earth, they would have the opportunity to gain a sense of meaning and value that could give order and purpose to their lives.

The certainty of nature, the renewal evident in the recurrent cycles of sunrise and sunset and the endless flow of rivers to the sea, could be a powerful source of meaning for the central characters of *The Sun Also Rises*. Certainly the novel presents Jake's generation as lost and embittered. But it attributes this loss to, as Love puts it, "a narrowly anthropocentric point of view." By adopting a wider perspective and paying attention to the renewal and intricate order visible in the natural world, Jake and his companions could gain a greater sense of purpose in their lives. The novel urges the acceptance of humans as a part of the natural world. As Stegner says, "we need to demonstrate our acceptance of the natural world. We need the spiritual refreshment that being natural can produce" (149). This is the message the novel is designed to communicate; *The Sun Also Rises* is an effort to guide the lost generation home.

Why should this novel, which urges us to remember that nature is larger than humanity, and that the life cycles of the planet will continue long after we are gone, make such extensive reference to pastoral? And why should a pastoral novel be "a very sinister book?" The pastoral is, in many instances, a highly imitative form, less concerned with depicting the natural world than with following literary precedent. When John Milton writes in "Lycidas" of "fresh woods and pastures new" he is referring to new poetic projects rather than actual woods or pastures (1796). As such, the pastoral leads us not closer to nature, but farther away from it. In addition, Milton consciously imitates his predecessors, who wrote in imitation of Virgil, who wrote in imitation of Theocritus. Pastoral is among the tamest of literary forms, and the most vital aspect of the natural world is its wildness. Love points out a major objection leveled by contemporary ecocritics against pastoral:

> Pastoral as a genre works upon the principles of harmony and reconciliation. It emphasizes resemblances and points of accommodation, often drawing the opposing worlds of nature and society into that characteristic meeting point of cultured or humanized nature, the garden. Implicit in this strategy of reconciliation, however, is a factor that has diminished the relevance of pastoral in contemporary thinking. That factor, which must be addressed if pastoral is to retain its critical authority for the present and the future, is its tendency to devalue wild nature, wilderness, the old, wild Arcadia, which from the time of the softened pastorals of the Roman poets until very recently, has been seen as an untenable extreme. (85)

In presenting the pastoral convention as a dead form, Hemingway calls attention to the ways in which the pastoral vision can obscure the complexity, vitality, and unpredictability of the natural world.

In depicting the vaunted Arcadia as a garden landscape, in placing highest value on land made subject to human utility, the pastoral shows its endorsement of agriculture. Love notes that "the word *pastoral* derives from the Latin *pastor*, for shepherd, and the original meaning refers to shepherds, herdsmen, and others directly involved in animal husbandry" (*Practical Ecocriticism* 80). In recent years a number of ecologically concerned writers have blamed farming for significant environmental damage. For instance, Dana Phillips observes, "environmental historians now argue that human degradation of the environment is due as much, if not more, to the ancient and ongoing development of agriculture as it is to more recent human innovations like heavy industry" (252). Pastoral, at least in its most conventional versions, valorizes the garden landscape, depicts an anthropocentric vision of the natural world, and endorses the subjugation of wild lands to human uses.

The novel's criticism of the pastoral vision is related to its treatment of the bullfight, or to adopt the term Allen Josephs prefers, *toreo*. Josephs calls *toreo* the "moral axis" of the novel and links it to the novel's criticism of modern life. "The primitive savagery of the *plaza de toros* was tantamount to Hemingway's embracing an ancient mystery and rejecting much of what passed for modern western values," Josephs says (153). The tameness and safety of the middle ground of pastoral is concurrent with the modern western values of 1924, the "American technological culture" which Stegner says American literature indicts for its vulgarity and commercialism. *Toreo* is valued in this novel because it provides a connection to wildness, the wildness that originally lay at the core of pastoral. Because the pastoral depicts a garden-variety relationship between humanity and nature, and an air of calm leisure exudes from the pastorals of Theocritus, Virgil, and their later imitators, the violence of *toreo* may seem quite out of place in pastoral. But the tradition out of which Virgilian pastoral grew had a vital connection to the wildness of nature, through its connection to the cult of Pan. As Love explains, borrowing from Phillipe Borgeaud's *The Cult of Pan in Ancient Greece* (1988):

> The Greek god Pan is an Arcadian and, for the Greeks, Arcadia symbolized the original life. The ancient Arcadians were seen in Greek life as rough, bestial, wild primitives who occupied their barren and forbidding region as "Pre-Selenians," that is, older than the time when the moon rose for the first time. "The Arcadians are autochthons, . . . integrally connected with the earth from which they were born." They were identified with animals, herding, and

hunting, and their chief divinity, Pan, was half-animal, half-man, copulating with animals as well as humans. (*Practical Ecocriticism* 75; Love's quotes are from Borgeaud)

Through its connection to Pan, the tame pastoral reveals a hint of wildness at its core. This connection to wildness makes *toreo* a central component of the novel's critique of pastoral. As Hemingway reports in a letter, *toreo* is "the one thing that has, with the exception of the ritual of the church, come down to us intact from the old days" (*SL* 237). *Toreo* stands outside modern western values, an ambassador from a world and time that accepted, celebrated, and even sacralized the wildness in nature.

The novel emphasizes the wildness of *toreo*. Despite the mastery of the matador, despite the high level of technique the matador brings to the performance, the bull is a wild beast, and the matador's control over him is limited. *Toreo* is a confrontation with wild nature, embodied in the bull, and the bull does not always lose. Terry Tempest Williams, in a keynote address she gave to the 1996 Hemingway Society convention on "Hemingway and the Natural World," describes her first experience of a bullfight in Spain:

> As the first bull charged into the arena, every hair on my arm raised. *I recognized wildness.* And then the carefully orchestrated ritual began.... My reaction went beyond thought, I felt something, something old and deep and archaic, right down to my bones. I saw an ancient story of love and loss, life and death, the paradoxical nature of both. I understood on some level the need to witness death over and over again. (12–13; my emphasis)

The narrative voice of *The Sun Also Rises* emphasizes the danger and unpredictability of the bullfight. When Jake's party first sees the running of the bulls, Cohn reports "One of the bulls got into the crowd in the ring and tossed six or eight people" (*SAR* 164). Jake witnesses the goring of a Spanish man running with the crowd ahead of the bulls:

> As the bulls passed, galloping together, heavy, muddy-sided, horns swinging, one shot ahead, caught a man in the running crowd in the back and lifted him in the air. Both the man's arms were by his sides, his head went back as the horn went in, and the bull lifted him and then dropped him. (200)

Jake values the wildness of *toreo*. This reverence for wild nature, this devotion to a ritual that honors wildness, is what draws Jake to Pamplona each summer. It sets him apart from his fellow expatriates and links him to the spiritual brotherhood of aficionados. By placing *toreo* at the heart of the novel, Hemingway is creating a broader, more complex form of pastoral, a wilder strain of pastoral.

The Sun Also Rises, despite the abundance of critical attention it has received, has never been appreciated for its engagement with ecological concerns. Yet the novel plays an important role in Hemingway's effort to expose and interrogate the limitations of conventional depictions of the natural world. As such, the novel is an attempt to revitalize the potential of literature to help humanity own its connection to nature.

Notes

1. This essay is a revision of a paper presented at the conference of the Association for the Study of Literature and Environment at the University of Oregon in June 2005. I am grateful for the comments and suggestions of my beloved companion Annette Steigerwald.

2. The influence of the Agassiz method of nature study on Hemingway's concern with careful observation and honest reporting is examined in Susan Beegel's "Eye and Heart: Hemingway's Education as a Naturalist." Beegel also treats the influence of the debate over the "nature-faker" controversy that played out in the popular press during Hemingway's childhood and which involved two figures that Hemingway admired, Theodore Roosevelt and John Burroughs. Roosevelt and Burroughs expressed outrage over popular writers who reported as true such obviously invented incidents as a porcupine escaping predators by rolling into a ball and tumbling down a hill, or a woodcock treating its broken leg by making a cast of clay.

3. Several critics briefly mention pastoral in their studies of *The Sun Also Rises*, particularly in reference to the fishing scene in Chapter XII, but none note the extensive use Hemingway makes of pastoral allusion throughout the novel. Among those who mention pastoral are George D. Murphy, Jackson J. Benson, Richard B. Hovey, and Wendy Martin. William Empson, though he does not discuss the novel in particular, links Hemingway's characters to the simple shepherds of pastoral. Empson says "The purpose behind a Hemingway character is to carry to the highest degree the methods of direct reporting—his stoical simple man is the type who gets most directly the sensations anyone would get from the events. This is a very general method for stories of action and has a touch of pastoral so far as it implies 'the fool sees true'" (16). Empson seems to fall prey to the view of Hemingway as "the dumb ox" propagated by Wyndham Lewis. Love applies the term "pastoral" to "Big Two-Hearted River," but not to *The Sun Also Rises*, though he does describe the shift "from pastoral to tragedy" as "the indispensable Hemingway note" (*Practical Ecocriticism* 118–119).

4. Another indication that Jake sees similarities between himself and Cohn comes in Chapter 16, after the bitter argument between Cohn and Mike. Jake says, "Everybody behaves badly . . . give them the proper chance." To which Brett replies, "you wouldn't behave badly." Jake responds, "I'd be as big an ass as Cohn" (*SAR* 185).

Jake often conceals his similarity to Cohn by retreating to anti-Semitism, emphasizing Cohn's identity as a Jew as a way to insist on this narrow point of difference between them (see also Jeremy Kaye's recent article in *The Hemingway Review*). When Cohn first sees Brett, Jake reports "I saw Robert Cohn looking at her. He looked a great deal as his compatriot must have looked when he saw the promised land" (*SAR* 29). Jake's criticism of Cohn's admiration for *The Purple Land* serves a similar evasive purpose.

5. Robert McIlvane reads the allusion to *The Purple Land* as a key to the character of Cohn. He says, "Parallels between Richard Lamb and Robert Cohn are interesting and significant, especially since Hemingway strongly implies that Cohn associated himself with Lamb and longed to go to South America to have similar adventures. A reading of *The Purple Land* certainly enables the reader of *The Sun Also Rises* to have a clearer understanding of the attitudes motivating Robert Cohn's inappropriate conduct among the twentieth-century expatriates in Paris" (n. pag.). McIlvane notes no similarity between Cohn and Jake, nor does he make any connection to pastoral.

6. Leo Marx says "One has only to consider the titles which first come to mind from the classical canon of our literature—the American books admired most nowadays—to recognize that the theme of withdrawal from society into an idealized landscape is central to a remarkably large number of them. Again and again, the imagination of our most respected writers—one thinks of Cooper, Thoreau, Melville, Faulkner, Frost, Hemingway—has been set in motion by this impulse" (10). While Marx notes the pastoral convention of escape in Hemingway, he does not specifically discuss *The Sun Also Rises*.

7. Yet another connection to classical pastoral in this scene is Bill's emphasis on Jake's role as an expatriate. The first *Eclogue* of Virgil depicts a dialogue between two shepherds: Tityrus, who sits happily playing on his pan-pipe, and the dispossessed farmer Melibeous who passes by, having been cast into exile. Jake may be seen as exiled from the United States.

8. Marx comments, "Among the more effective of the traditional counters to the pastoral dream have been certain stylized tokens of mortality" (25).

9. C. Harold Hurley examines the implications of the allusions to Bryant and Bryan in *The Sun Also Rises*, concluding: "Bill seems to indicate that William Jennings Bryan's conservative stance on religion and science, when held up for critical examination by skeptical minds . . . can no longer suffice in the modern world, just as the Power that dwelt a century earlier in the forests, streams, and prairies of William Cullen Bryant's polished lines can no longer minister to men and women living in the third decade of the twentieth century" (85).

10. Some critics differ with Hays and Krueger on the significance of the title. Robert A. Martin sees the title of the novel as "forming a metaphorical connection between the characters and the events" (100). He says "Hemingway's use of the title serves to reinforce the thematic pattern of the sun's predictable course by contrasting the unpredictable course of human nature and the pointless circularity of the lives of the characters" (100). Frederic Svoboda sees the title as highly significant. In his study of the manuscripts of the novel, Svoboda notes that the novel as first published included another verse of Ecclesiastes: "Vanity of vanities, saith the Preacher, vanity of vanities, all is vanity." But Hemingway cut this verse from the quotation in the third printing of the novel, "which tends to confirm that he very consciously decided to set the second quote as a more optimistic alternative to Stein's statement ["You are all a lost generation"]" (108).

Works Cited

Beegel, Susan F. "Eye and Heart: Hemingway's Education as a Naturalist." *A Historical Guide to Ernest Hemingway*. Ed. Linda Wagner-Martin. New York: Oxford UP. 53–92.

Benson, Jackson J. *Hemingway: The Writer's Art of Self-Defense*. Minneapolis: U of Minnesota P, 1969.

Borgeaud, Philippe. *The Cult of Pan in Ancient Greece*. Trans. Kathleen Atlass and James Redfield. Chicago: U of Chicago P, 1988.

Bryant, William Cullen. *The Poetical Works of William Cullen Bryant*. Ed. Parke Godwin. 2 vols. 1883. New York: Russell and Russell, 1967.

Clark, Suzanne. "Roosevelt and Hemingway: Natural History, Manliness, and the Rhetoric of the Strenuous Life." In Fleming. 55–67.

Empson, William. *Some Versions of Pastoral*. 1935. London: Penguin, 1995.

Fleming, Robert ed. *Hemingway and the Natural World*. Moscow, Idaho: U of Idaho P, 1999.

Hays, Peter L. "Catullus and *The Sun Also Rises*." *The Hemingway Review* 12.2 (Spring 1993): 15–23.

Hemingway, Ernest. *Dateline: Toronto. The Complete Toronto Star Dispatches, 1920–1924*. Ed. William White. New York: Scribner's, 1985.

———. *Ernest Hemingway: Selected Letters, 1917–1961*. Ed. Carlos Baker. New York: Scribner's, 1981.

———. *Green Hills of Africa*. New York: Scribner's, 1935.

———. *The Sun Also Rises*. New York: Scribner's, 1926.

Hovey, Richard. *Hemingway: The Inward Terrain*. Seattle: U of Washington P, 1968.

Hudson, W.H. *The Purple Land*. 1885. New York: Random-Modern Library, 1926.

Hurley, C. Harold. "But Bryant? What of Bryant in Bryan?: The Religious Implications of the Allusion to 'A Forest Hymn' in *The Sun Also Rises*." *The Hemingway Review* 20.2. (Spring 2001). 76–89.

Gifford, Terry. *Pastoral*. London: Routledge, 1999.

Josephs, Allen. "*Toreo*: The Moral Axis of *The Sun Also Rises*." *The Hemingway Review* 6.1 (Fall 1986). Rpt. in *Modern Critical Interpretations: Ernest Hemingway's The Sun Also Rises*. Ed. Harold Bloom. New York: Chelsea House, 1987. 151–167.

Kaye, Jeremy. "The 'Whine' of Jewish Manhood: Re-Reading Hemingway's Anti-Semitism, Re-Imagining Robert Cohn." *The Hemingway Review* 25.2 (Spring 2006): 44–60.

Krueger, Kurt J. "A Logotherapeutic Approach to Teaching *The Sun Also Rises*." *Teaching Hemingway's The Sun Also Rises*. Ed. Peter L. Hays. Moscow: U of Idaho P, 2003. 325–352.

Love, Glen A. "Revaluing Nature: Toward an Ecological Criticism." *Western American Literature* 25.3 (November 1990). Rpt. in *The Ecocriticism Reader*. Ed. Cheryll Glotfelty and Harold Fromm. Athens: U of Georgia P, 1996. 225–240.

———. *Practical Ecocriticism: Literature, Biology, and the Environment*. Charlottesville: U of Virginia P, 2003.

Martin, Robert A. "Hemingway's Sun as Title and Metaphor." *The Hemingway Review* 6.1 (Fall 1986). 100.

Martin, Wendy. "Brett Ashley as New Woman in *The Sun Also Rises*." In *New Essays on The Sun Also Rises*. Ed. Linda Wagner-Martin. Cambridge: Cambridge U P, 1987. 65–82.

Marx, Leo. *The Machine in the Garden: Technology and the Pastoral Ideal in America*. Oxford: Oxford UP, 1964.

McIlvane, Robert. "Robert Cohn and *The Purple Land*." *Notes on Modern American Literature* 5.2 (Spring 1981): Item 8. N. pag.

Milton, John. "Lycidas." *The Norton Anthology of English Literature.* Ed. M. H. Abrams, et al. New York: Norton, 2000. 1791–1796.

Murphy, George D. "Hemingway's Waste Land: The Controlling Water Symbolism of *The Sun Also Rises.*" *Hemingway Notes* 1.1 (Spring 1971): 20–26.

Phillips, Dana. *The Truth of Ecology: Nature, Culture, and Literature in America.* Oxford: Oxford UP, 2003.

Sambrook, James. *English Pastoral Poetry.* Boston: Twayne, 1983.

Stegner, Wallace. *The Sound of Mountain Water: The Changing American West.* 1969. New York: Penguin, 1997.

Svoboda, Frederic. *Hemingway and The Sun Also Rises: The Crafting of a Style.* Lawrence: UP of Kansas, 1983.

Theocritus. *Idylls and Epigrams.* Trans. Daryl Hine. New York: Atheneum, 1982.

Virgil. *Virgil's Works: The Aeneid, Eclogues, Georgics.* Trans. J. W. Mackail. New York: Random, 1950.

Williams, Terry Tempest. "Hemingway and the Natural World: Keynote Address, Seventh International Hemingway Conference." In Fleming. 7–17.

PHILIP MELLING

Cultural Imperialism, Afro-Cuban Religion, and Santiago's Failure in Hemingway's
The Old Man and the Sea

At a critical moment in his battle with the sharks in *The Old Man and the Sea*, Santiago reaches under the stern for an oar handle "sawed off to about two and a half feet in length" and "from as high up as he could raise the club" he hits a *galano* across "the base of the brain" (*OMATS* 105). The shark slides down the fish, but other sharks appear and Santiago is left to wonder how much damage he could have inflicted if he had "used a bat with two hands" (106). His desire for a baseball bat is of crucial importance. Instead of wanting to dramatize an indigenous style with sacred tools (the symbolic, wooden axe of the Afro-Cuban god Chango comes to mind) Santiago wishes to replicate the actions of an American hero whose baseball exploits were the stuff of adventure in the local tabloids—Joe DiMaggio. Santiago's actions in the boat bring DiMaggio's personal history to mind. A fisherman's son from San Francisco, DiMaggio as a boy sneaked away from home to practice his batting technique with "a broken oar as a bat on the sandlots nearby" (Talese 246). Santiago lacks DiMaggio's genius with the bat but his actions are those of a baseball scholar and a dutiful fan. During World War II, DiMaggio "was the most talked-about man in America" and in one of the popular hits of the day, Les Brown's band reminded the fans how important the baseball star was to the war effort. As the song cried out: "Joe . . . Joe . . . DiMaggio . . . we want you on our side" (Talese 251).

From *The Hemingway Review* 26, no. 1 (Fall 2006): 6–24. Copyright © 2006 by the Ernest Hemingway Foundation.

157

Santiago's fixation with Joe DiMaggio is not a casual one. Carefully nurtured, it is a creation of the movies, radio programs, newsreels, and mass circulation newsprint which, during the post-war period, became an integral feature of the new diplomatic landscape of the United States. Nearly "all the techniques later employed for influencing cultures" outside the U.S., says Reinhold Wagnleitner, "were tested in Latin America" during the 1930s and 1940s. "The Latin American strategy," initially designed to counter fascist influence, became the "central basis" for "later American cultural policies" in the fight against Communism. "The obvious appeal of popular culture" he argues, was based on "a Madison Avenue approach" and under the Department of State popular culture became "one of America's potent weapons" in the battle to win the hearts and minds of Latin America (Wagnleitner 62, 63).

One result, agrees Julio Garcia, director of the Havana Film and Television School, was the "colonial decimation" of the Latin American film industry,

> The American studios claimed it was due to market forces, but of course it wasn't. . . . In the 1930s and 1940s there were lots of great films being shown in our cinemas, then it dropped right off. . . . If we wanted some of their hits they would force us to take nine other films of lower quality. The glossy-produced films with big budgets were always put in the best cinemas, so Latin films screened in the less well-kept theatres. The public therefore assumed their own films were inherently inferior. (quoted in Payne 10)

Cultural imperialism buttressed economic imperialism during these years and cultural diplomacy, often conducted through the work of multinationals, lay at the heart of American foreign policy (Payne 10).

Jeremy Tunstall has shown that 75% of films watched by Cubans in 1948 were Hollywood productions (289). The newspaper industry also operated in a similar way. Between 1949 and 1963, America's export of books and printed material to Latin America multiplied ten-fold. Under the Media Guaranty Program (1948–1967), mass circulation newsprint became a daily feature of Latin American life (Wagnleitner 74). During these years, ordinary Cubans like Santiago were weaned away from their traditional faiths and, as Emily S. Rosenberg has written, "gravitated to the simplified messages of popular culture" (215): the language of American sport, music, film, and entertainment, all potent weapons in the fight against Communism. Latin American audiences were pandered to by a celebrity culture which did nothing to "combat injustice, poverty and ignorance," but "offered ethnocentric solutions disguised as internationalist ones ... dignified by the name of rationality" (Rosenberg 86). Mass culture may have been democratic "in the sense that it appealed to a cross section of the social classes," but, as Rosenberg notes, it was oligarchic and "carefully contrived and narrowly controlled" as an instrument of economic and cultural influence (36). Furthermore, even though Cuban society at this time included a substantial black population, the role models presented to Latin American audiences were uniformly white. Few if any discussed the morality of such intervention, let alone the moral, economic, and political stagnation of Cuba in the 1950s that America's support for Batista helped create.

These were the issues at the back of Hemingway's mind when he told the people of San Francisco de Paula who met him at Havana airport in 1959 that his sympathies were with the Revolution and that he did not want to be "considered a Yankee" (Fuentes 274). We must set his comment against Santiago's advising young Manolin to "have faith in the Yankees" (*OMATS* 14), a remark made at a time when the Yankees in question, the New York Yankees baseball club, had a reputation for racial profiling. Under its manager, Casey Stengel, the Yankees club in the 1950s was well-known for its opposition to players of color and notorious for its refusal to field a multi-ethnic squad. Stories in the media about the "racism" of the "Yankee organization" were commonplace, writes Jules Tygiel, citing Jackie Robinson's description of "the Yankees management" as "prejudiced" (294, 295). Despite the fact that *The Old Man and the Sea* was written at a "high point" in a cultural movement that stressed the importance of *barroquismo* (an expression that incorporated a diversity of styles) and a philosophy of resistance to North American culture and art, Santiago's advice disqualifies him as an agent of *lo cubano* or Afro-Cuban cultural perspectives resisting the hegemonic influence of the United States (Martinez 289, 281).

Transmitted on Cuban television in the weeks following Hemingway's receipt of the Nobel Prize, a rarely seen interview reveals his desire to preserve the integrity of Cuban life.[1] In carefully considered, colloquial Spanish Hemingway tells how he has always tried to engage with the local community and "understand the sea" and its "influence" on the daily life of those who use it. The presence of the sea, he stresses, is what he has "tried to put into [his] writing ... especially the sea on the north coast of Cuba" and its interactions, over the years, with settlement and culture. Hemingway also talks about the fishing village of Cojímar and the importance he attaches to its survival: "a very serious thing" he says, in a rapidly changing world. Cojímar's situation may be "serious" because of the decline in the local fishing industry, together with the effects of increased competition and the rising costs of both inshore and deep-sea fishing methods.

However, there are also issues of history to consider and cultural practices not in decline. For example, Hemingway had an extensive interest in anthropology dating back to his reading of James Frazer's *The Golden Bough* in the 1920s. In the library at the Finca Vigía, he also kept a copy of *Cultural Anthropology* by Melville Herskovitz and may have been influenced by the views of Herskovitz on family life and religious faith (Brasch and Sigman Item 3079). Herskovitz argued that the coastal settlers of the Caribbean islands had evolved through a practice of "transculturation" (Duany 22), an historical process incorporating the characteristics of African and European culture. This type of collaboration, claims Herskovitz, grew out of the relationship between faiths and religions of African origin—Santería, Payo Malombo, Payo Monte, Abakuá—and the Catholic Church. These diverse beliefs harmonized around the practice of saint worship. Santería, one such hybrid form of religion, says Diana H. Gonzalez-Kirby, "flourished rapidly" in the "minor" communities of northern and western Cuba. Villages like San Francisco de Paula and Cojímar were a living example of "the syncretisation of African belief" (Gonzalez-Kirby 42).

In 1949 Hemingway asked Malcolm Cowley to send him a copy of Margaret A. Murray's *Witch-Cult in Western Europe*, noting what he called the "considerable witch-craft practised in the neighbourhood especially in Guanabacoa" (*SL* 681). What Hemingway probably meant by "witch-craft" were contemporary vestiges of the religion originally practiced by Yoruba slaves brought to Cuba from southwestern Nigeria in large numbers between 1820 and 1860. During the 19th century, Santería emerged as a compromise faith bringing together Yoruba beliefs and various facsimiles in the Catholic Church. According to Rafael Martinez and Charles Wetli, in Santería each god or goddess—Yemaya, goddess of the sea; Eshu, the trickster deity; Eleggua, the orisha who controls the laws of chance; Ochosi, the god of the hunt; Babalu-aye, patron of the sick and elderly—was twinned with a Catholic saint and given control of "a specific domain" and the "unique powers" peculiar to it (33). In Santería, the most significant African deities are the Seven African Powers, many of whom are represented as protectors of those who rely on the sea or live in close proximity to it (Martinez and Wetli 33).

Although there is little evidence to suggest that he was a formal practitioner, Hemingway was intrigued by Santería. It suited his superstitious nature—the dressing-up, the out-of-body experiences and precognition, the rabbits' feet and occasional fondness for earrings, the need to touch wood three times, the use of numbers, and the prayers for help (Fuentes 84). At the Finca, Hemingway showed a fondness for the "divine mascots" and figurative statues that, according to Migene Gonzalez-Wippler, are often suggestive of primordial life in Santería. He was also fond of different types of stones, especially the *chinas pelonas* and *otanes* used to attract the attention of the orishas and thought to contain magnetic properties. In apparent emulation of a common practice in Santería, Hemingway carried his favorite stones around with him as if he was seeking the approval of a "spiritual guide" and acknowledging the orisha with a "good-luck charm" (Gonzalez-Wippler 1982, 18).

Stones and shells are important to an understanding of Santería. "The power of the orishas," say Rafael Martinez and Charles Wetli, resides in stones and Santería's ceremonial structures recognize the need to propitiate the gods through ritual acts such as the bathing and feeding of stones or the placing of stones close to the body (33). In Santería, ritual power is "seated" in stones, agrees Joseph Murphy, and transferred to the "head of the devotee" at the moment of initiation. "The juxtaposition of head and stones" lies at "the heart of the Santería mysteries," particularly in the ceremony of *"asiento."* Here, the transfer of power from orisha to initiate is dramatized when stones are placed over the head of a novice (*iyawo*). The act of "seating" the stone fixes "knowledge" inside the head, enlightening those who require the benefit of its "spiritual power" (Murphy 87). Hemingway scholar Larry Grimes says that stones were allegedly placed above the entrance to the Finca during the time Hemingway lived there. If true, this may suggest that Hemingway sought power through ritual practice, "seating" the stone at the head of his house in order to signify spiritual favor (Grimes).

Hemingway's desire to acquaint himself with the history of witchcraft contrasts sharply with Santiago's interest in baseball scores in the local newspapers. The contrast between Santiago's needs and Hemingway's intensifies the further we go beyond sight of land (where the protection offered by Joe DiMaggio has no power). As the journey progresses, DiMaggio's influence is in inverse proportion to the spiritual potency of the African Powers. In Santería, each orisha requires a ritual of propitiation in the form of a sacrificial offering (blood, corn, coffee, or water), before the "devotee's problems" can be addressed in the material world. Interestingly, Santiago's world contains all the "magical properties" on which the orishas spiritually depend, including herbs, blood, wood, and stone (Murphy 134). Santiago is given what Joseph Murphy calls "unique" opportunities to honor the gods, but even though their demands are modest, he turns them down (116). Santiago avoids all contact with the *ebos* of Santería and those sacrificial moments when "gifts" are made available—a broken oar, deep water, yellow weed—as a route to propitiation (Murphy 15).

On his return to his village at the novella's end, even though he is physically exhausted and possibly dying, Santiago still plans to hunt again. He tells Manolin:

"We must get a good killing lance and always have it on board. You can make the blade from a spring leaf from an old Ford. We can grind it in Guanabacoa. It should be sharp and not tempered so it will break. My knife broke." (*OMATS* 115)

This passage illustrates the distance that exists between Santiago as a commercial fisherman at a time of crisis and the Adamic solitary whom critics have invested with "mythic beliefs."[2] Rather than propitiate the orishas and invoke their power to subdue a rude and lawless world, Santiago seeks a weapon made from a cast-off American auto part for aid in vanquishing sharks. He has yet to learn that in Santería, only an orisha such as Oggun—father of sacrificial acts and an ironworker symbolized by a sacrificial knife and the spilling of blood—can change the sharks' behavior. And Oggun can only bestow his gifts through spiritual devotions and ritual acts of propitiation of the kind Santiago fails to perform.

Santiago also ignores Olokun, the great orisha of "sea depths who protected the ancestors on their terrible journey from Africa" (Murphy 1–2). In Santería, Olokun is honored with a song:

Olokun, Owner of the Ocean
Grandfather Olokun
We bow before you father Olokun
(Murphy 1–2)

But Santiago does not "bow." He has "strange shoulders" (*OMATS* 15) which served him well in his early life as a child-adventurer to Africa and later as an arm wrestler when he fought the Negro from Cienfuegos. But Olokun is propitiated with simple things—shells, stones, cigars, rum, and acts of salutation—not feats of strength. Protection can be sought by utilizing basic commodities of everyday life such as coffee and paper. Santiago has an abundance of both—the paper he sleeps on, the coffee he drinks—but does not use either material to invoke the African Powers.

Santería is a "hybrid" religion, a "syncretism of black and white worlds" available to all people, irrespective of race and gender, and offering "opportunities" for propitiation through symbols, icons, objects, and dates (Murphy 116). Yet Santiago's life is a drama of missed opportunity and deliberate avoidance. On the one hand, he regards the eating of turtle meat as morally abhorrent. On the other, he eats turtle eggs "all through May" in preparation for "the truly big fish" that run "in September and October" (*OMATS* 34). The decision he makes is inconsistent as well as intriguing. Santiago relies on eating turtle eggs for strength rather than propitiating Yemaya with turtle meat (the *guemilere*), as he should do on her feast day (8 September). Nor does he sacrifice to Agallu and Oshun, the orishas that protect seas and rivers (Murphy 41). The avoidance seems wilful as Santiago goes to sea during hurricane season and needs all the help he can get. Santiago has "no mysticism about turtles"; instead, he relishes their voracious energy and wishes he could share their physical powers. Combative behavior and physical strength are important to him but spiritual appeasement isn't.

Santiago's Darwinism is moderated by a sentimental attitude toward marine life and the moral polarities that define natural adversaries and conflicts. He loves the loggerhead turtles who eat the poisonous Portuguese man o' war jellyfishes that foul his lines and sting "like a whiplash" (*OMATS* 33). The marlin who are his "friends" and "brothers" are enemies of the sharks that bring "*salao*" (7). The spiritualities that govern the sea are of secondary importance to the secular qualities of animals and the characteristics he ascribes to them. Physiological processes, moral innateness, blood lines, and transfusions of energy, not religious belief, are the reasons why Santiago eats turtle eggs to cure the "welts and sores on his arms and hands" (*OMATS* 32–3). Strangely, he does not invoke Babalu-aye, the African orisha who heals "skin diseases," especially leprosy and the skin cancer from which Santiago suffers (Martinez 34). In Santería, Babalu-aye is represented as an impoverished old man who like Santiago lives alone in a wooden shack. The patron saint of those with arthritic problems, Babalu-aye can be propitiated with everyday things like pennies and water. Santiago could easily access this orisha, but does not even try.

If propitiation has any meaning for Santiago, it lies outside an Afro-Cuban community of saints. Instead, he seeks assistance from imperial faiths old and new as well as from celebrities in popular culture and popular Catholicism. His idea of partnership is non-egalitarian, based on a concept of self-help and private alliance with baseball stars and Catholic saints whose elite status inspires devotion. In Santiago's world, the "church" of baseball is not dissimilar to that of Rome (Chidester 219–238). The appeal of each relies on deference and the excitement generated by ritual events in metropolitan centers of power. African deities fall outside this particular theater. Faced with a choice between a Catholic icon or a facsimile of African or rural origin, Santiago prefers the Christian one. For this reason, he says "ten Our Fathers and ten Hail Mary's" (*OMATS* 60) to bring luck when he hooks the marlin, and then claims he will make a pilgrimage to the Virgin de Cobre should he bring the fish in. In Santería, the Virgin of Cobre corresponds with the orisha Oshun, patroness of love and sister of Yemaya, goddess of the sea. Santiago does not disclose the correspondence, but instead tells us that "he is not religious" (*OMATS* 60). It is difficult to explain the remark, bearing in mind that the man who makes it is a Cuban fisherman and that Havana Harbor, its fishermen and sailors, are protected by the Virgin de Regla and her twin, Yemaya. Santiago remains silent on the correspondence between saint and orisha, as if he is unable to embrace the "mental bridge" offered by Santería to those who "live," as Joseph Murphy puts it, "in two worlds" (121). Santiago has, it appears, no interest in the syncretism of a conquered race. Instead, he pledges an allegiance (of sorts) to the Catholic Church and the inspiration he receives in the newspapers from saints of baseball such as Joe DiMaggio.

Resisting the influence of the African Powers—Yemaya, Eshu, Eleggua, and Ochosi—Santiago shows no interest in the talismanic properties of stones, beads, and cowry shells. On the contrary, he sees in baseball an antithesis to *Afro Cubanismo*. He venerates players of light skin, not just Joe DiMaggio, but Mike Gonzalez and Adolfo Luque, "white" Cubans who, because of their skin color, were given dispensation to play in the majors during and after World War I. Crucially, he ignores dark-skinned Cubans and black players excluded from the majors but welcomed in Cuba and the Caribbean. In Cuban baseball, says Donn Rogosin, "race mattered little" and blacks and whites "competed as equals" in the winter leagues (154). During this period, "the extensive, sustained interaction between Cuban and Negro league baseball ... was of enormous significance" (Rogosin 155, 156). The Negro leagues hosted the Cuban Stars, comprised of both dark and light-skinned Cubans, some of whom, like Mike Gonzalez, also played in the major leagues. In Cuba, blacks and whites from the United States frequently played alongside each other. Cuba "became a traditional and important conduit of baseball information between white and black American players" (Rogosin 156). It created a racially-mixed community and gave black players such as John Henry Lloyd, Ray Dandridge, Willard Brown, and Willie Wells the opportunity to become full-time professionals and compete on equal terms with white players like Ty Cobb.

Santiago's racial attitudes come alive in his memory of arm-wrestling with a Negro in a tavern at Casablanca. The contest is remembered at a point in the story when Santiago is at a low ebb. It is his second day at sea without sleep. He has eaten little and is unable to haul the marlin back from the depths to which it has taken the line. Rather than invoke the orishas, he turns to his memory "to give himself more confidence." The decor of the tavern interior—the walls are "painted bright blue" and made of wood—contrasts with the "huge," menacing shadow cast by the Negro and the way the shadow moves on the wall as the hanging lamps shift in the breeze. This arm-wrestling match with "the strongest man on the docks" takes place over a day and a night and only concludes when the "negro" is beaten, his hand forced "down and down until it rested on the wood." The "negro" is a "great athlete" but he ends up ruined psychologically, his "confidence" "broken." Santiago, therefore, gains in "confidence" at the expense of the black community (*OMATS* 64–66).

If the breaking of a "fine" individual is necessary to ensure the triumph of Darwinism, the underlying need is to affirm the importance of protectorate power in the Caribbean. The belief that white individuals can invigorate themselves at the expense of people of color reminds us of how imperialism came of age in the United States. At the end of the 19th century, the United States developed an empire and acquired new lands through a process of pacification and physical control. Territory was acquired and traditional loyalties broken, says Walter L. Williams, as "religions and ceremonies" were "suppressed by government agents." This is true not only of American Indian lands but also of Africa and Asia, he argues, where swarms of "missionaries" promoted "new ways of thinking" thereby weakening "native confidence in their old ways of doing things" (237). According to Anders Stephanson, "empire as civilized domination showed the historical necessity of establishing order by means of force in the unruly sphere and thus allowing 'waste spaces' to be used in the 'interest of humanity'" (106).

Santiago mimics this procedure and puts an end to a putative *negrismo* by describing the contest with the "negro" as "finished" (*OMATS* 66). His opponent is no longer "the strongest man on the docks" and among the dockworkers, traditionally the best sports fans in Cuba (Rogosin 161); Santiago has become *El Campéon* (66). Santiago breaks the spirit of the black community by ruining, in a public demonstration, the crowd appeal of their unofficial leader. He has stayed the course because of his splendidly exceptional talent, unlike the "negro" who is now "broken" (66). Crowd control is a by-word for success.

As he contemplates "the darkness of the sea" under his boat, Santiago invokes the "great DiMaggio" (64), a god-like figure who popularizes the imperial project of conquering others through force of will. DiMaggio has triumphed in adversity—despite the bone spur in his heel—and led the Yankees to their 84th win of the season against the Washington Senators. He appeals to Santiago because, unlike the black baseball player, Jackie Robinson, he lives outside what Lisa Brock calls "the African cultural constellation" (25). Not only is DiMaggio "great," he appears to inhibit the spread of blackness in the wider baseball community.

The impact of Africa in *The Old Man and the Sea* is not only displaced by narratives of white power, it is also subsumed by a memory of adolescence. On the morning of his fishing trip Santiago is awakened by "the land breeze" that comes "very early" and is redolent with the "smell of Africa" in the "morning." The wilderness Santiago wants to remember—"the long golden beaches" "the high capes," "the great brown mountains," the sound of the surf, the native boats (*OMATS* 22)—is an example of what environmentalist critic William Cronon describes as the "romantic sublime," a form of subdued "primitivism" in which the "pristine sanctuary" is never "quite" what it appears. Cronon defines this type of wilderness as neither a "virgin place" nor an "uninhabited land," but one already contaminated by the presence of "civilization." Africa has been made safe for people like Santiago: its beaches tamed not by boys who sail from Tenerife on square-rigged ships, but slave masters and slave ships. The young lions he sees at dusk are his pets; he loves them as he loves Manolin, but only because they lack all semblance of adult desire and predatory aggression, natural attributes. Santiago's beach, as Cronon might put it, "hides its unnaturalness behind a mask that is all the more beguiling because it seems so natural" (76–80).

This version of Africa has no meaning for the people of Cuba nor does it reveal the way in which slave societies were willing and able to come to terms with the sea's meaning in the aftermath of their forced emigration. Santiago's Africa—virgin land, the game preserve as romantic retreat—is, in Cronon's words, a place where we "wipe clean the slate of our past and return to the tabula rasa that supposedly existed before we began to leave our marks on the world." The irony, as Cronon points out, is that only those "whose relation to the land (is) already alienated" are able to "hold up wilderness as a model for human life in nature." By imagining that their "true home is in the wilderness," they "forgive" themselves for "the homes" they "actually inhabit." The "flight from history" becomes an "antidote to the human self" (80).

We are given a clue on how Santiago's own "flight" will unfold the moment he smells the Trade Winds. These winds begin life in the equatorial regions of Africa and help create a system of currents that flow westwards to the Caribbean and feed eventually into the Gulf Stream. To the west of North Africa these winds form a river of seawater, the North Equatorial Current. In the 18th and 19th centuries this current was instrumental in facilitating the transportation of slaves from the sub-Saharan regions—the Gold Coast, the Bight of Benin, the Niger Delta—to the New World. The Atlantic waters that Santiago fishes are suffused, therefore, not only with the memory of slavery and the routes by which slaves might arrive in Cuba, but also with the high levels of mortality that occurred at sea and the trauma that accompanied a two-month-long voyage. "Cuba", says Herbert S. Klein, was "the largest slave colony ever created in Spanish America" and by the end of the 19th century "had become a major importer" of slaves "in its own right" (38, 197).

From the perspective of Santería, the sea emerged as an Africanized place, the natural domain of the orisha Olokun, a Yoruba sea god with male and female personifications that determine the sea's character. This sea is also rife with the spirit presences of the ancestors, whose lives and deaths must be acknowledged. Here are the souls of black folk who have the ability to rise up and walk on water, as they do in August Wilson's play *Joe Turner's Come and Gone*; here are the victims of slavery who "died bad" and demand recognition in Toni Morrison's novel *Beloved* (188). When Santiago ignores these presences he does so at his peril, especially as the dream that wakes him comes from a "breeze" with an African "smell" (*OMATS* 22). What Santiago does with this dream proves his undoing. He entertains a vision of Africa that is of no use in helping him complete the task to which he is firmly committed. He dreams of an Africa that seems attractive because of its cinematic and pictorial appeal. This is an Africa of boats and breezes from which slavery has been erased, as have the slave religions and the role they should occupy for any Cuban fisherman who looks to Africa for his inspiration.

We are reminded of this at a quiet moment when Santiago takes a "forward" position in the boat and, head bowed, dreams of a time when he saw the lions of Africa in "the evening off-shore breeze." "In the early dark" the lions come down onto the beach and in the dream he feels "happy" as the ship lies at anchor (*OMATS* 75). The dream, however, does nothing to pacify the marlin. Indeed, the Gulf Stream is the worst place to go to replace the heritage of African slavery with a vision of the sublime. Santiago is admonished: "the jerk of his right arm coming up against his face and the line burning out through the right hand." The fish jumps repeatedly. There is "a great bursting of the ocean." The speed of the line taken by the fish cuts his hands "badly" (76). We contrast this with the blood that comes "out from under the fingernails" when Santiago arm-wrestles the Negro from Cienfuegos. The strike exposes the folly of dreaming at sea.

Santiago does not know "what started" the fish (77). He can not explain the marlin's change from a fish that is "calm" and "strong" to one that appears to react aggressively to an image of Africa that lacks human presence and human remains (78). Because Santiago's sleeping position mimics the religious greeting known as *foribale* (salutation) in Santería, the jolt he receives comes as a warning to those who believe in virtual faiths. The thump disputes his romanticized vision of Africa as a place of tame wilderness, the colonized Africa of civilized recreation and safari. It's as if, in the darkness below, the fish takes on the personality of the rebellious slave, punishing the man who promotes that vision with a blow to the face. The action clearly illustrates the distance that has opened up between Santiago and Hemingway, who, throughout his time in Cuba, bore witness to the spiritual significance of its waters.

Hemingway shared his belief in channels of energy and streams of life with the Yoruba people who came to Cuba from Nigeria and the Western

Sudan. For the Yoruba, spiritual life was governed by the God *Olodumare*, the "ultimate expression of force" who channelled his energy through a "divine current" a "blood" stream of "cosmic life" known as "*ashe*" (Murphy 8). These ideals appealed to Hemingway, who appears to have seen little difference between divine current and physical current. For Hemingway, the sea was a primordial place and the currents of energy circulating in the Atlantic were an embodiment of what the Yoruba saw as "the ultimate destiny of all creation" (7).

Hemingway's earliest writing about the Gulf Stream and the wandering fish that travel the globe to swim in it appears in his *Esquire* articles of the 1930s. In the most famous of these, "On the Blue Water: A Gulf Stream Letter," written in April 1936, Cuba is portrayed as the meeting place of transoceanic streams and currents that have been in motion since men first "went on (them) in boats" (*BL* 228). In another article, written in August 1934, "Out in the Stream: A Cuban Letter," Hemingway describes the fish that live hundreds of fathoms below the surface and travel thousands of miles in response to the flow of "current" and "counter current." The words "connected" "connection," and "circuit" suggest that the fish "follow" "the warm currents of all the oceans." The sense of connection to this wilderness endows the fisherman with a state of feeling that transcends mere "hunting" (*BL* 171, 172). In "On The Blue Water" Hemingway knows that the fish are more than physical specimens. They are "strange and wild things of unbelievable speed and power and [a] beauty . . . that is indescribable." The act of being "fastened to the fish as much as he is fastened to you" generates a divine energy, an appreciation of the cosmic life in the sea (231).

In "On the Blue Water," Hemingway writes that "the Gulf Stream and the other great currents are the last wild country there is left." And because all factual knowledge of the sea is at best provisional, "no one knows" the actual domain of the "unexploited." When the fish strikes, the primal "scream" of the reel creates an unimaginable "thrill," one "that needs no danger to make it real." The fish that takes the line may leave you "at the end of five hours" with nothing but "a straightened-out hook." Throughout this period, the fisherman has direct contact with the supernatural and is required to acknowledge the simplest of questions: "who can say what you will hook sometime?" (*BL* 228–230).

Hemingway's answer—a giant marlin or swordfish compared "to which the fish we have caught are pygmies" (*BL* 230)—brings to mind a spiritual role model whose "great weight" is reminiscent of the Yoruba God, *Olodumare*, "owner" and source of "all destinies" and the "pulse of life and death. . . . incarnated in the world as force" (Murphy 7–8). In Santería, this force is dramatized through orishas of great power and extravagance that express their meaning in theatrical terms. Hemingway, in a similar vein, describes how a great fish "throws a column of spray like a shell lighting" and its "shoulders smash out of the water" as it "bursts" into life. The use of military imagery suggests Hemingway's willingness to rise to the challenge of the "indescribable" ("On the Blue Water," *BL* 231–232). Here, what is "strange and wild" from a western perspective is instantly recognizable from an African one. If the sea is a theater, the fish is an emissary of Chango, a warrior deity whose life principle is one of "force" and whose "dance posture" evokes a state of physical "aggression" through "violent acrobatics" (Murphy 42–3; Bailey 49). Chango, whose early life was spent at sea, is a ruler of thunder, lightning, and explosive fire reminding us of the marlin's "speed" and "force." Hemingway, "fastened" to the fish, is connected "intimately" to its "savage power." The "friction" of the line "against the water" generates, he says, a new awareness of the life below him ("On the Blue Water," *BL* 231, 229). In terms of Santería, the line is alive with "divine current" a conductor whose "receptivity" puts the fisherman firmly in touch "with spiritual beings" (Murphy 8).

Santiago, on the other hand, resists the spiritual instruction of water. He lets "the current do a third of the work," but is loath to recognize supernatural circuitry (*OMATS* 276–7). As the fish runs from the boat and performs its acrobatics in the water, the speed of the line cuts his hand. His back is burned and he loses feeling in his left hand; the effect is similar to an electric shock. The surge of explosive energy combines temporary paralysis—"There was a moment when I could not find you" (78), he tells the hand—with heightened awareness. Santiago is pulled "down" (76), as he has been on other occasions, into a praying position. The word "friction" (77) is used to signify the electromagnetic power that fish can generate when they travel on what Hemingway in "Out in The Stream" calls "certain circuits" (*BL* 172).

Hemingway was probably aware of the Gulf Stream's electromagnetic properties, discussed by oceanographer Henry Chapin in his study of the Gulf Stream, *The Ocean River*. Co-authored with Frederick G.W. Smith and published by Charles Scribner's Sons (Hemingway's publisher) in 1952, the same year as *The Old Man and the Sea*, *The Ocean River* "gives a good picture of the state of understanding about the Stream in Hemingway's time," says Susan Beegel. "It's hard to imagine he was not aware of it," she adds, especially because Hemingway's library at the Finca shows he kept up with Chapin's work, owning a copy of a later book, *The Sun, the Sea, and Tomorrow: Potential Sources of Food and Energy from the Sea* (Brasch and Sigman item 6163) and subscribing to *Sea Frontiers*, a journal of oceanography begun by Chapin in 1954. Chapin's interest in electromagnetism and sea currents recurs throughout his writing. In *The Ocean River* he puts it thus:

Currents of water in their passage through the salt water generate electricity, though in very small amounts. . . . Sea water, itself an electrical conductor, develops an electric current in its passage across the earth's magnetic field, and the greater the speed of the stream, the greater the electricity produced. (144)

Hemingway's apparent decision to experiment with the idea of an electric shock in *The Old Man and the Sea* invites us to consider the supernatural charge that water possesses in African religion. If Santiago is aware of this charge he doesn't let on. The fish shocks him and wakes him up but there is no spiritual awakening. Blood seeps from Santiago's hand and he immerses it in salt water to cleanse the wound. But in doing this, he misses once again an important opportunity to acknowledge the sea before the sharks arrive. In *African Magic in Latin America*, Migene Gonzalez-Wippler describes blood as an important offering given to the orishas to "replenish their powers." Blood offerings, he explains, are "the most important and indispensable" form of energy because they are "released" as "living energy" and, as such, able to nourish "the spiritual world" (Gonzalez-Wippler 200–1). Santiago's rinsing of his bleeding hand lacks devotion. With the hand "bled . . . clean" (*OMATS* 92), Santiago does not acknowledge the owners of fortune, *Los Ibelli*, the divine twins of Santería, nor does he intend to propitiate the spiritual world with sacrificial blood. Later in the novella, the marlin's spilled blood will settle like a dark cloud in the sea and bring sharks, perhaps because it has not been returned to the sea with sacred intent—the traditional custom in Santería—to "replenish" the energies lost with the death of the marlin and the discharge of electrical power (Martinez 34).

As the recipient of current, Santiago draws energy out of the water but prefers to recognise other "conductors" (Murphy 8). When he says that "it would be wonderful" to fish "with a radio" (*OMATS* 45), he signals his interest in networks of power and information that originate in the United States. His need to be stimulated by American broadcasts reassures him far more than Old World "circuits." The irony is considerable. Baseball, as expressed through the medium of the World Series, allows him to avoid any contact with Africa and its "human line of continuity with the past" (Murphy 9).

For Nadine Gordimer, Cuba and Africa have a shared "African bloodstream" and a relationship whose long history is based on "trade, ideas, values and culture" (7). In Santería the "bloodstream" of the sea commemorates that relationship in ceremonies that dramatize "the moral *ashe* of the ancestors" and the powers the sea bestows on the orishas (Murphy 11). The sea is a place of ceremonial instruction where the orishas "guide" and "admonish" as they see fit. In return, "the community of the present" can "look to the past for moral example" (Murphy 10). It is strange, therefore, that when Santiago takes a blow in the mouth and receives an indication that an offence has been committed, he is indifferent to the sign. The risk he takes in refusing to propitiate the orishas of the sea is close to willful.

At least Santiago is consistent throughout the novella. When he starts his journey he rows "out over that part of the ocean that the fisherman called the great well." The well goes to a depth of "seven hundred fathoms where all sorts of fish congregated because of the swirl of the current made against the steep walls of the floor of the ocean." The well is both oceanographic site and historical deposit where the "wandering fish" have fetched up, their journey shaped by a maritime process that belongs to an ancient world (*OMATS* 25). "The great well" has a special significance in Santería. Migene Gonzalez-Wippler, in his book, *The Santería Experience*, says that the presence of Yemaya is always much "stronger in very deep waters." In Santería, "anything that falls within these waters is lost forever. . . . unless Yemaya is offered a prize in exchange for her bounty." Yemaya's "demands" are always "modest" and pennies or syrup or candles, for example, are normally "enough" to propitiate her. "The value of the gift" is always secondary to the particular "faith" that underlies it (Gonzalez-Wippler 8–9).

Santiago is not prepared to "please" Yemaya with simple gifts. The sea, to him, is whimsical. Its personality is lunar—"feminine," which makes "la mar" emotionally unstable. She kills the terns and sea swallows for no good reason and is inconsiderate to the small birds with their "sad voices" "who are made too delicately for the sea." She is "kind and very beautiful," but unpredictable and cruel. The sea's mind can not be fathomed. She "gave or withheld great favours," we are told, "and if she did wild or wicked things it was because she could not help them" (*OMATS* 26).

Santiago's sea is fickle, ruled by chance and "the wild or wicked things" (26). Because the sea is emotional it is best understood in references that imply control: Darwinism, baseball scores, bats, knives. Rather than fathom the ways of the sea by propitiating Eleggua (the trickster deity) or Chango (controller of force), Santiago describes the sea as a woman unable to help herself and indiscriminate in the way she chooses to bestow her "favours" (26). Ignoring the protection of Olokun, the orisha of sea depths in African folklore, Santiago subjects the sea to a mythology based on personal control. The problem is that the ability to dominate physically bears little relationship to the protection given the slaves who arrived on their terrible journey to the New World. Santiago's offense could not be worse. At moments of crisis, he purposely avoids the deep-sea gods and the help available from them through acts of propitiation.

In Hemingway's work, those who have offended the sea rarely escape its retribution. Like the orishas in Santería, his sea is "fierce" and "generous," yet willing to "criticise the behaviour of the living and hold them to the highest moral standards," should they offend (Murphy 9). The sea has a moral and providential presence in the novel. Yet, at the end of his journey, Santiago is keen to exonerate himself. If the fish is lost, at least he has managed to kill "many sharks" and ruin "many others." If he has failed he has done so in an epic quest, one that allows him to live briefly in the shadow of Joe DiMaggio. If he goes "too far" outside the circle prescribed by DiMaggio it is only because, as he tells himself, baseball is his sustenance and he does not want to "think" beyond it (*OMATS* 106). Santiago shares DiMaggio's "pain"; his movements are restricted, his hands torn and bloodied from the fight. But he also emulates DiMaggio's strength. "Do you believe the great DiMaggio would stay with a fish as long as I will stay with this one?" he wonders—as if he has come of age in the *Ligas* and the *galanos* have become the *Tigres of Detroit*. Sometimes the fetishism knows no bounds: "I must be worthy of the great DiMaggio who does all things perfectly," he says a little earlier (64).

In *The Old Man and the Sea*, the quest for human perfectibility in baseball is not transferable to the spiritual landscape of the Caribbean. The popular idea of the stadium as a "church" where the primacy of Yankee life is affirmed by a theology of rules, scores, and batting averages, the play of demi-gods, and the papacy of managers like Adolfo Luque, comes undone in a black Atlantic. Santiago worships America from afar. He can not attend Yankee Stadium or witness for himself the "sacred memory" of ceremonial space (Chidester 222). The way he worships is virtual yet all-consuming, the product of radio programs, magazine articles, newspapers, and the same kind of cultural diplomacy that all American governments have lent their support to since World War II.

Notes

1. The video of this interview, "A Day with Hemingway, A 'Sato' Cuban," was made available to the author in VHS format by Guidmar Venegas Delgado, c/o Cuban State Television, at the 10th International Ernest Hemingway Colloquium, Havana, Cuba, 23–25 May 2005.

2. One of the earliest uses of mythic tropes in a reading of *The Old Man and the Sea* can be found in a letter written by Malcolm Cowley to Ernest Hemingway on 3 August 1952 (quoted in Fuentes 391).

Works Cited

Bailey, James A. *The Yoruba of Southwestern Nigeria and Santería in the Southeastern United States: History, Culture, Rituals and Ceremonies of an Afro-Cuban Cult*. New Bern, NC: Godolphin House, 1991.

Beegel, Susan. E-mail to author. 6 July 2004.

Brasch, James D. and Joseph Sigman, comps. *Hemingway's Library: A Composite Record*. New York and London: Garland, 1981.

Brock, Lisa and Digna Castenada Fuentes, eds. *Between Race and Empire: African-Americans and Cubans before the Cuban Revolution*. Philadelphia: Temple UP, 1990.

Chapin, Henry and Frank G. Walton Smith. *The Ocean River: The Story of the Gulf Stream*. 1952. London: Victor Gollancz, 1953.

———. *The Sun, the Sea, and Tomorrow: Potential Sources of Food, Energy, and Minerals from the Sea*. New York: Scribner's, 1954.

Chidester, David. "The Church of Baseball, the Fetish of Coca-Cola, and the Potlatch of Rock 'n Roll." In *Religion and Popular Culture in America*. Eds. Bruce Forbes and Jeffrey Mahan. Berkeley: U of California P. 2001. 219–237.

Cronon, William. *The Trouble with Wilderness; or, Getting Back to the Wrong Nature*. New York: W.W. Norton, 1995.

Duany, Jorge. "Reconstructing Cubanness: Changing Discourses of National Identity on the Island and in the Diaspora during the Twentieth Century." In Fernández and Betancourt. 17–43.

Fernández, Damian J. and Madeleine Camara Betancourt, eds. *Cuba, The Elusive Nation: Interpretations of Identity*. Gainesville: UP of Florida, 2000.

Firmat, Gustav Peret. *Life on the Hyphen: The Cuban-American Way*. Austin: U of Texas P, 1994.

Fuentes, Norberto. *Hemingway in Cuba*. Trans. Consuelo E. Corwin. Secaucus, NJ: Lyle Stuart, 1984.

Gonzalez-Kirby, Diana H. "Santería: African Influences on Religion in Cuba." *Negro History Bulletin* 48 (July–September 1985): 39–44.

Gonzalez-Wippler, Migene. *African Magic in Latin America*. New York: Doubleday, 1973.

———. *The Santería Experience*. Englewood Cliffs, NJ: Prentice Hall, 1982.

Gordimer, Nadine. "Back to the Laboratory". *The Guardian* [London]. 25 January 2003. 7.

Grimes, Larry. Conversations with the author. 7–12 June 2004.

Hemingway, Ernest. *By-Line: Ernest Hemingway*. Ed. William H. White. 1967. Harmondsworth: Penguin, 1970.

———. *Ernest Hemingway: Selected Letters, 1917–1961*. Ed. Carlos Baker. London: Granada, 1981.

———. *The Old Man and the Sea*. 1952. London: Jonathan Cape, 1953.

Hemingway, Hilary and Carlene Brennen. *Hemingway in Cuba*. New York: Rugged Land, 2003.

Herskovitz, Melville Jean. *Cultural Anthropology*. New York: Knopf, 1955.

Kinnamon, Keneth. "Hemingway and Politics." In *The Cambridge Companion to Hemingway*. Ed. Scott Donaldson. Cambridge: Cambridge UP, 1996. 170–197.

Klein, Herbert S. *The Atlantic Slave Trade*. Cambridge: Cambridge UP, 1999.

Martinez, Juan A. "*Lo Blanco-Criollo as lo Cubano*: The Symbolisation of a Cuban National Identity in Modernist Painting of the 1940s." In Fernández and Betancourt. 277–292.

Martinez, Rafael and Wetli, Charles V. "Santería: A Magico-Religious System of Afro-Cuban Origin." *American Journal of Social Psychiatry* 2/3 (1982): 32–38.

Morrison, Toni. *Beloved*. New York: Knopf, 1987.

Murphy, Joseph M. *Santería: African Spirits in America*. Boston: Beacon, 1988.

Murray, Margaret Alice. *The Witch-Cult in Western Europe: A Study in Anthropology*. Oxford: Clarendon, 1921.

Payne, Chris. "A Vatican for Film Makers." *The Guardian* [London]. 28 November 2003. 10–11.

Rogosin, Donn. *Invisible Men: Life in Baseball's Negro Leagues.* New York: Atheneum, 1983.

Rosenberg, Emily S. *Spreading the American Dream: American Economic and Cultural Expansion, 1890–1945.* New York: Hill and Wang, 1982.

Stephanson, Anders. *Kennan and the Art of Foreign Policy.* Cambridge: Harvard UP, 1989.

Talese, Gay. "The Silent Season of a Hero." *Esquire.* July 1966. Rpt. in *Fame and Obscurity.* New York: Ivy, 1993. 224–264.

Thomas, Hugh. *Cuba: The Pursuit of Freedom.* 1971. London: Picador, 2001.

Tunstall, Jeremy. *The Media are American: Anglo-American Media in the World.* London: Constable, 1978.

Tygiel, Jules. *Jackie Robinson and his Legacy: Baseball's Great Experiment.* New York: Vintage, 1984.

Wagnleitner, Reinhold. "Propagating the American Dream: Cultural Policies as Means of Integration." *American Studies International* 24.1 (April 1986): 60–84.

Williams, Walter L. "American Imperialism and the Indians." In *Indians in American History.* Ed. Frederich E. Hoxie. Arlington Heights, IL: Harlan Davidson, 1988. 231–251.

Wilson, August. *Joe Turner's Come and Gone: A Play in Two Acts.* 1988. New York: Penguin, 1992.

Zoss, Joel and John Bowan. *Diamonds in the Rough: The Untold History of Baseball.* London: Macmillan, 1989.

DONALD A. DAIKER

"Brett Couldn't Hold Him": Lady Ashley, Pedro Romero, and the Madrid Sequence of The Sun Also Rises

The central event in Ernest Hemingway's *The Sun Also Rises* occurs when the novel's narrator and protagonist, Jake Barnes, arranges for the woman he loves but cannot have, Lady Brett Ashley, to begin a sexual liaison with the young Spanish bullfighter Pedro Romero. Jake's decision to bring Brett to Romero has both immediate and future consequences. Its immediate result is that Robert Cohn, desperately in love with Brett himself, calls Jake a "damned pimp" (*SAR* 194).[1] When Jake responds by swinging at him, Cohn knocks Jake out cold and then goes on to pummel Mike Campbell, Brett's fiancé. Cohn next attacks Romero. "He nearly killed the poor, bloody bull-fighter" (205), Mike tells Jake. But although Cohn knocks Romero down "about fifteen times," the bullfighter, unlike Jake and Mike, will not stay down:

> .... he wanted to fight some more. Brett held him and wouldn't let him get up. He was weak, but Brett couldn't hold him, and he got up. (206)

The longer range consequences of Jake's pandering include Mike's increased drunkenness, Cohn's tearful apology and departure from Pamplona, Jake's becoming so depressed that he gets drunker than ever before, and—most significantly—Brett's going off to Madrid with Romero.

From *The Hemingway Review* 29, no. 1 (Fall 2009): 73–88. Copyright © 2009 by the Ernest Hemingway Foundation.

Virtually every reader of *The Sun Also Rises* would, I believe, accept the accuracy of the above summary. Disagreement arises about what happens next in the novel. What happens, that is, between Brett and Romero once they reach Madrid? We know that they stay together in the Hotel Montana, and we know that they are there for no more than three days and nights.[2] By the time Jake arrives at Brett's hotel—less than four full days after she and Romero have left Pamplona—Romero is gone and gone for good. Most readers of *The Sun Also Rises* are convinced—mistakenly, I believe—that Romero is gone because Brett has sent him away. Many commentators believe not only that Brett ends the relationship but that her sending Romero away is her most moral and commendable act in the novel. Stanley Edgar Hyman writes that "the key action of the book is Brett's renunciation of Romero for the boy's own good, the first truly unselfish act in her life" (31). "In giving up Romero," Frederic Joseph Svoboda writes, "Brett has acted more responsibly than we have seen before" (27). Linda Patterson Miller describes Brett's sending Romero away as "her personal breakthrough" (179). For Milton A. Cohen it is "her first brave act in the story, the first in which she renounces her sexual magic and debasing power" (303). Robert W. Lewis writes that Brett "selflessly drives him [Romero] away" (75), and Gerry Brenner finds in Brett's behavior evidence of "genuine moral growth" (50). There seems to be critical consensus, then, on what Earl Rovit calls "Brett's famous act of self-abnegation, her decision to send Romero away because she will not be 'one of these bitches that ruins children'" (155).

But even among those who agree that Brett rather than Romero has ended the affair, there is growing recognition of the complexity of Brett's character. For Lawrence Broer, Brett is not only "Hemingway's most complex and provocative female character" but "one of the most elusive and richly enigmatic figures in modern literature" (139). Linda Patterson Miller argues that critics have ignored "the complexity of Brett's character and the intricate role she plays in the novel ..." ("Brett Ashley" 170). Delbert Wylder points to "the subtlety with which Hemingway treats some of the deeper aspects of Jake's and Brett's rather complicated relationship, and particularly the characterization of Lady Brett Ashley" (90). A major reason why Brett is both elusive and enigmatic, why in Miller's words she "resists formulaic readings" ("In Love with Papa" 10), is, as Jackson J. Benson explains, that "Hemingway treats her with a delicate balance of sympathy and antipathy" (36). So while understanding Brett and her complex motivations will not be easy, a close, analytic reading of the Madrid sequence will show that it is Romero who has left Brett and not the other way around.

What we know about Brett and Romero in Madrid we know directly only from Brett herself. Because Romero is gone and never heard from again, we learn about their short time together only from what Brett reveals to Jake during their conversations—first in her room at the Hotel Montana, next at the bar of the Palace hotel, then at Botín's restaurant, and finally during a taxi ride along Madrid's Gran Via. But how we understand and interpret Brett's words—and whether we find her story credible—will be colored by her behavior, especially her body language, by Jake's responses to what Brett is telling and showing him, and by our judgment of her trustworthiness as a narrator.

Although there may be no earlier instances in the novel of Brett's outright dishonesty, she often makes statements that are simply not true. She fibs when she tells Cohn that she's promised the next dance to Jake and then that she and Jake have a date in Montmartre (*SAR* 30). Then, to convince Jake to leave the *bal musette* with her, Brett tells him that Georgette, the woman he brought there, is "well taken care of" (31). Brett is wrong: soon after Jake and Brett leave, Georgette becomes involved in a "frightful row" with the patronne's daughter (36). Brett is equally mistaken, but with far graver consequences, when she tells Jake that she thought her going off with Robert Cohn would be "good for him" (89). Brett is wrong again when she tells Jake that "Michael and I understand each other" (148), implying that Mike understands and accepts her affair with Cohn when actually Brett's infidelities—first with Cohn and then with Romero—destroy Mike emotionally. But what Brett tells Jake in Madrid is not simply wrong or mistaken; what Brett says about her relationship to Romero is a lie. Brett knows it is a lie, and it does not take long for Jake to realize it is a lie, although he never lets on that he knows. Brett tells Jake that she ended the relationship with Romero when her words, her actions, and Jake's responses show that it was in fact Romero who left.

In Madrid, as earlier in Pamplona, "Brett couldn't hold him" (*SAR* 206). Clearly, the primary meaning here of "Brett couldn't hold him" is that Brett does not have the physical strength to hold Romero *down*, to prevent him from getting up off the floor to continue fighting with Cohn. But an equally clear secondary meaning is that Brett is unable to hold *on to* Romero, to prevent him from eventually leaving her. This latter meaning dominates *The Torrents of Spring*, the parody Hemingway wrote and published while he was writing and revising *The Sun Also Rises*. In *Torrents*, Hemingway uses the phrase "hold him" no fewer than 29 times to characterize the relationship between Scripps O'Neil, the story's protagonist, and his elderly wife Diana. "He was her man and she would hold him" (*TOS* 43), Diana vows; "That was all that mattered now. To hold him. To hold him. Not to let him go. Make him stay" (42). But by the end of the book Scripps has left: "She couldn't hold him. She couldn't hold him. She couldn't hold him" (82).

When Jake arrives at Brett's hotel room, it is immediately clear that she is in desperate straits. Brett's desperation was signaled earlier by her having sent Jake not one but two identically worded telegrams: "COULD YOU COME HOTEL MONTANA MADRID AM RATHER IN TROUBLE BRETT (*SAR* 243)." Brett's use of the word "rather" underlines her desperation because, in her British idiom, "rather" does not have the American meaning of "to a certain extent" or "somewhat." Both the Oxford English Dictionary and the *American Heritage Dictionary* point to the chiefly British usage of "rather" as an intensive, as an emphatic affirmative, and that is how Brett has used the word earlier in the novel. When Jake says that Brett knows where to find drinks in his apartment, Brett answers, "Rather" (61), meaning "certainly" or "absolutely." When Brett is asked whether Romero will fight after his beating by Cohn, she responds, "Rather" (210), meaning he assuredly will. Thus when Brett describes herself as "rather in trouble," she is telling Jake that she is in deep and even debilitating difficulty.

Jake's understanding that Brett is deeply distressed is confirmed as soon as he reaches the Hotel Montana. There the maid says that Brett wants to see him "now, at once," and moments later Brett calls out, "Come in. Come in" (*SAR* 245), the repetition in each instance signaling how desperately she needs Jake. As soon as Jake enters, Brett exclaims "Darling!" in obvious tones of relief and, apparently with her eyes and body language, invites Jake to her bed to comfort her with an embrace. Jake immediately notices that Brett's hotel room is "in that disorder produced only by those who have always had servants" (245), an indication that Jake has started to understand his subservient role in Brett's life, at least as Brett sees it. Brett's characteristic response to the messes she creates is to leave them for others to clean up. She flicks cigarette ashes on the rug in Jake's Paris apartment until Jake finds "some ash-trays and spread them around" (64). When her dalliance with Romero so angers Mike that he deliberately upsets a café table, crashing beer and shrimp to the ground, Brett says, "Let's get out of this" (211) and leaves. Throughout *The Sun Also Rises*, the conditions of rooms consistently correspond to the emotional states of their occupants. Mike's room at the Hotel Montoya is "in great disorder" with bags open, clothing "strewn around," and "empty bottles beside the bed" (214). By contrast, because Jake is trying to put his post-fiesta life back together, his room in San Sebastian is tidy and orderly with bags unpacked, clothes hung up, and books stacked neatly on a bedside table (238). Brett's disordered room points to her disordered life and psyche now that Romero has left her.

Brett will not admit to Jake that Romero has walked out on her. And because, as Delbert Wylder has observed, "Brett does not understand herself very well" (93), she initially may not even admit it to herself. Because no other male in the novel has yet resisted Brett's beauty and charm, Romero's may have been her first such rejection. But in response to questions, Brett provides enough information to enable Jake to figure things out. Although at first Brett says, "I made him [Romero] go," her subsequent disclosures suggest that Romero left on his own. Brett's first painful admission occurs when she acknowledges that "It was rather [absolutely, totally] a knock his being ashamed of me. He was ashamed of me for a while, you know" (*SAR* 246). Apparently Romero grew ashamed of Brett's short hair—she wears it "brushed back like a boy's" (30)—and wanted her to grow it out in order to look "more womanly" (246). Brett goes on to tell Jake that Romero "got over that. He wasn't ashamed of me long" (246). But she later undermines her assertion when she says of Romero, "he'd have gotten used to" her personal appearance. (247). Her use of the conditional *would* strongly implies that Romero had not gotten over being ashamed of her by the time he leaves. And if Romero "really wanted" to marry her, as Brett claims, that marriage could only occur, Brett acknowledges, "After I'd gotten more womanly" (246), something that will never occur. When Jake asks, "What was it about being in trouble?" Brett answers, "I didn't know whether I could make him go" (246). Her language—especially the conditional *could*—makes clear that she never had the chance to ask Romero to go because he left on his own. Even so, in an attempt to prevent Jake from grasping the truth of her situation, she quickly changes the subject from "trouble" to "money."

There are other good reasons besides the inconsistencies in Brett's story, to believe that Romero has dumped her. Brett's acute depression seems unaccountable if she has been the one to end the relationship. Brett has been upset before—"Oh, darling, I've been so miserable," she told Jake in Paris (*SAR* 32)—but that is nothing compared to her deep despair in Madrid. Not only does she admit she's "had such a hell of a time" (245), but Brett is "trembling" and "crying," something that didn't happen earlier (245, 247). Jake goes on to say, "I could feel her crying. Shaking and crying" (247). Moments later Jake can still feel Brett "crying," and even after he comforts her by stroking her hair, she is still "shaking" (247). Only after the first sip of a Martini is Brett's hand steady enough to lift her glass (248).

Hemingway suggests in two further ways that Brett's crying, shaking, and general depression is the result of Romero's decision to leave her. The first sign is Brett's refusal to look at Jake. As long as the two remain in the hotel room where she and Romero have lived together, Brett will not look into Jake's eyes. Elsewhere in *The Sun Also Rises* and in other work by Hemingway, an inability to look directly at someone is a sign of dishonesty, deception, or an unwillingness to accept painful truth. In "The End of Something," the story of Nick Adams's breakup with his girl friend Marjorie, Nick is "afraid to look at Marjorie" because he does not want to tell her that he doesn't love her any more (*CSS* 81). When Nick eventually does tell her, he still cannot look at her face, only at her back. This link between looking away and deception or denial continues in *The Sun Also Rises*. When the innkeeper at Burguete announces outrageously high room rates to Jake, she "put her hands under her apron and looked away from me"; when Jake protests, she "just took off her glasses and wiped them on her apron" (*SAR* 115). When Jake and Brett are alone in his Paris apartment, Jake lies "face down on the bed" because he refuses to acknowledge that he and Brett cannot live together (61). To emphasize this point, Jake repeats it: "I was lying with my face away from her. I did not want to see her" (62). When Cohn, rejected by Brett, lies "face down, on the bed in the dark" (197), looking away again constitutes a reluctance to acknowledge unpleasant truth. Moments later Cohn is still "face down on the bed, crying" (197). Brett's looking away from Jake in Madrid is both a sign that she does not want to face up to rejection and an indication that she does not believe the story she is telling Jake. Significantly, just after Brett tells Jake that sending Romero away makes her "feel rather good" and "rather set up" (247), she cannot look Jake in the eye. At this precise point in her story, Brett "looked away" and "wouldn't look up." Moments later she still "would not look up" (247). Brett refuses to admit that Romero has abandoned her, but Jake—having been in her position earlier—puts his arms around her, holds her close, and gently strokes her hair in acknowledgment of her need to deny the truth of Romero's rejection.

The credibility of Brett's assertion that she made Romero leave is further undercut by her lack of self-control during the Madrid sequence.[3] One sign is her constant swearing. Brett resorts to profanity no less than ten times in four pages, whereas Jake swears only once at the very beginning of the scene. In *The Sun Also Rises*, profanity is often a sign of anger, pain, or distress. For example, when Bill asks about Brett, Jake admits that he has been in love with her "Off and on for a hell of a long time," but that he doesn't "give a damn any more" although he'd "a hell of a lot rather not talk about it" (*SAR* 128). Jake's swearing is also a sign of anger when he says, "[W]hat the hell is it to Frances?" (14), "To hell with you, Brett Ashley (152)," "Oh, to hell with Cohn" (226), and, on receiving Brett's telegrams, "Well, that meant San Sebastian all shot to hell" (243). Significantly, Hemingway eliminated the profanity from the novel's original last line—"'Yes,' I said. "'It's nice as hell to think so'"—because he did not want to imply a loss of control on Jake's part (*SAR: Facsimile* 616). Hemingway considered the use of profanity essential to his novel. When his Scribner's editor Maxwell Perkins asked him to eliminate some of the profanity, Hemingway resisted fiercely—but with a touch of humor: "I've tried to reduce profanity but I reduced so much profanity when writing the book that I'm afraid not much could come out. Perhaps we will have to consider it simply as a profane book and hope that the next book will be less profane or perhaps more sacred" (*SL* 213).

Brett's inability to stop talking about Romero is a further sign of her loss of control. Again and again, Brett begs Jake to drop the topic of her relationship to the bullfighter:

> "Oh, hell!" she said, "let's not talk about it. Let's never talk about it." (*SAR* 245)

> "Oh, let's not talk about it." (246)

> "Don't let's ever talk about it. Please don't let's ever talk about it." (247)

> "But, oh, Jake, please let's never talk about it." (247)

When Brett herself insists on bringing up Romero after each such plea, Jake finally says, "I thought you weren't going to ever talk about it." Brett's response is a telling one: "How can I help it?" (249). Just as she had earlier been helpless to prevent his leaving her, Brett cannot help talking about Romero.

Brett's two references to Mike Campbell, the man she deserted in Pamplona to run off with Romero, make sense only if Romero left Brett, rather than the other way around. In the throes of disappointment after telling Jake that Romero "wanted to marry me, finally," Brett says, "I can't even marry Mike" (*SAR* 246). The key word here is *even*, reflecting Brett's sense that Mike isn't much but she doesn't deserve even that. Brett's second reference to Mike signals her loss of self-worth yet more sharply. The draft manuscript version reads this way:

> "I'm going back to Mike," I could feel her crying as I held her close.
> "He's so damned nice and he's so very awful. He's my sort."
> (*SAR: Facsimile* 603)

Hemingway revised the final sentence by adding two key words: "He's my sort of thing" (*SAR* 247). In calling Mike, and by extension herself, a "thing," Brett reveals—as Debra Moddelmog points out—"her inner turmoil and ambivalence" (158).

But Brett's comment also registers the depth of her self-loathing brought on by Romero's rejection. Mike had earlier referred to Brett as a "thing" (*SAR*

85), but had done so light-heartedly, evoking a smile from Brett. By contrast, her use of the term echoes Romero's disdainful view of the bullfighter Marcial as "the sort of thing he knew all about" (219), as something beneath notice or regard. Hemingway uses the word "thing" in an equally insulting way in both "The Mother of a Queen" where the reprehensible bullfighter Paco, whose mother's body is dumped into a bone heap because he refuses to pay for her grave, is labeled a "thing" (*CSS* 318) and in "A Clean, Well-Lighted Place" where the insensitive younger waiter says that "An old man is a nasty thing" (*CSS* 289). By likening herself to a "thing," Brett powerfully reveals her self-contempt.

Brett's self-loathing is an additional indication that she has not behaved virtuously in Madrid, especially when her words are understood in the context of the novel's definition of morality. In Chapter XIV, the novel's expository and thematic center, Jake defines "immorality" as "things that made you disgusted afterward" (*SAR* 152); by implication, then, morality consists of things that make you feel good afterwards.[4] *Death in the Afternoon*, Hemingway's first-person treatise on bull-fighting published just six years after *The Sun Also Rises*, makes it clear that Jake's standards are his creator's as well: "So far, about morals, I know only that what is moral is what you feel good after and what is immoral is what you feel bad after . . ." (*DIA* 4). Because Brett feels bad after Romero has left—as her crying, trembling, repeating herself, looking away, losing control, and calling herself a "thing" demonstrate conclusively—she has not acted morally by Jake's or Hemingway's standards. If Brett had indeed sent Romero away, if she had "realized. . . . right away" that he "shouldn't be living with any one" (*SAR* 245), if she had performed the act of "virtuous renunciation" that Earl Rovit and other critics ascribe to her, then she should genuinely be feeling "all right" and "rather good" and "rather set up" (246–247). But she doesn't. She feels rotten because she knows that Romero walked out on her, and she has no reason for self-congratulation.

One further sign of Brett's depressed emotional state is the complete absence, in Book III, of her wonderful humor and what Lorie Watkins Fulton calls her "subtle wit" (68). In Book I, in Paris, Brett had joked with Jake about his bringing a prostitute to the *bal musette* as being "in restraint of trade" (*SAR* 30) and with Count Mippipopolous about her career (68). In Book II, she tells Mike not to be "indecent" because there are "ladies at this bar" (85), humorously implying that she is not one. Even in Pamplona Brett jokes about having "the wrong type of face" (212) for church and about Romero's green trousers. But in Book III, in Madrid, Brett never attempts a joke and never exercises her wit. Instead, she is too depressed even to appreciate Jake's humor and irony. So when Jake speculates that Romero wanted to marry Brett in order to become "Lord Ashley," Brett doesn't catch the joke. She responds not with a laugh or a smile but only, more seriously, with "No. It wasn't that" (246).

Brett's mood lightens a bit when Jake takes her away from the room she had shared with Romero to the bar of the Palace Hotel, although even here Brett cannot stop talking about the bullfighter. Once again—actually for the fifth time—she acknowledges her powerlessness in relation to Romero: "How can I help it?" she asks Jake (*SAR* 249). Brett attempts to buoy her fallen spirits by convincing herself that she deserves credit "for deciding not to be a bitch" (249), but because it was Romero who left her, she has made no such decision at all.

During the final scenes of the novel—first at Botín's restaurant and then in a Madrid taxi—Romero is an invisible presence for both Jake and Brett. Mark Spilka is absolutely right in asserting that Romero "dominates the final conversation between the lovers, and so dominates the closing section" (*SAR* 256). For Jake, Romero is an unseen but powerful mentor guiding Jake's conduct toward Brett, the bull in his life.[5] For Brett, Romero is present in several manifestations. At Botín's, Brett projects onto Jake the enduring love and commitment that she sought from Romero but did not receive. Brett thinks Jake is purposely getting drunk—four times she tells him, "Don't get drunk" (250)—because she believes that, in contrast to the departed Romero, Jake truly loves her and still pines for her. While Jake still cares for Brett as a friend—that is why he rescues her in Madrid and, knowing "she can't go anywhere alone" (107), arranges "for berths on the Sud Express for the night" (247)—he no longer harbors romantic fantasies about their marrying or living together. Brett, it becomes increasingly clear, is completely unaware of Jake's change.

Consumed by rejection and self-centered as always, Brett tells Jake detail after detail about Romero[6]—his age, his date of birth, his schooling, his learning English, his women. In her hotel room and through three Martinis at the Palace she never once inquires about the fiancé she abandoned in Pamplona or asks Jake a single question about himself. Not until they've completed a full meal at Botín's does Brett ask Jake a personal question and even then it is a superficial one: "'How do you feel, Jake?' Brett asked. 'My God! what a meal you've eaten'" (*SAR* 249).[7] Thus when Brett tells Jake, "You don't have to [get drunk]" and goes on to assure him, "You'll be all right" (249), she is uttering platitudes and clichés.

Brett knows nothing, for instance, of Jake's recuperation and self-restoration in San Sebastian.[8] A key implication of Brett's sending telegrams to Paris and Pamplona when Jake is actually in San Sebastian is that Brett does not know where Jake has been—literally or metaphorically. Brett's telegraphing Jake in Paris with the request that he meet her in Madrid underscores both her desperation and her dependence upon Jake: the train ride from Paris to Madrid would have taken Jake a full 28 hours.[9] So although it's true that Jake is—and will be—"all right," Brett has no means of knowing it. That's why Jake challenges her with the question, "How do you know?" (*SAR* 249). In Madrid, Jake is not what Brett had expected. He is not the loving, doting, and accepting romantic that he used to be and that Romero proved not to be. He is not the Romero substitute Brett desires.

Brett herself has not changed appreciably. As Michael Reynolds observes, Brett in Madrid "is no different than she is when we first meet her" (23). Brett "never ate much," and so even at "one of the best restaurants in the world" like Botín's, "Brett did not eat much" (*SAR* 249), a detail that links her to the sick and defeated Belmonte who "ate very little" (225) and distances her from the happy, self-assured Count Mippipopolous, whose motto is "I always like a good meal" (64). Brett's last spoken words make clear that she is the same Brett who, earlier on the dance floor at Zelli's in Paris, had told Jake, "Oh, darling . . . , I'm so miserable" (70). Brett's final statement, spoken as she and Jake ride in a taxi along Madrid's Gran Via, both echoes her earlier expression of what Kenneth Lynn calls her "unquenchable unhappiness" (325) and constitutes her final—this time subtle—reference to Romero: "Oh, Jake," Brett said, "we could have had such a damned good time together" (*SAR* 251).

Brett feels sorry for herself because Romero has left her, and so for the first and only time in the novel she permits herself to indulge in the might-have-been with Jake Barnes. But Romero has not left Jake, who will have none of Brett's self-pity.[10] By responding "Isn't it pretty to think so?" Jake once and for all dismisses Brett's fantasies as foolishly sentimental (*SAR* 251). Brett will be surprised and pained by Jake's refusal to share her fantasy, but because Romero has "wiped out that damned Cohn" (246), she is free to return to Michael who, like Brett herself, is both awful and nice. Like Romero, who literally pays the bill at the Hotel Montana, Jake literally—as well as metaphorically—pays his bill for having Brett as a friend by purchasing them tickets on the Sud Express.[11] Brett herself doesn't "have a sou to go away" with (246). The train will take her back to San Sebastian, where Mike is waiting at a pub in nearby Saint Jean de Luz.[12] Thanks to Jake's friendship—and money—Brett is no longer "rather in trouble."

Because it was Romero's decision to end their relationship, Brett cannot be credited with what Kurt Krueger has called a "self-transcendent deed" (343) and Doris Helbig an act of "charity or agape" (103). Nor has she achieved the "moral triumph" (25) that Spilka attributes to her. Lady Ashley at the end of the novel is the same complex, interesting, charming, self-centered, and frustrated woman she has been all along. As the novel draws to a close, she greets Jake in Madrid with "Darling! I've had such a hell of a time" (*SAR* 245), just as she greeted him in Paris at the novel's beginning with "Oh, darling, I've been so miserable" (32). But Jake is not the same. He has learned and grown. As H. R. Stoneback accurately notes, "One of the main thrusts of the novel is to differentiate between Jake's character and behavior and Brett's, to draw distinctions . . ." (292). The final and most important distinction is that while Brett, unable to hold onto Pedro Romero, is sorrowfully and reluctantly returning to Mike, Jake is—thanks to the same Pedro Romero—now leading his life "all the way up" (18) and beginning a new phase of that life without the burden of Lady Brett Ashley.

Notes

1. All quotations from *The Sun Also Rises* are from the Scribner 2003 edition and are cited parenthetically in the text.

2. Although Benson labels it "two weeks of adultery" (40), Brett and Romero could have been living together no more than three full days. Mike says that Brett had left Pamplona and "gone off with the bull-fighter chap" on the last day of the fiesta (*SAR* 227). The next day—Day Two—Jake says good-bye to both Mike and Bill Gorton, spends the night in Bayonne, France, and hears nothing from Brett. The following day—Day Three—Jake crosses the border to San Sebastian, Spain, where he spends the night, again with no word from Brett. But at mid-morning the next day—Day Four—Jake receives two telegrams from Brett announcing that she is "rather in trouble" and asking him to come to the Hotel Montana in Madrid (242). By the next morning—Day Five—when Jake arrives at the Hotel Montana, Romero is gone, and Brett tells Jake that Romero "only left yesterday"—that is on Day Four (245). There is strong reason to believe that it was Romero's departure that prompted Brett to wire Jake with a call for help. In any case, Brett and Romero could have been together for no more than three full days.

3. Hemingway emphasizes the importance of control throughout *The Sun Also Rises*. In the opening chapter, Robert Cohn's lack of emotional control, in contrast to his physical prowess in the boxing ring, is suggested by the passive voice: he "was married by the first girl who was nice to him," his mother "settled an allowance on him," and he is later "taken in hand" by another woman who "led him quite a life" (*SAR* 13–15). In the closing chapter of Book II Hemingway presents Cohn's opposite, Pedro Romero, whose bullfighting is "so slow and so controlled" (221). The marked contrasts between Cohn and Romero invite the reader to explore issues of control in the book's concluding chapter, especially the Madrid sequence.

4. Hemingway's most serious and important utterances are often cloaked by humor or understatement. In Chapter XIV Jake announces his philosophy of life, what Rovit calls "the value center of the novel" (149): "Enjoying living was learning to get your money's worth and knowing when you had it." But then he immediately qualifies it with "It seemed like a fine philosophy. In five years, I thought, it will seem just as silly as all the other fine philosophies I've had" (*SAR* 152). By the same token, Jake undercuts his own definition of immorality—"things that made you disgusted afterward"—with humor: "What a lot of bilge I could think up at night" (152).

5. For informative discussions of Romero's impact upon Jake, see Donald Daiker ("Affirmative Conclusion"), Terrence Doody, Dewey Ganzel, and Allen Josephs.

6. Significantly, Brett says not one single word about Romero's bullfighting, supporting James Nagel's assertion that "her interest in Pedro is sexual, and not a case of admiration of his craft" ("Brett" 97). Lawrence Broer, by contrast, mistakenly asserts that "Brett . . . becomes seriously involved in the meaning of the bullfight . . ." (*Spanish Tragedy*, 53).

7. Jackson Benson rightly notes Brett's failure to acknowledge Jake "as a human being with emotions" except for a question and a request designed as "feelers toward confirming whether the old sentimental magic is still working on Jake. . . ." (40–41).

8. For insightful commentary on the significance of Jake's stay in San Sebastian, according to Svoboda "one of the most heavily revised sections of the novel" (40), see Steinke ("both the experience and his untroubled attentiveness to it are cleansing and exhilarating" [133]), E. Miller Budick ("His swim at San Sebastian is not just a ritual immersion. It is a vital confrontation with sexuality and with death" [330]), Ellen Andrews Knodt ("Jake is now ready for Brett's telegram" [35]), and H. R. Stoneback ("Jake has been to the bottom over the Brett-Cohn affair, but now, eyes wide open, having no illusions, he has come out the other side of that 'dark shadow' . . ." [281].

9. "We left Paris one morning and got off the train at Madrid the next noon," Hemingway reported in "Bull Fighting a Tragedy," a 1923 article for *The Toronto Star Weekly* (*BL* 79).

10. Benson writes that to Brett, "Jake is a valuable piece of property, a home base for self pity that she can return to until the loss of Romero, or whoever it might be, has lost its poignancy" (42). For the case that by the end of the novel Jake has dispensed with self-pity and is now fully in control of himself, Brett, and their relationship, see Daiker (2007), Rovit (147–162), and Carole Gottlieb Vopat ("With pity and irony, compassion and control, Jake breaks the circle . . ." [104]).

11. After Hemingway moved from Paris to Toronto in the late summer of 1923, he wrote to his father, "We made a mistake to come back here. But the only way to do with mistakes is to pay for them and get out of them as soon as possible" (*SL* 100). Jake Barnes follows the exact same course.

12. Hemingway's unfinished sequel to *The Sun Also Rises*, a nine-page afterword probably written the year after the novel's publication, shows Brett and Michael back together. Cataloged under the title "Jimmy the Bartender," the sketch depicts Jake Barnes at the Dingo Bar in Paris when Lady Brett walks in with Mike Campbell. Jake is not surprised. See Fleming.

Works Cited

Benson, Jackson J. *Hemingway: The Writer's Art of Self-Defense*. Minneapolis: U Minnesota P, 1969.

Brenner, Gerry. *Concealments in Hemingway's Works*. Columbus: Ohio State UP, 1983.

Broer, Lawrence R. *Hemingway's Spanish Tragedy*. University, AL: U Alabama P, 1973.

———. "Intertextual Approach to *The Sun Also Rises*." In *Teaching Hemingway's The Sun Also Rises*. Ed. Peter Hays. Moscow: U Idaho P, 2003. 127–146.

Budick, E. Miller. "*The Sun Also Rises*: Hemingway and the Art of Repetition." *University of Toronto Quarterly* 56:2 (1986/7): 319–331.

Cohen, Milton A. "Circe and Her Swine: Domination and Debasement in *The Sun Also Rises*." *Arizona Quarterly* 41:4 (1985): 293–305.

Daiker, Donald A. "The Affirmative Conclusion of *The Sun Also Rises*." 1974–75. In *Critical Essays on Ernest Hemingway's The Sun Also Rises*. Ed. James Nagel. New York: G. K. Hall, 1995. 74–88.

———. "Jake Barnes as Teacher and Learner: The Pedagogy of *The Sun Also Rises*." *The Hemingway Review* 27:1 (Fall 2007): 74–88.

Doody, Terrence. "Hemingway's Style and Jake's Narration." 1974. In *Ernest Hemingway: Seven Decades of Criticism*. Ed. Linda Wagner Martin. East Lansing: Michigan State UP, 1998. 103–117.

Fleming, Robert E. "Second Thoughts: Hemingway's Postscript to *The Sun Also Rises*." In *Critical Essays on Ernest Hemingway's The Sun Also Rises*. Ed. James Nagel. New York: G. K. Hall, 1995. 163–169.

Fulton, Lorie Watkins. "Reading Around Jake's Narration: Brett Ashley and *The Sun Also Rises*." *The Hemingway Review* 24:1 (Fall 2004): 61–80.

Ganzel, Dewey. "*Cabestro* and *Vaquilla*: The Symbolic Structure of *The Sun Also Rises*." *Sewanee Review* 76 (1968): 26–48.

Helbig, Doris A. "Confession, Charity, and Community in *The Sun Also Rises*." *South Atlantic Review* 58:2 (1993): 85–110.

Hemingway, Ernest. *By-Line: Ernest Hemingway*. Ed. William White. New York: Bantam, 1967.

———. *The Complete Short Stories of Ernest Hemingway: The Finca Vigía Edition*. New York: Scribner's, 1987 .

———. *Death in the Afternoon*. New York: Scribner's, 1932.

———. *Ernest Hemingway: Selected Letters, 1917–1961*. Ed. Carlos Baker. New York: Scribner's, 1981.

———. "Jimmy the Bartender." Item 530. The Ernest Hemingway Collection. John F. Kennedy Library. Boston, MA. 1–2.

———. *The Sun Also Rises*. 1926. New York: Scribner, 2003.

———. *The Sun Also Rises: A Facsimile Edition*. Ed. Matthew J. Bruccoli. Detroit, MI: Archive of Literary Documents, 1990.

———. *The Torrents of Spring*. 1926. New York, Scribner's, 1987.

Hyman, Stanley Edgar. *Standards: A Chronicle of Books for Our Time*. New York: Horizon, 1966.

Josephs, Allen. "*Toreo*: The Moral Axis of *The Sun Also Rises*." *The Hemingway Review* 6.1 (Fall 1986): 88–99.

Kinnamon, Keneth. "Hemingway, the Corrida, and Spain." 1959. In *Ernest Hemingway's The Sun Also Rises: A Casebook*. Ed. Linda Wagner-Martin. Oxford: Oxford U P, 2002. 81–98.

Knodt, Ellen Andrews. "Diving Deep: Jake's Moment of Truth at San Sebastian." *The Hemingway Review* 17.1 (Fall 1997): 28–37.

Krueger, Kurt J. "A Logotherapeutic Approach to Teaching *The Sun Also Rises*." In *Teaching Hemingway's The Sun Also Rises*. Ed. Peter Hays. Moscow: U Idaho P, 2003. 325–352.

Lewis, Robert W. "Tristan or Jacob?" 1965. In *Brett Ashley: Major Literary Characters*. Ed. Harold Bloom. New York: Chelsea House, 1991. 63–75.

Lynn, Kenneth S. *Hemingway*. New York: Simon and Schuster, 1987.

Miller, Linda Patterson. "Brett Ashley: The Beauty of It All." In *Critical Essays on Ernest Hemingway's The Sun Also Rises*. Ed. James Nagel. New York: G. K. Hall, 1995. 170–184.

———. "In Love with Papa." In *Hemingway and Women: Female Critics and the Female Voice*. Eds. Lawrence Broer and Gloria Holland. Tuscaloosa: U Alabama P, 2002. 3–22.

Moddelmog, Debra A. "Contradictory Bodies in *The Sun Also Rises*." 1999. In *Ernest Heming-way's The Sun Also Rises: A Casebook*. Ed. Linda Wagner-Martin. Oxford: Oxford UP, 2002. 155–165.

———. "Brett and the Other Women in *The Sun Also Rises*." In *The Cambridge Companion to Hemingway*. Ed. Scott Donaldson. Cambridge: Cambridge UP, 1996. 87–108.

Reynolds, Michael S. *The Sun Also Rises: A Novel of the Twenties*. Boston, MA: Twayne, 1988.

Rovit, Earl. *Ernest Hemingway*. New Haven, CT: Twayne, 1963.

Spilka, Mark. "The Death of Love in *The Sun Also Rises*." 1958. In *Ernest Hemingway: Cri-tiques of Four Major Novels*. Ed. Carlos Baker. New York: Scribner's, 1962. 18–25.

Steinke, Jim. "Brett and Jake in Spain: Hemingway's Ending for *The Sun Also Rises*." *Spectrum* 27: 1–2 (1985): 131–141.

Stoneback, H. R. *Reading Hemingway's The Sun Also Rises: Glossary and Commentary*. Kent, OH: Kent State U P, 2007.

Svoboda, Frederic Joseph. *Hemingway and The Sun Also Rises: The Crafting of a Style*. Law-rence: U P of Kansas, 1983.

Vopat, Carole Gottlieb. "The End of *The Sun Also Rises*: A New Beginning." 1972. In *Brett Ashley: Major Literary Characters*. Ed. Harold Bloom. New York: Chelsea House, 1991. 96–104.

Wylder, Delbert E. "The Two Faces of Brett: The Role of the New Woman in *The Sun Also Rises*." 1980. In *Critical Essays on Ernest Hemingway's The Sun Also Rises*. Ed. James Nagel. New York: G. K. Hall, 1995. 89–94.

Chronology

1899	Born Ernest Miller Hemingway on July 21 in Oak Park, Illinois.
1917	Graduates from Oak Park High School; works as a reporter for the *Kansas City Star*.
1918	Enlists in Red Cross Ambulance Corps; wounded in Italy on July 8.
1920	Begins writing for the *Toronto Star* newspapers.
1921	Marries Elizabeth Hadley Richardson; moves to Paris.
1923	Attends first bullfight in Spain; publishes *Three Stories and Ten Poems*; moves to Toronto; son John (Bumby) is born.
1924	Returns to Paris; publishes *In Our Time* in Europe.
1925	Publishes *In Our Time*, which adds 14 short stories to the earlier vignettes, in America.
1926	Publishes *The Torrents of Spring* and *The Sun Also Rises*.
1927	Divorces Hadley Richardson; marries Pauline Pfeiffer; publishes *Men Without Women*.
1928	Moves to Key West, Florida; son Patrick is born.
1929	Publishes *A Farewell to Arms*.
1931	Son Gregory is born.
1932	Publishes *Death in the Afternoon*.

1933   Publishes *Winner Take Nothing*; begins first African safari.

1935   Publishes *Green Hills of Africa*.

1937   Begins covering the Spanish Civil War for the North American Newspaper Alliance; publishes *To Have and Have Not*.

1938   Publishes *The Fifth Column and the First Forty-nine Stories*.

1940   Publishes *For Whom the Bell Tolls*; divorces Pauline Pfeiffer; marries Martha Gellhorn; buys Finca Vigía estate in Cuba.

1944   Serves as war correspondent in Europe; suffers concussion in serious auto accident.

1945   Divorces Martha Gellhorn.

1946   Marries Mary Welsh.

1950   Publishes *Across the River and into the Trees*.

1952   Publishes *The Old Man and the Sea*.

1953   Awarded Pulitzer Prize for *The Old Man and the Sea*; begins second African safari.

1954   Suffers major injuries in two plane crashes in Africa; receives Nobel Prize for Literature and Award of Merit from the American Academy of Arts & Letters.

1961   Commits suicide in Ketchum, Idaho, on July 2.

1964   *A Moveable Feast* is published.

1970   *Islands in the Stream* is published.

1986   *The Garden of Eden* is published.

1999   *True at First Light: A Fictional Memoir* is published.

2005   *Under Kilimanjaro*, first unabridged version of *True at First Light*, published.

Contributors

HAROLD BLOOM is Sterling Professor of the Humanities at Yale University. Educated at Cornell and Yale universities, he is the author of more than 30 books, including *Shelley's Mythmaking* (1959), *The Visionary Company* (1961), *Blake's Apocalypse* (1963), *Yeats* (1970), *The Anxiety of Influence* (1973), *A Map of Misreading* (1975), *Kabbalah and Criticism* (1975), *Agon: Toward a Theory of Revisionism* (1982), *The American Religion* (1992), *The Western Canon* (1994), *Omens of Millennium: The Gnosis of Angels, Dreams, and Resurrection* (1996), *Shakespeare: The Invention of the Human* (1998), *How to Read and Why* (2000), *Genius: A Mosaic of One Hundred Exemplary Creative Minds* (2002), *Hamlet: Poem Unlimited* (2003), *Where Shall Wisdom Be Found?* (2004), and *Jesus and Yahweh: The Names Divine* (2005). In addition, he is the author of hundreds of articles, reviews, and editorial introductions. In 1999, Professor Bloom received the American Academy of Arts and Letters' Gold Medal for Criticism. He has also received the International Prize of Catalonia, the Alfonso Reyes Prize of Mexico, and the Hans Christian Andersen Bicentennial Prize of Denmark.

GEORGE MONTEIRO is a professor emeritus at Brown University. He edited *Critical Essays on Ernest Hemingway's* A Farewell to Arms for G. K. Hall. He is the author and/or editor of many other books as well, covering such authors as Henry James, Elizabeth Bishop, Robert Frost, and Fernando Pessoa. He also is a translator.

DONALD E. HARDY is a professor at the University of Nevada, Reno. His work includes two books on Flannery O'Connor.

191

MARGOT NORRIS is a professor at the University of California, Irvine. She is the author of *Writing War in the Twentieth Century*. Her research field is Modernism.

ROBERT PAUL LAMB is a professor at Purdue University. He is the author of *Art Matters: Hemingway, Craft, and the Creation of the Modern Short Story* and coeditor of *A Companion to American Fiction, 1865–1914*.

NORMAN FRIEDMAN authored *Form and Meaning in Fiction* as well as texts on E. E. Cummings. He also coauthored *Poetry: An Introduction to Its Form and Art*.

SUSAN F. BEEGEL is an affiliate associate professor at the University of Idaho. She is the editor of *The Hemingway Review*. She is the author of *Hemingway's Craft of Omission* and *Hemingway's Neglected Short Fiction*.

DAVID SAVOLA is an instructor at Northern Michigan University. He also has been a visiting assistant professor at Wittenberg University.

PHILIP MELLING is a professor in the American studies Department at Swansea University, where he also is graduate student director. He is working on the monograph *Hemingway and Imperialism*. He has been granted access to the archived research of one of the pioneers of Hemingway research in Cuba, a founding director of the Ernest Hemingway Museum.

DONALD A. DAIKER is professor emeritus at Miami University in Ohio. He has published essays on *The Sun Also Rises* and several books on writing as well.

Bibliography

Beegel, Susan F., ed. *Hemingway's Neglected Short Fiction: New Perspectives*. Ann Arbor, Mich.: UMI Research Press, 1989.

Benson, Jackson J., ed. *New Critical Approaches to the Short Stories of Ernest Hemingway*. Durham: Duke University Press, 1990.

Berman, Ronald. *Fitzgerald, Hemingway, and the Twenties*. Tuscaloosa: University of Alabama Press, 2001.

————. *Modernity and Progress: Fitzgerald, Hemingway, Orwell*. Tuscaloosa: University of Alabama Press, 2005.

————. *Translating Modernism: Fitzgerald and Hemingway*. Tuscaloosa: University of Alabama Press, 2009.

Broer, Lawrence R., and Gloria Holland, eds. *Hemingway and Women: Female Critics and the Female Voice*. Tuscaloosa: University of Alabama Press, 2002.

Cheatham, George. "Margot Macomber's Voice in Hemingway's 'The Short Happy Life of Francis Macomber.'" *Soundings: An Interdisciplinary Journal* 83, nos. 3–4 (Fall–Autumn 2000): 739–64.

Clifford, Stephen P. *Beyond the Heroic "I": Reading Lawrence, Hemingway, and "Masculinity."* Lewisburg, [Pa.]: Bucknell University Press, 1998.

Fleming, Robert E., ed. *Hemingway and the Natural World*. Moscow, Idaho: University of Idaho Press, 1999.

Gaggin, John. *Hemingway and Nineteenth-Century Aestheticism*. Ann Arbor, Mich.: UMI Research Press, 1988.

Gajdusek, Robert E. *Hemingway in His Own Country*. Notre Dame, Ind.: University of Notre Dame Press, 2002.

Grant, David. "Hemingway's 'Hills Like White Elephants' and the Tradition of the American in Europe." *Studies in Short Fiction* 35, no. 3 (Summer 1998): 267–76.

Ibanez, Beatriz. "Hemingway's Ethics of Writing: The Ironic Semantics of 'Whiteness' in 'The Snows of Kilimanjaro.'" *North Dakota Quarterly* 70, no. 4 (Fall 2003): 94–118.

Idema, Henry, III. *Freud, Religion, and the Roaring Twenties: A Psychoanalytic Theory of Secularization in Three Novelists: Anderson, Hemingway, and Fitzgerald.* Savage, Md.: Rowman & Littlefield Publications, 1990.

Johnston, Kenneth G. *The Tip of the Iceberg: Hemingway and the Short Story.* Greenwood, Fla.: Penkevill Publishing Co., 1987.

Leonard, John. "'A Man of the World' and 'A Clean, Well-Lighted Place': Hemingway's Unified View of Old Age." *The Hemingway Review* 13, no. 2 (Spring 1994): 62–73.

Lewis, Robert W., ed. *Hemingway in Italy and Other Essays.* New York: Praeger, 1990.

Macdonald, Scott. "Hemingway's 'The Snows of Kilimanjaro': Three Critical Problems." *Studies in Short Fiction* 11 (1974): 67–74.

Meyers, Jeffrey, ed. *Ernest Hemingway: The Critical Heritage.* London; New York: Routledge, 1997, 1982.

Miller, Paul W. "Hemingway vs. Stendahl, or Papa's Last Fight with a Dead Writer." *The Hemingway Review* 19, no. 1 (Fall 1999): 127–40.

Moddelmog, Debra A. *Reading Desire: In Pursuit of Ernest Hemingway.* Ithaca, N.Y.: Cornell University Press, 1999.

Morgan, Kathleen. *Tales Plainly Told: The Eyewitness Narratives of Hemingway and Homer.* Columbia, S.C.: Camden House, 1990.

Nagel, James, ed. *Ernest Hemingway: The Writer in Context.* Madison: University of Wisconsin Press, 1984.

Pavloska. Susanna. *Modern Primitives: Race and Language in Gertrude Stein, Ernest Hemingway and Zora Neale Hurston.* New York; London: Garland, 2000.

Piep, Karsten H. *Embattled Home Fronts: Domestic Politics and the American Novel of World War I.* Amsterdam, Netherlands: Rodopi, 2009.

Rovit, Earl, and Arthur Waldhorn, ed. *Hemingway and Faulkner in Their Time.* New York: Continuum, 2005.

Rudat, Wolfgang E. H. *A Rotten Way to Be Wounded: The Tragicomedy of* The Sun Also Rises. New York: P. Lang, 1990.

Sanderson, Rena, ed. *Hemingway's Italy: New Perspectives.* Baton Rouge: Louisiana State University Press, 2006.

Schnitzer, Deborah. *The Pictorial in Modernist Fiction from Stephen Crane to Ernest Hemingway.* Ann Arbor, Mich.: UMI Research Press, 1988.

Smiley, Pamela; "Gender-Linked Miscommunication in 'Hills Like White Ele-phants." *The Hemingway Review* 8, no. 1 (Fall 1988): 2–12.

Spilka, Mark. *Hemingway's Quarrel with Androgyny.* Lincoln: University of Nebraska Press, 1989.

Stoltzfus, Ben. *Hemingway and French Writers.* Kent, Ohio: Kent State University Press, 2010.

Strychacz, Thomas. *Dangerous Masculinities: Conrad, Hemingway, and Lawrence.* Gainesville: University Press of Florida, 2008.

Vernon, Alex. *Soldiers Once and Still: Ernest Hemingway, James Salter, & Tim O'Brien.* Iowa City: University of Iowa Press, 2004.

Wagner, Linda W., ed. *Ernest Hemingway: Six Decades of Criticism.* East Lansing: Michigan State University Press, 1987.

Wagner-Martin, Linda W., ed. *Ernest Hemingway: Seven Decades of Criticism.* East Lansing: Michigan State University Press, 1998.

Acknowledgments

George Monteiro, "Ernest Hemingway, Psalmist." From *Journal of Modern Literature* 14, no. 1 (Summer 1987): 83–95. Copyright © 1987 by Indiana University Press.

Donald E. Hardy, "Presupposition and the Coconspirator." From *Style* 26, no. 1 (Spring 1992): 1–11. Copyright © 1992 Northern Illinois University Department of English and College of Liberal Arts & Sciences.

Margot Norris, "The Novel as War: Lies and Truth in Hemingway's *A Farewell to Arms*." From *Modern Fiction Studies* 40, no. 4 (1994): 689–710. Copyright © 1994 Purdue Research Foundation. Reprinted with permission of the Johns Hopkins University Press.

Robert Paul Lamb, "Hemingway and the Creation of Twentieth-Century Dialogue." From *Twentieth-Century Literature* 42, no. 4 (Winter 1996): 453–80. Copyright © 1996 by *Twentieth-Century Literature*. Revised for *Art Matters: Hemingway, Craft, and the Creation of the Modern Short Story*. Copyright © 2010 Louisiana State University Press.

Norman Friedman, "Harry or Ernest? The Unresolved Ambiguity in 'The Snows of Kilimanjaro.'" From *Creative and Critical Approaches to the Short Story*, edited by Noel Harold Kaylor Jr. Copyright © 1997 by the Edwin Mellen Press.

Susan F. Beegel, "Santiago and the Eternal Feminine: Gendering *La Mar* in *The Old Man and the Sea*." From *Hemingway and Women: Female Critics and the Female Voice*, edited by Lawrence R. Broer and Gloria Holland. Copyright © 2002 by the University of Alabama Press.

David Savola, "'A Very Sinister Book': *The Sun Also Rises* as Critique of Pastoral." From *The Hemingway Review* 26, no. 1 (Fall 2006): 25–46. Copyright © 2006 by the Ernest Hemingway Foundation.

Philip Melling, "Cultural Imperialism, Afro-Cuban Religion, and Santiago's Failure in Hemingway's *The Old Man and the Sea*." From *The Hemingway Review* 26, no. 1 (Fall 2006): 6–24. Copyright © 2006 by the Ernest Hemingway Foundation.

Donald A. Daiker, "'Brett Couldn't Hold Him': Lady Ashley, Pedro Romero, and the Madrid Sequence in *The Sun Also Rises*." From *The Hemingway Review* 29, no. 1 (Fall 2009): 73–88. Copyright © 2009 by the Ernest Hemingway Foundation.

Every effort has been made to contact the owners of copyrighted material and secure copyright permission. Articles appearing in this volume generally appear much as they did in their original publication with few or no editorial changes. In some cases, foreign language text has been removed from the original essay. Those interested in locating the original source will find the information cited above.

Index

Characters in literary works are listed by first name followed by the title of the work in parentheses.